Defending Public Schools

Defending Public Schools

Volume III

Curriculum Continuity and Change in the 21st Century

EDITED BY
KEVIN D. VINSON AND E. WAYNE ROSS

Praeger Perspectives

Westport, Connecticut
London

Library of Congress Cataloging-in-Publication Data

Defending public schools.
p. cm. — (Praeger perspectives)
Includes bibliographical references and index.
Contents: v. 1. Schooling and the rise of the security state / edited by David A. Gabbard and E. Wayne Ross — v. 2. Teaching for a democratic society / edited by Kathleen R. Kesson and E. Wayne Ross — v. 3. Curriculum continuity and change in the 21st century / edited by Kevin D. Vinson and E. Wayne Ross — v. 4. The nature and limits of standards based reform and assessment / edited by Sandra Mathison and E. Wayne Ross.
ISBN 0-275-98295-5 (set : alk. paper) — ISBN 0-275-98296-3 (v. 1 : alk. paper) — ISBN 0-275-98297-1 (v. 2 : alk. paper) — ISBN 0-275-98298-X (v. 3 : alk. paper) — ISBN 0-275-98299-8 (v. 4 : alk. paper)
1. Education and state—United States. 2. Public schools—United States. I. Gabbard, David. II. Ross, E. Wayne, 1956– III. Series.
LC89.D46 2004
379.73–d22 2004050549

British Library Cataloguing in Publication Data is available.

Library of Congress Catalog Card Number: 2004050549
ISBN: 0-275-98295-5 (set)
0-275-98296-3 (vol. I)
0-275-98297-1 (vol. II)
0-275-98298-X (vol. III)
0-275-98299-8 (vol. IV)

First published in 2004

Praeger Publishers, 88 Post Road West, Westport, CT 06881
An imprint of Greenwood Publishing Group, Inc.
www.praeger.com

Printed in the United States of America

The paper used in this book complies with the Permanent Paper Standard issued by the National Information Standards Organization (Z39.48–1984).

10 9 8 7 6 5 4 3 2 1

To
Paula and Olivia
K.D.V.

and

Gail McCutcheon
E.W.R.

Contents

General Editor's Introduction: Defending Public Schools, Defending Democracy

E. Wayne Ross

WHY DO PUBLIC SCHOOLS NEED TO BE DEFENDED?

Why do public schools need to be defended? This may be the first question some readers have about this multivolume collection of essays, and it's a good one. Certainly, the title suggests schools are under attack, and they are. Public schools in the United States have always carried a heavy burden as one of the principal instruments in our efforts to create an ideal society. For example, public schools have been given great responsibility for equalizing gender and racial inequalities, providing the knowledge and skills that give everyone an equal opportunity to experience the "American Dream," producing a workforce with skills that enable U.S. corporations to compete effectively in the global marketplace, and preparing citizens to be effective participants in a democratic society, just to name a few.

Critics of public schools come from across the political spectrum, but it is important to understand the reasons behind the various criticisms of public schools. The diverse responsibilities of public schools present a huge challenge to educators, and even when schools are performing well, it is difficult, if not impossible, for them to deliver all the expected results when their mission necessarily entails contradictory purposes. For example:

- Should schools focus on increasing equity or increasing school performance (e.g., student test scores)?
- Should the school curriculum be limited to the development of students' cognitive

processes, or do schools have a responsibility for supporting the development of the whole person?
- Should public schools serve the interests of the state, or should they serve the interests of local school communities?
- Should schools prepare a workforce to meet economic needs identified by corporations, or should they prepare students to construct personally meaningful understandings of their world and the knowledge and skills to act on their world?
- Should schools be an instrument of cultural transmission with the goal of preparing students to adopt (and adapt to) the dominant culture, or should schools function as an engine for social and cultural change, reconstructing society based upon principles of progress aimed at amelioration of problems?

It is important not to view the contradictory goals of public education as merely "either/or" questions as presented above. The terrain of public schooling, as with all aspects of the human endeavor, is too complex to be reduced to dualisms.

PUBLIC SCHOOLS IN A DEMOCRACY[1]

In his magnum opus *Democracy and Education*, John Dewey—widely regarded as America's greatest philosopher—states that all societies use education as means of social control in which adults consciously shape the dispositions of children. He continues by arguing that "education" in and of itself has no definite meaning until people define the kind of society they want to have. In other words, there is no "objective" answer to the question of what the purposes and goals of public schools should be.

The implication of Dewey's position is that we—the people—must decide what we want our society to be and, with that vision in mind, decide what the purposes of public education should be. The challenge then is assuring that a pluralism of views on the nature and purposes of public schools is preserved in the process of defining what they should be. This is the problem of democracy. It also explains why public schools are the object of criticism from various points along the political spectrum (e.g., from liberals and conservatives) as schools become the context in which we work out, in part, our collective aims and desires and who we are as a people.

Our understanding of what happens (as well as what various people would like to see happen) in U.S. public schools can be enhanced by taking a closer look at our conceptions of democracy and how democracy functions in contemporary American society.

Democracy is most often understood as a system of government providing a set of rules that allow individuals wide latitude to do as they wish. The first principle of democracy, however, is providing means for giving power to the people, not to an individual or to a restricted class of people. "Democracy," Dewey said, is "a mode of associated living, of conjoint communicated experience."[2] In this conception, democratic life involves paying attention to the multiple implications of our actions on others. In fact, the primary responsibility of democratic citizens is concern with the development of shared interests that lead to sensitivity to the repercussions of their actions on others. Dewey further characterized democracy as a force that breaks down the barriers that separate people and creates community.

From a Deweyan perspective, democracy is not merely a form of government nor is it an end in itself; it is the means by which people discover, extend, and manifest human nature and human rights. For Dewey, democracy has three roots: (a) free individual existence, (b) solidarity with others, and (c) choice of work and other forms of participation in society. The aim of a democratic society is the production of free human beings associated with one another on terms of equality.

Dewey's conception of democracy contrasts sharply with the prevailing political economic paradigm—neoliberalism. Although the term *neoliberalism* is largely unused by the public in the United States, it references something everyone is familiar with—policies and processes that permit a relative handful of private interests to control as much as possible of social life in order to maximize their personal profit.[3] Neoliberalism is embraced by parties across the political spectrum, from right to left, and is characterized by social and economic policy that is shaped in the interests of wealthy investors and large corporations. The free market, private enterprise, consumer choice, entrepreneurial initiative, and government deregulation are some important principles of neoliberalism.

Neoliberalism is not new. It is merely the current version of the wealthy few's attempt to restrict the rights and powers of the many. Although democracy and capitalism are popularly understood (and often taught) as "birds of a feather," the conflict between protecting private wealth and creating a democratic society is conspicuous throughout U.S. history. The framers of the U.S. Constitution were keenly aware of the "threat" of democracy. According to James Madison, the primary responsibility of government was "to protect the minority of the opulent against the majority." Madison believed the threat to democracy was likely to increase over time as there was an increase in "the proportion of those who will labor under all the hardships of life and secretly sigh for a more equal distribution of its blessing."[4]

In crafting a system giving primacy to property over people, Madison and the framers were guarding against the increased influence of the unpropertied masses. The Federalists expected that the public would remain compliant and deferential to the politically active elite—and for the most part that has been true throughout U.S. history. Despite the Federalists' electoral defeat, their conception of democracy prevailed, though in a different form, as industrial capitalism emerged. Their view was most succinctly expressed by John Jay—president of the Continental Congress and first Chief Justice of the U.S.

Supreme Court—who said that "the people who own the country ought to govern it." Jay's maxim is a principle upon which the United States was founded and is one of the roots of neoliberalism.

For over two hundred years, politicians and political theorists have argued *against* a truly participatory democracy that engages the public in controlling their own affairs; for example, founding father Alexander Hamilton warned of the "great beast" that must be tamed. In the twentieth century, Walter Lippman warned of the "bewildered herd" that would trample itself without external control, and the eminent political scientist Harold Lasswell warned elites of the "ignorance and stupidity of the masses" and called for elites not to succumb to the "democratic dogmatisms" about people being the best judges of their own interests.

These perspectives have nurtured a neoliberal version of democracy that turns citizens into spectators, deters or prohibits the public from managing its own affairs, and controls the means of information.[5] This may seem an odd conception of democracy, but it is the prevailing conception of "liberal-democratic" thought—and it is the philosophical foundation for current mainstream approaches to educational reform (known collectively as "standards-based educational reform"). In spectator democracy, a specialized class of experts identifies what our common interests are and thinks and plans accordingly. The function of the rest of us is to be "spectators" rather than participants in action (for example, casting votes in elections or implementing educational reforms that are conceived by people who know little or nothing about our community, our desires, or our interests).

Although the Madisonian principle that the government should provide special protections for the rights of property owners is central to U.S. democracy, there is also a critique of inequality (and the principles of neoliberalism)—in a tradition of thought that includes Thomas Jefferson, Dewey, and many others—that argues that the root of human nature is the need for free creative work under one's control.[6] For example, Thomas Jefferson distinguished between the aristocrats, "who fear and distrust the people and wish to draw all powers from them into the hands of the higher classes," and democrats, who "identify with the people, have confidence in them, cherish and consider them as the most honest and safe . . . depository of the public interest."[7]

Dewey also warned of the antidemocratic effects of the concentration of private power in absolutist institutions, such as corporations. He was clear that as long as there was no democratic control of the workplace and economic systems, democracy would be limited, stunted. Dewey emphasized that democracy has little content when big business rules the life of the country through its control of "the means of production, exchange, publicity, transportation and communication, reinforced by command of the press, press agents and other means of publicity and propaganda." "Politics," Dewey said, "is the shadow cast on society by big business, the attenuation of the shadow will not change the substance." A free and democratic society, according to Dewey, is one where people are "masters of their own . . . fate."[8]

Therefore, when it comes to determining the purposes of public schools in a democracy, the key factor is how one conceives of what democracy is and, as illustrated earlier, there are longstanding contradictions about the nature of democracy in the United States. In the contemporary context, mainstream discourse on the problems and the solutions for public schools has been based upon the principles of neoliberalism and manifest in standards-based educational reform, the subject of many of the contributions to *Defending Public Schools.*

WHY ARE WE DEFENDING PUBLIC SCHOOLS?

The editors and authors of *Defending Public Schools* are not interested in defending the status quo. Each contributor is, however, very interested in preserving public schools as a key part of the two-centuries-old experiment that is American democracy. Public schools are in a centripetal position in our society and, as result, they always have been and will continue to be battlegrounds for conflicting visions of what our society should be.

We believe that public schools serve the public, "We, the people." We believe that schools should strengthen our democracy in the sense that our ability to meaningfully participate in the decision-making processes that impact our communities and our lives is enhanced, not constricted. Educational resources need to be directed toward increasing people's awareness of the relevant facts about their lives and increasing people's abilities to act upon these facts in their own true interests. Since the 1980s and even before, the purposes of public schools have been by the interests of the state and of concentrated private/corporate power, as follows from what I described earlier, as neoliberalism. We believe that public education ought to serve public interests, not the interests of private power and privilege.

At a time when our democracy and many of the liberties we hold dear are in crisis, we propose that the preservation of public schools is necessary to reverse antidemocratic trends that have accelerated under standards-based educational reforms, which intend to transform the nature and purposes of public schools and our society. Each of the volumes in *Defending Public Schools* takes on a different aspect of education, yet these volumes are bound together by the underlying assumption that preserving public schools is a necessary part of preserving democracy. The following ten points provide a synopsis of what defending public schools means to us:

1. The statist view of schools treats teachers as mere appendages to the machinery of the state and seeks to hold them accountable to serving the interests of state power. Linked as it is to the interests of private wealth, this view defines children's value in life as human resources and future consumers. Education

should foster critical citizenship skills to advance a more viable and vibrant democratic society. Schools should be organized around preparing for democratic citizenship through engagement with real-world issues, problem solving, and critical thinking, and through active participation in civic and political processes. Informed citizenship in a broad-based, grassroots democracy must be based on principles of cooperation with others, nonviolent conflict resolution, dialogue, inquiry and rational debate, environmental activism, and the preservation and expansion of human rights. These skills, capacities, and dispositions need to be taught and practiced.

2. The current system uses "carrots and sticks" to coerce compliance with an alienating system of schooling aimed at inducing conformity among teachers and students through high-stakes testing and accountability. This system alienates teachers from their work by stripping it of all creative endeavors and reduces it to following scripted lesson plans. We believe that teaching is a matter of the heart, that place where intellect meets up with emotion and spirit in constant dialogue with the world around us. We call for the elimination of high-stakes standardized tests and the institution of more fair, equitable, and meaningful systems of accountability and assessment of both students and schools.
3. Current federal educational policy, embodied in the No Child Left Behind Act, sets impossible standards for a reason. Public access to institutions of learning helps promote the levels of critical civic activism witnessed during the 1960s and 1970s that challenged the power of the state and the corporations that it primarily serves. The current reform environment creates conditions in which public schools can only fail, thus providing "statistical evidence" for an alleged need to turn education over to private companies in the name of "freedom of choice." In combination with the growing corporate monopolization of the media, these reforms are part of a longer-range plan to consolidate private power's control over the total information system, thus eliminating avenues for the articulation of honest inquiry and dissent.
4. The current system of public schooling alienates students by stripping learning from its engagement with the world in all of its complexity. It reduces learning to test preparation as part of a larger rat race where students are situated within an economic competition for dwindling numbers of jobs. We believe that educational excellence needs to be defined in terms of teachers' abilities to inspire children to engage the world, for it is through such critical engagement that true learning (as opposed to rote memorization) actually occurs. Students living in the twenty-first century are going to have to deal with a host of problems created by their predecessors: global warming and other ecological disasters, global conflicts, human rights abuses, loss of civil liberties, and other inequities. The curriculum needs to address what students need to know and be able to do in the twenty-first century to tackle these problems—and it needs to be relevant to students' current interests and concerns.
5. Teachers matter. Teaching is a public act that bears directly on our collective future. We must ensure the quality of the profession by providing meaningful forms of preparation, induction, mentoring, professional development, career advancement, and improved working conditions. High learning standards should serve as guidelines, not curricular mandates, for teachers. Restore teacher control, in collaboration with students and communities, over decision mak-

ing about issues of curriculum and instruction in the classroom—no more scripted teaching, no more mandated outcomes, no more "teacher-proof" curricula. Local control of education is at the heart of democracy; state and nationally mandated curriculum and assessment are a prescription for totalitarianism.

6. In the past two decades, the corporate sector has become increasingly involved with education in terms of supplementing public spending in exchange for school-based marketing (including advertising space in schools and textbooks, junk fast-food and vending machines, and commercial-laden "free" TV). We believe that students should not be thought of as a potential market or as consumers, but as future citizens.
7. All schools should be funded equally and fully, eliminating the dependence on private corporate funds and on property taxes, which create a two-tiered educational system by distributing educational monies inequitably. Include universal prekindergarten and tuition-free higher education for all qualified students in state universities.
8. Children of immigrants make up approximately 20 percent of the children in the United States, bringing linguistic and cultural differences to many classrooms. Added to this are 2.4 million children who speak a language other than English at home. Ensure that the learning needs of English language learners are met through caring, multicultural, multilingual education.
9. Citizens in a pluralistic democracy need to value difference and interact with people of differing abilities, orientations, ethnicities, cultures, and dispositions. Discard outmoded notions of a hypothetical norm, and describe either *all* students as different, or none of them. All classrooms should be *inclusive,* meeting the needs of all students together, in a way that is just, caring, challenging, and meaningful.
10. All students should have opportunities to learn and excel in the fine and performing arts, physical education and sports, and extracurricular clubs and activities in order to develop the skills of interaction and responsibility necessary for participation in a robust civil society.

In the end, whether the savage inequalities of neoliberalism—which define current social and national relations as well as approaches to school reform—will be overcome depends on how people organize, respond, learn, and teach in schools. Teachers and educational leaders need to link their own interests in the improvement of teaching and learning to a broad-based movement for social, political, and economic justice, and work together for the democratic renewal of public life and public education in America.

***

I would like to acknowledge the many people who have contributed to the creation of *Defending Public Schools.*

Each of my coeditors—David Gabbard, Kathleen Kesson, Sandra Mathison and Kevin D. Vinson—are first-rate scholars, without whom this project could never have been completed. They have spent untold hours conceiving of, writing for, and editing their respective volumes. I have learned much from them as educators, researchers, and as advocates for more just and democratic schools and society.

I would also like to acknowledge the truly remarkable contributions of the chapter authors who have provided *Defending Public Schools* with cutting-edge analysis of the most recent educational research and practice. I know of no other work on issues of public schooling that brings together a comparable collection of highly respected scholars, researchers, and practitioners.

I would be terribly remiss not to acknowledge the tremendous support and invaluable advice I have received from my editor, Marie Ellen Larcada. *Defending Public Schools* was initially envisioned by Marie Ellen, and she has been an essential part of its successful completion. Additionally, I would like to thank Shana Grob who, as our editorial assistant, was always attentive to the crucial details and made editing these four volumes a much more manageable and enjoyable job.

Thanks also to the folks who inspire and support me on a daily basis, comrades who are exemplary scholars, teachers, and activists: Perry Marker, Kevin Vinson, Steve Fleury, David Hursh, Rich Gibson, Jeff Cornett, Marc Bousquet, Heather Julien, Marc Pruyn, Valerie Pang, Larry Stedman, Ken Teitelbaum, Ceola Ross Baber, Lisa Cary, John Welsh, Chris Carter, Curry Malott, Richard Brosio, and Dave Hill.

Lastly, words cannot express my love for Sandra, Rachel, and Colin.

Defending Public Schools: Curriculum and the Challenge of Change—An Introduction

KEVIN D. VINSON AND E. WAYNE ROSS

Increasingly, American public schools have been placed under unprecedented scrutiny and have been held up to immense, even dangerous, criticism. No doubt, the recent emphasis on the No Child Left Behind (NCLB) Act and its related stress on standards-based educational reform (SBER—especially high-stakes standardized testing) has played a major role here. Moreover, and perhaps for some surprisingly, such criticism has come from the entirety of the pedagogical-political spectrum, both the Left and the Right—that is, contemporary public school negativity has drawn from arguments grounded across the ideological gamut.

All of this, of course, has special relevance to curriculum. The Rightist critique developed, in its modern guise, most directly, in our view, from the 1983 publication of *A Nation at Risk*; arguably, therefore, NCLB (and related reforms) is its direct descendant. *A Nation at Risk* maintained that the growing "mediocrity" of American public schools was causing an alarming degree of political and economic failure—that is, that underperforming schools were threatening the economic and political status of the United States in a world that was increasingly and competitively globalizing.

Quite simply, the specifics of this conservative critique today (see Oberle and Vinson, this volume) are that:

1. standards are too low;
2. schools replicate and extend the worthless theories of the "educational establishment";

3. public education is a monopoly;
4. content is neglected in favor of process and "self";
5. progressivism rules to the detriment of more effective direct instruction;
6. cultural relativism trumps traditional values;
7. parents' roles have been usurped by "educrats"; and
8. public schools seek to solve problems by "throwing money" at them when this is not necessarily the correct—or even a reasonable—solution.

For many of us who wish to defend public schools and schooling, these criticisms are clearly preposterous. If anything, the opposite of this perspective is the case. Perhaps, for example, schools are *underfunded,* educational experts—including teachers, students, and parents—have *too little* influence (given the increasing role of corporate and government leaders), and curriculum and instruction are *too traditional* (in their emphases on nationalistic, fact-based content and so-called Judeo-Christian ideologies). In any event, this line of condemnation aimed toward public schools is, at the very least, (1) off-base (in many cases, anyway), (2) unfair, and (3) deserving of a rigorous and substantive resistance or reaction.

On the other hand, the traditional liberal critique—perhaps founded in large measure in the progressive movement popularized during the early part of the twentieth century—suggests that schools:

1. stifle freedom and creativity in favor of conformity and discipline;
2. are dominated by non-educators (e.g., corporations/corporate leaders, politicians);
3. are too centrally controlled;
4. focus overwhelmingly on fact-based, standardized content to the detriment of student needs and interests;
5. are hypertraditional in terms of purpose, curriculum, instruction, and assessment;
6. emphasize homogeneity over the more significant issues of diversity and difference;
7. neglect neighborhoods and local communities; and
8. are underfunded.

While, to a large degree, we are more sympathetic to the Left/liberal viewpoint, we also accept that many currently employed public classroom teachers are doing everything they can to counteract these conditions and claims. To the extent to which such criticisms indeed are valid, often they are merely the reproductive dictates of the systematic powers that be.

Regardless of opinions and of contingent and evolving political climates, any discussion of curriculum today—the early twenty-first century—must take into account the meanings and consequences of NCLB and SBER, for this conjoined "movement" frames the development and actualization of contemporary schooling in all its assorted aspects. As we have previously asserted, as currently posited and understood, NCLB/SBER is simultaneously (1) antidemocratic, (2) oppressive, (3) inauthentic, and (4) disciplinary/conformative.[1] To make matters worse, the intentions of NCLB/SBER remain consistent with and reinforce the educational, blended agendas of both political-pedagogical liberals and political-pedagogical conservatives (in what we have termed the "will-to-standardize" or the "standardization imperative"), especially in a power-based and hierarchical manner. Nonetheless, it remains the dominant setting within which modern-day curriculum work occurs. Thus, no matter what, it must be taken seriously.

GENERAL THEMES

One point—if not *the* point—of this book is to defend public schools against the vast array of current criticism from both the Right and the Left and to decide whether there are any real, meaningful differences (at least between traditional conservatives and liberals) in their various complaints and their variously construed and affected results and agendas. As such, the chapters in the volume address a multiple range of contemporary concerns relative to American public schooling and education.

Defending Public Schools: Curriculum Continuity and Change in the 21st Century aims to support public schools specifically with respect to the curriculum as it exists—and could or should exist—today. Although critical, the authors here generally are critical principally via the conditions and limitations imposed on schooling by those who control its complex and power-laden (post-) modern functionings (e.g., governments, corporations) and not of public schooling—overarchingly—or its underlying and productive ideals per se. That is, although we know, of course, that not all teachers are good teachers and not all the curricular and instructional decisions they make are good decisions, we still support their continuing and remarkable efforts—as well as those of parents, students, and administrators—especially as they strive to do their very and underappreciated best under frequently less than optimal—and even less than supportive—circumstances (to say, in our view, the least).

To this end, each chapter included in this volume incorporates a number of related ideas and addresses several connected and timely themes. The authors all, for instance, offer a *critique* of the contemporary state of public schooling. While, initially, this might seem rather incompatible or inconsistent with the goal of *defending* public schools, in fact it really is not. For, in each case, the authors advance a discussion of both positive and negative characteristics and do so with the knowledge and optimism that education—particularly the curriculum—can, and should, be better. Certainly we—teachers, our children, and society at large—deserve nothing less than an honest and sincere appraisal.

Second, each chapter pursues alternatives. In other words, the authors present not simply criticisms but also concrete suggestions regarding how contemporary American public schooling might improve and how, more fundamentally, it, structurally, might reach its commendable and laudable historical and foundational goals.

Lastly, *Defending Public Schools: Curriculum Continuity and Change in the 21st Century* extends *hope*, because, in the end, each of the contributing authors is a long-term, dedicated, and quintessential advocate of public education. Each believes, centrally and wholeheartedly, that (1) the purposes of public schooling are essential and admirable; (2) we—in terms of both schooling and society—can always do more; and (3) the fundamental aims of publicly supported schooling—the advancement of democracy, opportunity, equality, freedom, and justice—and its practice as constructed today ought to be of principal concern to all American citizens. No matter what one's beliefs or attitudes, the future of society is inextricably linked not only to public schooling but also to our children and their everyday lives and life chances.

THE CHAPTERS

The authors in part I of this volume provide an overview of the history, context, and future of the public school curriculum. Obviously, the subject matters, and each author investigates the ways in which the core content in public schools is constructed within particular historical and sociopolitical contexts, and assesses the current and future status of these subjects within the curriculum of public schools.

The arts in education have seldom enjoyed a central role in the curriculum of public schools, and educators have often relied on arguments outside the arts to prove their worth within the curriculum. In chapter 1, Rita L. Irwin argues that the arts are worth defending for a variety of reasons, with the most noteworthy residing within the arts themselves. Even though our public schools could be strengthened with more resources, both financial and human, they need to be recognized for the strengths they already bring to the learning enterprise. Irwin illustrates how learning in and through the arts provides an education that opens minds to alternative ways of thinking and being, to the process of creating one's self, to nurturing a sense of excitement and passion for learning, and to appreciating the diversity of cultures in which we live. Using the arts to strengthen learning in other subject areas could be considered a valuable secondary outcome, but for Irwin (and many other educators) the primary reasons for including the arts within the curriculum reside within the qualities of the artistic experiences themselves.

In chapter 2, Perry M. Marker observes that, for more than a century, the social studies curriculum has been relatively unchanged, and yet, ironically, for more than a century, social studies has had an identity crisis. Society has changed remarkably since 1916 when the report of the National Education Association Committee on Social Studies—which still defines much of the social studies curriculum—was issued. From transportation to technology, from social life to sexual mores, life at the turn of the twenty-first century would be virtually unrecognizable to those living in 1916. Incredibly, during the same period of time, the social studies curriculum has remained virtually static. Marker describes contemporary social studies as ensnared in a history-centered, discipline-bound, nonpartisan, and moribund curriculum, designed for a particular time and society; situated at a particular intersection of class, race, and gender; and immersed in an ethic influenced by the industrial revolution and capitalism. This chapter explores the past, present, and future of social studies in contemporary American society.

In her chapter on "Literacy Research and Educational Reform," Martha Rapp Ruddell describes how popular (and some professional) opinion today holds that literacy achievement in the United States has suffered an ongoing downward spiral since a mythical golden period of high achievement, that the cause of this downward trend was the widespread and thoughtlessly careless use of instructional practice not supported by research, and that the current "research-based" instruction—heavily steeped in systematic phonics and skills-first reading and writing instruction—is the answer to all the literacy achievement "problems" that need to be fixed. Indeed, the latest federal education policy, the No Child Left Behind Act of 2001, not only endorses such instruction but also mandates yearly standardized testing of all children above second grade to "assure" that skills have been learned. Contrary to this view, Ruddell presents a history of American literacy instruction that is marked by periods in which new concerns about our children's literacy arose, followed by research efforts and instructional reforms that were undertaken to counter these concerns, and resulting subsequent periods where yet other questions surfaced. Ruddell illustrates how the questions asked in these cycles of periodic concern had direct influence on the research and instruction that followed. She further demonstrates the existence of a cyclical pattern of concern-research-reform that belies the notion that great waves of literacy instruction in this country were baseless, unresearched, and atheoretical. Ruddell's chapter traces the development of research and reform in American literacy instruction and highlights the ways in which public and professional concern shaped research trends and instructional practice. It provides an analysis of current reforms and the research base for those reforms.

With the possible exception of reading/language arts, no subject area enjoys as much, and as widespread, approval for inclusion in the school curriculum as does mathematics. Whether viewed as one of "the basics" (i.e., one of the "3 Rs"), as problem-solving, as skill acquisition, as intellectual/applied process, or as the learning of specific content knowledge (etc.), mathematics maintains support from across the pedagogical and ideological spectrum—from essentialists to progressives, from traditionalists to radical educational critics. And yet, simultaneously, it is a discipline that faces frequent, sustained, and extensive challenges, both warranted and unwarranted. In their chapter, Cynthia O. Anhalt, Robin A. Ward, and Kevin D. Vinson raise and pursue the following questions: Historically, what has been the place and purpose of mathematics education? What is the current "state of the field" (e.g., best practice, standards, competing dominant views, and so on)? To what extent, and on what basis, is mathematics education currently under attack? What is exemplary about contemporary mathematics education? And where do we go from here? They conclude by considering both the positive and negative aspects of contemporary mathematics education, coming down, in the end, on the side that says that mathematics education deserves to be defended, that it is vital, and that it warrants a defense of vis-à-vis its special position relative to the often underrated status, standing, place, and development of the school curriculum and, more broadly, of American public education.

For over 100 years, what constitutes science in public schools has swung between an emphasis on content and an emphasis on process. In chapter 5, "Science in Public Schools: What Is It and Who Is It For?" Bruce Johnson and Elisabeth Roberts describe how these shifts have been closely related to changes in perceptions of the purpose of public schools. For science, the debate has been between preparing future scientists and helping all people understand science and its applications in and to their lives. Johnson and Roberts argue that current national education policy emphasizes both content and process, challenging schools to both prepare future scientists and ensure that all learners become scientifically literate. But to achieve this goal, science teaching must deemphasize facts and engage students to construct conceptual understanding and to reason scientifically. These lofty aims face harsh realities in the classroom. Systemic and political challenges, such as high-stakes testing and "structure of the disciplines" models, limit time for science in elementary schools and reinforce traditional pedagogy in high schools. Regardless, Johnson and Roberts remain optimistic. Public education can and should both prepare all students to understand what science is as well as provide the foundation needed for those who want to pursue science careers. Thus the primary purpose of science in public schools, they argue, should be science literacy for all.

In chapter 6, Four Arrows (aka Don Trent Jacobs) examines an issue that cuts across the entirety of the public school curriculum—"character education." In this chapter, he summarizes historical, contemporary, and reform issues pertaining to character education from a variety of directions, including a highly suggestive American Indian perspective that has been little understood in mainstream education. In assuming that it is most important for students to emerge from public schools with the ability to reflect spiritually, reason autonomously, and act virtuously for the greater good, Four Arrows presents indigenous worldviews full circle into the current conversation about school priorities while at the same time offering a concise overview of the journey.

Frequently when people think about contemporary U.S. public schooling, a particular set of dominant and dominating images comes to mind. Too often, the popular and "official" view is that all schools and classrooms are and should be the same—even across grade levels and subject areas. In fact, some of the harshest criticisms of public education center on its "unwillingness" or "inability" to change or to try different and alternate approaches. Even in this current age of standardization and conformity, certain powerful critics (ironically) condemn instruction, teachers, curriculum, and so on, for being too slow to experiment and to move away from "entrenched" and "ineffective" pedagogies. Moreover, those "experimental" and "nontraditional" efforts that do exist—for example, Montessori Schools—are commonly perceived either as elitist or as only implemented in private or parochial schools. In chapter 7, "Not the Same Old Thing: Maria Montessori—A Nontraditional Approach to Public Schooling in an Age of Traditionalism and Standardization," Elizabeth Oberle and Kevin D. Vinson examine Montessori education—both in theory and practice—as a reasonable, significant, and meaningful mode of *public* schooling, one that potentially challenges many of the condemnations levied by current pedagogical critics. Oberle and Vinson consider (1) the meanings of Montessori education, (2) the extent to which Montessori education has made impressive inroads vis-à-vis public schooling, (3) the advantages of public Montessori education, and (4) how an understanding of the relationships between Montessorianism and the goals of public education might help advocates defend the workings and successes of twenty-first-century American schooling—curriculum, instruction, assessment, and policy.

In part II of *Defending Public Schools: Curriculum Continuity and Change in the 21st Century*, the contributing authors take on enduring and critical issues that affect all subject matter areas. In chapters 8 and 9, Stephen C. Fleury and Steven L. Strauss examine the state regulation of knowledge and curriculum. In "The Military and Corporate Roots of State-Regulated Knowledge," Fleury argues that, depending on a person's ideological thermometer and occupational position, "the State regulation of knowledge" may characterize a finely honed process for ensuring that citizens have access to (and are protected with) the best knowledge available in society. For others, however, this phrase may evoke images of a myopic redundancy by legions of bureaucrats or oppressive manipulation by privileged groups. There is a political process for how something becomes "official knowledge," and increasing regulation of this process is tied to the interest of corporations and the military. Fleury describes how the decentralizing shift in state control, ostensibly deregulating knowledge, has unleashed economic and cultural forces that pragmatically enable the dominance of a Rightist ideology through texts and testing.

Corporate interests and the regulation of reading education is the subject of Strauss's chapter, "Extreme Takeover: Corporate Control of the Curriculum, with Special Attention to the Case of Reading." Corporate America has not been secretive about what it expects schools to accomplish in the field of reading. Through its Business Roundtable Education Task Force, it has made clear that it sees itself in a life-and-death struggle with Corporate Europe and Corporate Asia for control of the world's markets. It is pinning its very survival on a retooled U.S. labor force that possesses the highest possible levels of "twenty-first century literacy skills." These skills include data manipulation, information management, software troubleshooting, and, in general, the ability to "read instruction manuals." The attainment of such skills via schooling is the centerpiece of Corporate America's education agenda. Strauss describes how the federally mandated curriculum on reading, as expressed in No Child Left Behind, was lauded by the Business Roundtable, two of whose members are on President Bush's education advisory committee. The core component of the curriculum is intensive and direct instruction in phonics and phonemic awareness, in which young children process letters on a page and manipulate the resulting sounds to form words. To the authors of NCLB, this represents the most elementary form of information processing, the core skill that, through accumulated and aggressive drilling and backed up by high-stakes testing and accountability, becomes a more complex information processing skill, ultimately leading to the creation of a "twenty-first-century knowledge worker." Strauss argues that the formulation of the "neophonics" curriculum by federally funded scientists, and the mandating of this curriculum by Congress, indicates the extent to which corporate control of the reading curriculum is achieved by its control over the government and its research and scientific agencies.

Looks, body size, and sexual orientation are key elements in the make-it-or-break-it world of peer acceptance and popularity. These social markers are the cultural capital of adolescent society. In "The Body and Sexuality in Curriculum," Lisa W. Loutzenheiser pursues "sex, sexuality, and body image" as "the currency of adolescent culture" as she interrogates "the ways in which youth navigate their various identities and how schools make visible the terrain of normative behavior and the unattainable standards set by the dominant culture." Focusing on lesbian, gay, bisexual, transsexual, and queer (LGBTQ) young people, Loutzenheiser considers "social pressures," "familial pressures," "academic pressures," and other pertinent issues relative to sexuality and to sexual identities, specifically in terms of two "constructed vignettes" (centering on the fictional "Marion" and "George"). Following discussions of the misrepresentation of gender and sex, the nature of queer theory, and ways in which schools and educators can combat heterosexism and homophobia in the classroom, she concludes by arguing that "Turning a critical eye toward the normative and normalizing and exploring their place in the classroom through a lens of queer, queer theories, fluidity, and nonessentializing identity categories may offer all of those who think and theorize about teaching and learning a productive path toward working with, amongst, and across differences."

In chapter 11, "When Race Shows Up in the Curriculum: Teacher (Self-) Reflective Responsibility in Students' Opportunities to Learn," authors H. Richard Milner, Leon D. Caldwell, and Ira E. Murray explain pertinent issues around the influence and the intersection of race and curriculum. The authors argue that teachers need to develop the skills and knowledge necessary to reflect on their own experiences where race and the curriculum are concerned. They discuss how strategies for introspection can lead teachers to place a greater emphasis on racially inclusive classroom contents and practices and how interventions addressing color blindness and assumptions of Eurocentric universality could prove effective as teachers grapple with ways to better meet the needs of racially diverse students (pedagogically and philosophically). Milner, Caldwell, and Murray point out that students of color often operate in classrooms that do not meet their affective, social, and intellectual needs. As a result, many of these students become educationally marginalized, which exacerbates achievement gaps and myths of anti-intellectualism in nonwhite communities, especially African-American and Hispanic communities. They argue that the explication of race-based educational disparities infrequently includes discussions about the characteristics of teachers, such as racial identity or racial attitude. This chapter sheds light on this oversight and suggests strategies for increasing the awareness of racial attitudes in the discourse of and on curriculum development. With the ever-widening achievement gaps and their social and economic implications, the authors believe we can no longer afford to focus solely on the characteristics of the student without focusing on the characteristics of the teacher.

In their chapter on critical multiculturalism, Marc Pruyn, Robert Haworth, and Rebecca Sánchez explore their attempts to use a contraband-inspired—critical—pedagogy for social justice both within the social studies teacher education courses they teach and the K–12 classrooms where they most recently served as teacher-learner pedagogues. They review the foundations of the critical pedagogy movement—with particular emphasis on Latin America and North America—and then lead readers empirically through their efforts to enact the principles of a critical and contraband pedagogy for social justice relative to both K–12 and preservice learners in the diverse U.S.-México borderlands in southern New Mexico.

William B. Stanley's chapter, "Schooling and Curriculum for Social Transformation," reconsiders the status of perhaps the most contentious idea in education. Developing a curriculum for social transformation has had a long, troubled history. For over two centuries, various groups and individuals have proposed plans for using education to transform society in some substantive way; the effort continues. At least since Dewey's emergence as an influential curriculum theorist, curriculum for social transformation has generally been considered a "liberal," "progressive," or even "radical" approach to public education. But one could also argue that, in practice, education for social transformation has often been proposed to achieve conservative ends. The current No Child Left Behind legislation is only the most recent case in point. Stanley makes clear that part of the difficulty in analyzing the concept of social transformation is its ever changing and paradoxical nature. For once education is successful in achieving its socially transformative ends (progressive or conservative), it tends to shift to a social transmission or conservation focus. On a more fundamental level, curriculum for social transformation involves answering the basic question, "What, or whose, knowledge is of most worth?" In addition, we must examine who gets to answer such questions and on what basis. This chapter presents a reconsideration of these issues within the context of the current standards-based education reform movement. The analysis includes a rethinking of the role of ideology as it relates to curriculum reform as well as recent developments in critical approaches to curriculum theory.

CONCLUSIONS

Our overall goal—in fact, our deepest wish—is that this volume (as well as the others in the *Defending Public Schools* series) will be attractive to a broad sweep of those individuals and groups concerned with public education and with other engaged (enraged?), involved, and affected school-related stakeholders. Therefore, we have attempted to create this work in a way that will appeal across the board (that is, not just in a way interesting to professional educators or scholars). We hope that teachers, professors, parents, policymakers, and others will find what we have done both interesting and useful. For, in the end, almost everyone wants public schools to succeed. It is with these purposes in mind that we present this effort.

— I —

History, Context, and the Future of the Public School Curriculum

— 1 —

An Artful Curriculum/ A Curriculum Full of Life

RITA L. IRWIN

As I reflect upon my learning experiences in galleries, theaters, museums, and community centers, I find myself relearning what many of us know but gradually disregard under societal pressures. Being in artistically rich environments, as spectators or creators, calls us into experiencing the world in meaningful, holistic ways. In these environments, I am offered a chance to be transported into a space and time that causes me to feel, perceive, move, and contemplate in ways ordinary experiences do not allow or encourage. Instead, I am thrust into the wholeness of my being. I am fully alive. My senses are recharged, my imagination is ignited, my emotions are revealed, and my soul unexpectedly finds meaning or questions previously held meanings. I am transformed, created, and/or re-created into a new being, fully present.

Whereas artistically rich environments call us to experience the fullness of our humanity, many other environments are often limited to, or defined by, narrow forms of understanding. Educational environments, and particularly public schools, often are caught between creating environments that stress narrowly defined notions of high academic achievement and those that stress realizing our full potential as human beings. In the former, less attention is often given to knowing through our bodies, emotions, and spirits than knowing through our minds. Testing and rankings are used to measure competencies, and, ultimately, one's abilities. In the latter, multiple forms of understanding are sought to appreciate and critically reflect upon our world. As such, learning assessments are based upon contextual features, individualized learning portfolios, and criterion-based forms of evaluation. For me, an irony exists in this dichotomous view of learning. Whereas an artistically rich learning environment embraces academic learning in its entirety, an academically focused (narrowly defined) learning environment erases artistically rich conditions for learning. For me, an artful curriculum is a curriculum full of life. It is a curriculum that embraces all of our humanity and refuses to erase the conditions needed for every student to reach his or her full potential.

The arts in education have seldom enjoyed a central role in the curriculum of public schools. This has never been more evident than in our current circumstances. Over the last two decades, educators have been forced to justify the existence of arts programming within educational trends focused upon standardized measures of achievement. In an effort to convince decision makers of the centrality of the arts within education, educators have often relied on arguments outside the arts to prove the worth of the arts within the curriculum. A popular example is the philosophy that integrating the arts into the core curriculum strengthens learning in the core subjects. For instance, integrating art into a language arts lesson strengthens the quality and quantity of learning within the literacy experience. Although I am not denying this claim, in this chapter, I argue that the arts are worth defending for a variety of reasons, the most noteworthy residing within the arts themselves. It may be that the arts strengthen learning across all subjects in the curriculum, but their greatest contributions lie in their uniqueness within the learning enterprise and in their durability to humanity over time. Even though our public schools could be strengthened with more resources, both financial and human, schools and teachers who are incorporating the arts into their overall curriculum need to be recognized for the strengths they already bring to the learning endeavor. *Learning in the arts* provides an education that opens minds to alternative ways of thinking and being, to the processes of creating one's self, to nurturing a sense of excitement and a passion for learning, and to appreciating the diversity of cultures in which we live. *Learning through the arts* strengthens all subject areas and nurtures a project-based learning environment filled with the freedom to learn more than first conceived. Although learning through the arts may be used to justify many arts programs today, the results of such programming are limited by their secondary outcomes because the primary reasons for including the arts in the curriculum reside within the qualities of the artistic experiences themselves. Furthermore, *learning from the arts* offers us new ways to perceive all facets of our lives. To reimagine our very existence as an artistic event allows us to re-create our personal or public lives and the practices and events within them as artistically rendered, perceived, valued, and cherished. To lead an artful life and to conduct our lives in artful ways means taking responsibility for our feelings, movements, thoughts, and aspirations as we render our lives in perceptually significant and meaningful ways. What a powerful way to experience one's humanity.

LEARNING IN THE ARTS

All of us should consider how we might define the primary purposes of our educational institutions and, in particular, our public schools. I tend to agree with Maxine Greene, who claims that "the primary purpose of education is to free persons to make sense of their actual lived situations—not only cognitively, but personally, imaginatively, affectively—to attend mindfully to their own lives, to take their own initiatives in interpreting them and finding out where the deficiencies are and trying to transform them. And discovering somehow that there is no end to it, that there is always more to see, to learn, to feel."[1]

It is very possible that individuals could lead good lives without stepping into a gallery, museum, or concert hall, or knowing the collected works of well-known artists, musicians, dancers, and actors now and across time. However, it would be impossible to lead a good life without the arts. Every day, we are surrounded visually and audibly with the creative work of professional and amateur artists as well as the symbol systems from traditional and contemporary forms of cultural practices. We gather pleasure from these sensory sources of understanding. We create meaning from their inclusion in our existence. We adapt and change as a result of their influence. Whether these sensory sources come to us vicariously through television, advertising, music videos, movies, hit CDs, the Internet, or from live performances and exhibitions, we experience the arts and should have opportunities to experience the widest possible spectrum of the arts through our formal schooling. If we take the purpose of education to be that which I outlined earlier, then the arts underscore our abilities to make sense of our lives, cognitively, perceptively, imaginatively, and affectively. By being mindful of how the arts help us to understand, interpret, analyze, and judge our lives and the world around us, we discover the endless wonder of our collective creative potential. The arts are inexhaustible. When I encounter a work of art, I am provoked to consider an alternative to my previously held understandings. When I am in the presence of an original work of art, dance revue, or symphonic performance, I am forever changed. I come away surprised by the self-discovery or self-creation that has happened in the act of being present. Experiences such as these are made more powerful when we are able to view works of art firsthand, to be in their presence. Virtual witnessing can also be enlightening, but seeing the brushstrokes in a Van Gogh painting cannot be duplicated in a reproduction. The two experiences are quite different from one another. Then again, I also visit galleries over and over again so I can be in the presence of the same paintings again and again. Each time

I learn something new, see something I haven't seen before, and experience something I haven't experienced previously. The stained-glass windows in a local church do this for me, too. Whether it is the brightness of the sunshine flooding through their mosaics or the teachings of the clergy during the service, or the life experiences I bring to the event, each time I am in the presence of these windows I learn something new, see something different, and experience something I've never experienced before.

Learning in the arts provides a rich foundation to explore ideas, sensory qualities, open questions, and personal feelings through the use of materials and instruments in studio- and performance-based arts practices or through the use of texts (highlighting arts history, criticism, or aesthetics) in discourse-based arts practices. Nothing can replace learning in the arts. Consider this: Few people, if any, would send someone to see a movie for them. We intrinsically know the value of seeing the movie for ourselves. We know that the arts should be experienced, not relayed. Teachers who understand the arts provide us with the space to experience freedom and be fully alive. They also commit themselves to discovering what they can do to empower themselves as creators and transformers of the world so that they are better able to understand how to empower their own students. Teachers *and* students involved in making or performing the arts through painting, singing, acting, writing, and moving are inevitably energized to create something new. The freedom to create allows us to feel the fullness of being human while experiencing the confidence engendered through making connections between tradition and innovation. It's not hard to accept that the more we know, the more we understand, see, and hear. All those years of piano lessons gave me a deep appreciation for the skill and virtuosity of accomplished pianists playing Mozart concertos as well as the deep attentiveness I find listening to Jim Brickman play his solo renditions of romantic interludes. I may not play the piano myself, but I have a relationship with the piano, its penetrating sound and profound presence. Certainly all my art-making activities experienced during childhood stayed with me into adulthood. The sensations and perceptions I experienced enlarged my aesthetic understanding of the world, and increasingly, as I invested myself in the arts, I endeavored to leave my fingerprints upon the visual world. I resisted the unaesthetic myths of education limited to reading, writing, and 'rithmetic and embraced the aesthetic education found in and through the arts. Rather than denying the qualities found in good literature, I denied the rule-bound nature of the philosophy behind the 3Rs. Because I embraced an aesthetic education, I look at reading, writing, and arithmetic differently. Reading still touches me deeply as a result. In fact, let me recall a haunting book I read this summer entitled *The Lovely Bones*, by Alice Sebold. Through reading this book, I was forced to create meaning beyond the cognitive understanding of the events by creating renditions steeped in my intuition, imagination, and feelings. The text became an object of my experience as well as a metaphor for a related experience in my own life. Consciously, I grappled with life and death, sexual assault, images of betrayal, and the sounds of fear. I analyzed family dynamics during grief-stricken years of recovery. I felt, more deeply than before, the weight of time against the grain of loss. The aesthetic experience I had in reading this book of fiction created a bodily reaction and emotional sympathy set within a spiritual risk. Using my imagination, I was transported into the lives of others and discovered how their lives resonated with my own. The collective experience I came to feel grounded my sense of humanity within suffering. I am forever changed through the reading of this book. Whether as a child or as an adult, the arts have offered me opportunities to embrace my freedom to create and transform my realities.

In *The Arts and the Creation of Mind,*[2] Elliot W. Eisner argues eloquently for a wide range of arts experiences in our public schools. As the title suggests, the arts contribute to the creation of our minds, and they do so by evoking and provoking imaginative thinking that motivates individuals to work through their emotionally pervaded experiences. The arts transform our personal consciousness as well as our socially connected cultures by refining our senses and our abilities to represent our ideas. The very premise of his book is that the creation of mind is a process, an act of inquiry, a way of being and becoming in the world. For Eisner, the arts serve as models for creating the very best educational experiences possible.

Earlier, I shared how Greene defined the purpose of education. For Eisner, "education is the process of learning how to invent yourself."[3] At its very best, education, and I would dare say arts education, recognizes that "as I create, I create myself,[4] or as Eisner might say, as I learn and learn how to learn, I invent myself. This is a powerfully transforming understanding of the capacity we have as human beings to create and re-create the world anew each and every day. The power of the arts may be accepted, but how one goes about teaching the arts can be achieved in a variety of ways according to a variety of perspectives. This might seem strange to those outside of the public schools. Surely including the arts in the curriculum is a matter of having children and adolescents use a variety of materials and media, across learning modalities (e.g., visual-spatial, auditory, kinesthetic, numerical, linguistic) in developmentally appropriate ways. This seems pretty straightforward. However, there is more to this scenario. Whenever we choose to see something from one perspective, we are not seeing it from another, even within the arts. So as arts educators develop programs in the arts, they are inevitably creating them according to the way they see the arts, the way they feel empowered, and the way they feel the arts can best enhance the lives of their students. In so doing, they are creating an environment for education in the arts that emphasizes particular means and ends.

Without going into great detail, allow me to share with you eight approaches to arts education as outlined by Eisner.[5] *Discipline-based arts education* is organized around the creative, historical, critical, and aesthetic dimensions of arts practices and performances. Students learn to create artworks while also learning how to appreciate and judge exemplary works of art. Arts education taught through attention to our global *visual culture* is concerned with popular culture as well as the "fine arts" and pays particular attention to the cultural, political, and semiotic implications of the arts across our multicultural and transcultural societies. For those arts educators interested in *creative problem solving*, the field of design, exemplified by the German Bauhaus, educates students to become problem solvers for socially important tasks (e.g., product design, architecture). Arts educators concerned with releasing the human spirit through creative impulses focus their attention on *creative self-expression*. Whereas many arts education perspectives can be taught, this particular viewpoint suggests that self-expression cannot be taught, though the conditions for self-expression can be facilitated. Many who hold this viewpoint believe the arts counteract the repressive nature of most schooling practices. While several of these perspectives are concerned with the individual child developing from within, there are others primarily concerned with learning through the social milieu. Most notably, seeing *arts education as preparation for work* is an effort to justify the arts through their practical economic benefits for society. Advocates of this view suggest aesthetic experiences are nice to have but can be acquired outside of school. Arts education, on the other hand, should teach cooperation, skill development, confidence building, refinement of skills, and other attributes related to helping students become vocationally competitive. *The arts and cognitive development* is still another perspective. Educators concerned with learning how to discern subtle relationships among artistic elements in a work of art or who are interested in studying the symbol systems of various cultures are primarily interested in the cognitive character of an aesthetic education. *Using the arts to boost academic achievement* is a popular justification at the moment. Large-scale studies have been conducted in the United States[6] and in Canada[7] showing that the arts have an effect on some forms of academic achievement, in particular, computational skills in mathematics. Though these studies show that learning in the arts promotes stronger forms of engagements with learning across all subjects, the arts are justified for something other than what they are. Would we ever teach mathematics to create stronger arts programs? No. Then why would we justify teaching the arts to create stronger math programs? Arts educators aligned with this perspective have typically felt marginalized and use this justification as a last resort for advocating the inclusion of the arts in education. A closely related and popular perspective is called the *integrated arts*. Through this form of arts education, educators organize learning experiences around particular historical periods or cultural studies (e.g., World War II), design elements among the arts (e.g., rhythm), pursue interdisciplinary concepts across subject matter (e.g., patterns), and engage in problem solving within project-oriented studies in which the problem itself requires multiple disciplinary perspectives in order to arrive at a successful conclusion (e.g., designing an ecologically sustainable community). Although these eight approaches to arts education can exist as separate entities, they are more likely to be hybridized among several forms according to the beliefs of the teacher, the needs of the school and community, and the economic climate of the times. Given this, what are some principles for designing arts education programs? Eisner[8] and other leading arts educators encourage a combination of these rich approaches. I suspect most would agree with me when I say the arts should be valued for their distinctive qualities as they stimulate our need to create works of art through our personally unique forms of artistic intelligences as well as our need to interpret and assess works of art, and artful forms of inquiry and being alive, in a variety of cultures in and through time. Any arts programs attempting to nurture these attributes and qualities will go a long way toward developing the perceptual and imaginative capacities of our youth.

Encouraging the development of perceptual and imaginative capacities is an important element in arts education. Developing one's imaginative life through mindful awareness is a way for human beings to experience life in vivid detail and, arguably more important, to effect personal and social change. Greene, perhaps, says it best: "At a time of boredom, disenchantment, and passivity, few concerns seem as important to me as the concern for imagination, especially as that capacity can be released by encounters with the arts, and on whose release encounters with the arts depend."[9] Education that values the arts and nurtures learning in the arts provides an opportunity for students to never be bored, feel defeated, or succumb to a feeling of futility. Our imaginative capacities are almost magical, for they help us perceive in new ways that which is troubled, conflicted, and hopeless. Our imaginations use metaphors to awaken our sensibilities and perceptions as we connect with others through our passion and compassion. The arts call us to use images, sounds, and movements to think metaphorically about ideas in ways that may have previously seemed unconnected. This act of change, invention, metamorphosis, is what makes the arts so important to all learning activities.

LEARNING THROUGH THE ARTS

In order to truly know something, I need to "experience" knowing. This seems pretty commonsensical. Indeed, anything taught purely through rote learning denies the human need for experience. Despite this widespread understanding, rote learning is used worldwide. John Dewey,[10] an early twentieth-century philosopher and educator, advocated for learning through experience. Let's consider this: Why is it that most of us cannot retain facts we memorized for an exam? I suspect it's because we didn't experience that knowledge. When I have learned something through movement, emotional response, soulful attachment, or perceptual engagement, I have always retained my new knowledge. It stays with me. It means something to me. I understand it in very concrete ways. Schools and the curriculum found within our schools have something to learn from the arts and from venues that celebrate and challenge the arts because the arts embrace knowing through experience.

A recent Canadian study concludes that when students are involved in learning activities that include the arts, their mathematics achievement scores increase,[11] regardless of whether the arts were integrated into the actual mathematics activities. The nature of this finding is important. Arts education is not provided at the expense of mathematics. In other words, more mathematics instruction does not necessarily yield higher mathematics scores. The recent research suggests the opposite: A balanced curriculum, which includes the arts, actually strengthens *all* learning. Students engaged with their own learning are experiencing their own knowledge creation, discovering their own passions, and creating their own minds.

What can we learn *through* the arts? Because the arts permeate our existence as human beings, they are valued across all learning experiences. Let's see if their breadth and magnitude can even been summarized. The arts provide (a) pleasurable, sentimental, inspirational, informative, and surprising experiences; (b) far-reaching economic, social, and political influences; and (c) insights into society through skillful accomplishments, historical interpretations, and cultural characterizations. The arts also (a) communicate by generating, recording, and transmitting ideas; (b) act as cultural sources and resources by helping people form identities and recognize accomplishments while also destabilizing practices that are problematic; and (c) enhance our lives by making the ineffable tangible. In very general terms, the arts contribute to our personal efficacy as well as our interconnectedness with all living and spiritual entities. Does this summary say it all? Hardly. The arts always represent more than what can be said. We grasp understanding through the arts by seeing more, hearing more, feeling more, and being more than can ever be said or summarized. That is why learning through the arts is so seductive. The arts offer a vehicle for learning that permeates every aspect of our being and offers opportunities for personal and cultural transformations throughout the process. Learning through the arts provides a basis for experiential learning that is durable in and through time. By durable, I mean learning that I will remember—learning that lasts.

When I was in grade six, I studied Egypt as one of the important ancient civilizations on earth. To this day, I remember the murals we drew that represented the life and times of the people, how they dressed, the jewelry they wore, and the customs they had. I remember the patterns on their elegant headdresses, the sashes holding up their robes. I fondly think of the mummies we attempted to make while learning about their funerals and tombs. The ingenuity and skill required to create the pyramids have remained a wondrous miracle of the human spirit in my mind. Every time I see images of Egypt now I am transported back to that time when I learned how other cultures are valued for their differences. How did I learn that? I dare say it wasn't because someone told me to believe this but rather because I internalized this understanding. I came to appreciate the aesthetic appeal of their golden adornments, the commitment they had toward their gods, and the pride they held for their cultural traditions. I learned this through my own brief engagement with their ideas by visualizing, moving through, reading, and imagining who they were and what I could learn from them. Some day I hope to travel to Egypt to experience its contemporary culture, because deep down inside of me a spark of mystery still exists. As I reflect upon this and other experiences, I recognize that integration across subjects is a worthy goal in order to make learning durable. However, I also recognize that just as the arts benefit other subjects, so too do other subjects benefit the arts. They all work hand in hand through an emphasis upon aesthetic understanding, or a "deep engagement with the sensory experience of the material world."[12] In this way, the arts offer a profound opening for experiencing the world that cognitive detachment dismisses. We understand ourselves, our cultures, and our histories through our sensory and aesthetic experiences. "Work in the arts is not only a way of creating performances and products; it is a way of creating our lives by expanding our consciousness, shaping our dispositions, satisfying our quest for meaning, establishing contact with others, and sharing our culture."[13]

There are many occasions when teachers need and appreciate the involvement of artists in the delivery of integrative experiences. Artist residencies are becoming more and more popular within our schools. Although teaching artists can never replace arts teachers, partnerships between the two can yield exciting forms of collaboration. Even so, as accountability concerns are considered, administrators and teachers look to artist residencies for their match between the curriculum and standards set by their districts and boards and, ultimately, to the results they produce. Arts organizations responsible for the residencies are increasingly interested in working with teachers, administrators, and arts specialists in order to meet the needs of the schools and to ensure the success of the programs. Artist residencies tend to have three instructional purposes: to encourage students' interest in the arts, to support the development of students' knowledge and skills within the arts while integrating the arts into other subjects, and to provide professional development for teachers endeavoring to teach the arts.[14] Although some residencies might concentrate on one of these purposes, it is more likely that several purposes will be met. These experiences are expressly designed to provide learning in and through the arts, but they are also designed for *learning about the arts.* When artists spend time in schools, working with students and teachers, as well as performing their art forms, they are effectively teaching others about their work. I personally feel that learning through the arts is closely related to learning about the arts. Intense experiences with artists always seem to immerse students and teachers into projects that work across domains of learning and culminate with products or performances. In my own research into an artist residency program called *Learning through the Arts* ™, my research colleagues and I discovered that the foremost reason teachers and students are attracted to such a program has to do with the holistic nature of the arts themselves.[15] Even though teachers wanted to use the arts as a way for integrating subject matter content across disciplines, the most noticeable integration was far more foundational, yet elusive. Everyone wanted to have integrative experiences because they were learning holistically.[16] Put simply, they were involving their minds, bodies, emotions, and spirits. They engaged every part of their being in learning. Holistic learning[17] is essential for all learning, and the easiest way to ensure that learning is holistic is to embrace learning in *and* through the arts.[18] Once teachers and students are committed to learning holistically,[19] commitment can grow to an exploration of concepts from various disciplines in order to probe for intellectual depth.

Although learning holistically through the arts is certainly attractive to many, the greatest gains that might be realized are with disadvantaged students from a lower socioeconomic status (SES). James S. Catterall, Richard Chapleau, and John Iwanaga conducted a large study of over 25,000 students over ten years and analyzed the differences between socioeconomic groups. All students experienced great benefits, but they were especially noticeable for the low SES students, who experienced higher academic achievement and better attitudes toward school if they were involved in the arts long-term. "For low SES students, 43.8% of students highly involved in the arts scored in the top two quartiles in reading, compared to 28.6% for students with little or no arts engagement. When the entire student sample was considered, 70.9% of high arts students scored in the top 2 quartiles in reading, compared to 46.3% of the low arts students."[20] Catterall, Chapleau, and Iwanaga also found low SES students were twice as likely to be involved in the arts than other students scoring in the top quartiles. These results clearly show that the arts have a profound impact upon student learning, particularly for students who likely have little exposure to the arts outside of school. Learning through the arts has far-reaching benefits for all students in all subjects across the curriculum. Yet we cannot lose sight of the fact that the arts, as subjects themselves, have distinctive histories and have made distinctive cultural contributions that make learning in and about the arts just as important, if not more so, than learning through the arts.

LEARNING FROM THE ARTS

Education as a whole has much to learn from engagement in the arts. Learning in the arts and learning through the arts are both important to a vital educational program for all students. Yet there is one more twist of phrase to be considered: *learning from the arts.* What can the arts teach us about learning that will inspire excitement, passion, even a love affair with learning itself? The teaching of art, or for that matter the teaching of any subject, must be about the artistry of teaching. Eisner says, "By artistry I mean a form of practice informed by the imagination that employs technique to select and organize expressive qualities to achieve ends that are aesthetically satisfying."[21] As artists of teaching, teachers learn to see and reflect upon their practices in an effort to refine their work and to grasp the magnitude of the work they have created. The very best teachers approach their practices with artistry as if life itself were a work of art. It is with this idea that all of us can learn a great deal from the arts. Metaphorically speaking, living is a form of curriculum. Living becomes a curriculum full of life when we enact and embody an artful engagement with life itself. We create our futures, we create our minds, we create our cultures, and we create our experiences. To assume a learning disposition throughout life is to accept that, through learning, we invent ourselves personally and collectively.

Let me transport you into my studio for a brief excursion into my artistic life before I illustrate for you how I attempt to apply what I have learned from the arts to my teaching and my being. Last year I painted over twenty paintings around the theme of trees and, particularly, forests. I live on the edge of a magnificent cedar forest and when I am not consumed by the forest, I am often drawn to the rich variety of trees that line the boulevards. For quite some time I collected photographs during my walks through the forest and the groves of trees. During those occasions, I was consumed with noticing the relationships between the light filtering through the trees and the shadows on the forest floor, the connections among each distinctive green (emerald, chartreuse, lime, olive, etc.) and its placement in the setting, and the relationships between clusters of nearly perfect trees alongside a few tortured, fallen trees. I reflected upon the time of day, the crispness of the air, the duration of my immersion, and the variety of trails I pursued. Each time I walked, I knew I would find internal satisfaction as I found the freedom to contemplate and the time to imagine. Returning from these walks always felt like a spiritual aesthetic awakening. They were experiences I wanted to explore in other ways. As a painter, I chose to use the photos as visual studies for exploring my personal experiences with the forest. Through artistic inquiry, I sought to explore my emotional responses to these occasions by painting not just my memories but my relationships and experiences of being in the presence of these majestic entities. With each painting, I started by considering a photograph, noticing particular qualities in the images before responding emotionally. Then I let the image go so I could begin a new relationship with each painting. Working with paint and paper, I began to look beyond the taken-for-granted surface views and went to the underbrush, or the surfaces below the immediate surfaces. I built up layer upon layer of color and texture, light and shadow, shape and form. I was resolving a visual problem through dialogical relationships with each emerging image. Seldom, if ever, did the final images look "just like" the photograph. They were never intended to, though one could see a likeness or similarity. Rather, new experiences grew out of the collection of walks and photographs. These new experiences helped me to savor my experiences, to feel fully present in creating new understandings of myself and the world, and to contribute to the joy of others as they took in the visuality of each painting for themselves. Painting for me is all about joy, even though there are plenty of times in which I am frustrated when I have overpainted a section, and I can't seem to return to the magic of what I had moments earlier. There are other times when I am not certain of the intention of each piece— what is it that I am trying to convey? I have to work through each of these frustrations, and as I do, an aesthetic dialogue unfolds and I realize a new conversation has begun. I am learning something new again.

So what does this have to do with learning from the arts? As I reflect upon my walks as artistic events, just as my painting experiences are artistic performances, I find myself contemplating the qualities of what it means to be engaged in artistic inquiry and an aesthetic way of life. During these experiences, I learned and relearned there isn't one right answer. *How* something is communicated is just as important as *what* is communicated. I came to appreciate how my imagination transforms my understanding in unique and surprising ways and how my aesthetic sensibilities define my quality of life. I metaphorically came to understand how being purposefully flexible during my painting can also be used to enhance my work and play so I am not tied to particular results. I learned I am interested in relationships, not just among trees, or between colors, but among people. I learned to slow down and notice the particular in the taken-for-granted. Lingering in an experience becomes an act of joy, satisfaction, and humble appreciation, for the inherently rich qualities embedded in being experientially present. My artistic way of being reminded me of what life can be if I open the way for its unfolding vitality.

As I have reflected upon ideas like this over my career,[22] I have attempted to enact my teaching as an art form. At times, this has meant paying attention to the rhythms of each day and the lessons within, while being careful to attend to patterns of interactions and spatial relationships between individuals as well as between individuals and objects. I've attended to the colors and textures of my clothing, as well as to the colors in each classroom and the placement of images on the walls. I've become more attuned to the tonal qualities in my voice during discussions, debates, and casual conversations and particularly during the storytelling nature of my teaching activities. I allow my body to move through each classroom in ways that create interest in each lesson. I attempt to embody the freedom of movement I hope students will pursue. I have come to appreciate that lessons do not always go as planned but that what is more important is the quality of the dialogue, the learning environment, and the conditions for learning. These qualities have often sparked my attention to the ineffable, to that quality of experience that is difficult to talk about yet is easily recognizable by all who experience it.

Performing teaching as an art form calls teachers into a space of artistic work many seldom consider. Teachers who attend to their practice as an art form are often viewed as the teachers we remember years later, those teachers whose practices and processes make just as much difference, if not more, than the actual products of learning. People follow passion. Everyone wants to love what he or she does and who he or she is. When we experience teachers who are passionate about their own learning and their work, as learners we find ourselves motivated to learn, for we want what our teachers have. I remember teachers whose lessons inspired me. I remember how I felt when I anxiously wanted to learn not only in their classes but also outside of school when I could pursue the topics in my own way. I remember their joyful presence, their excitement for learning and teaching. I also remember much of what I learned in their classes. I don't know if they thought of themselves as artful teachers, but to me they were artful teachers inspiring me through an artful curriculum.

Learning in, through, and from the arts are important conceptions for the design of curriculum experiences in any learning environment at any age level. The possibilities for learning are endless if one considers the magnitude of these ways of learning. As I reflect upon treasured experiences in my studio or my many long walks in nature or my lingering visits with works of art, I am struck by the ways the arts have caused me to keep learning out of the sheer joy and excitement I feel for learning. These experiences might be my own, but we all have experiences that can be viewed, created, or interpreted through artistic or aesthetic lenses. Our public schools are important learning communities for providing the conditions for all students to experience the very best education by learning in, through, and from the arts. Schools that partner with artistic venues, such as galleries and museums, as well as artists, musicians, dancers, actors, poets, and storytellers, recognize the value of the arts as being larger than any one talented teacher. The arts belong to all of us, exist in multiple forms within our communities and our society at large, and should be considered essential to a balanced curriculum. After all, public schools are places where students can flourish as they realize their full human potential to think, feel, intuit, imagine, and act, as they engage in an artful curriculum, a curriculum full of life, a curriculum that embraces what it means to be humanly present.

— 2 —

Old Wine in a New Bottle: Twentieth-Century Social Studies in a Twenty-First-Century World

PERRY M. MARKER

Social studies educators at the beginning of the twenty-first century are at a crossroads very similar to their social studies colleagues at the turn of the twentieth century. The period from the 1870s to the 1920s in American culture saw the most dramatic changes in political economy, technology, and schooling that have ever taken place in American history. This period saw the emergence of a large urban society; immigration from Asia, southern and eastern Europe, and far-reaching developments in industrialism, monopolistic capitalism, and school reform.

The period from the late 1980s to the present has been described as the "information age." Rapid technological, economic, and political development has brought us the Internet, cell phone technology, personal computers, and instant global communications, to name but a few innovations. At the beginning of the twenty-first century, there is intense pressure to reform social studies education to meet our changing social, political, and economic demands. Social studies educators are in danger of reproducing the curriculum of 100 years ago, adopting and accepting an unyielding history-based and corporate-influenced curriculum that renders us resistant to change in our information age. Maintaining and sustaining a century-old, history-centered social studies curriculum is akin, in effect, to putting the same stale, old wine from the nineteenth-century *industrial* age into the shiny new bottles of the twenty-first-century *information* age.

SOCIAL STUDIES AND ITS INDUSTRIAL-AGE ORIGINS

For almost a century, the social studies curriculum has been relatively unchanged, yet, ironically, social studies has an identity crisis. With little agreement on its nature and purpose, the dominant perspective regarding social studies in the twentieth century rested with historians. This group of scholars has had the greatest influence, in fact, on what has happened in social studies classrooms. During the twentieth century, the social studies curriculum remained somewhat static and discipline-bound, its scholars trapped in what Barr, Barth, and Shermis called an endless maze, laboring "to project some order or pattern on the chaos around them."[1]

Amid this chaos, however, there is, at least, some order. There is general agreement, for instance, among social studies educators that the 1916 report of the National Education Association (NEA) Committee on Social Studies had a profound impact on the social studies curriculum. It was this group of educators, heavily influenced by the emergence of the industrial state, that produced the scope and sequence of courses that still define the contemporary social studies curriculum:

Grade K: Self, School, Community, Home
Grade 1: Families
Grade 2: Neighborhoods
Grade 3: Communities
Grade 4: State History, Geographic Regions
Grade 5: U.S. History
Grade 6: Western Hemisphere
Grade 7: World Geography or World History
Grade 8: U.S. History
Grade 9: Civics
Grade 10: World History
Grade 11: U.S. History
Grade 12: American Government

Yet few would argue that *society* has not changed since 1916. From transportation to technology, from social life to sexual mores, life at the turn of the twenty-first century would be unrecognizable to those living in 1916. Incredibly, during the same period, the social studies curriculum has remained virtually unaltered. Contemporary social studies is ensnared in a history-centered, discipline-bound, "nonpartisan," moribund curriculum. This century-old social studies curriculum was designed for a particular time and society, immersed in an ethic influenced by a burgeoning industrial age. The social studies was developed in and at a time when education was evolving from a century of rural, one-room schools to a modern, public system of education that supported a rising and powerful industrial-based economy. The development of a system of public education was heavily influenced by powerful businessmen who were leaders of U.S. industrialization. The spread of public school education in an age of industry enabled a whole generation of workers to become the literate labor force of the emerging manufacturing economy.

The creation of a factory-like system of public education in the twentieth century was not accidental.[2] Educators such as Franklin Bobbitt championed the application of F. W. Taylor's scientific management techniques to education and schooling. As Herbert Kliebard has stated, "he [Bobbitt] provided professional educators [and businessmen] in the twentieth century with the concepts and metaphors—indeed, the very language—that were needed to create an aura of technical expertise without which the hegemony of professional educators could not be established."[3] These forces were coalescing to exert an influence over the public schools and the social studies curriculum that would last throughout the twentieth century.

During the late nineteenth and early twentieth centuries, history was considered to be the central social studies discipline around which all others were organized. The emerging fields of economics, sociology, and political science were incorporated into university history departments. Barr, Barth, and Shermis have cogently described the influence the field of history exerted on the emergence of social studies at the end of the nineteenth century: "It is . . . understandable that the first committees making recommendations for public school social studies were comprised [sic] primarily of historians [and titans of industry] and were associated with the American Historical Association. The American Historical Association was organized in 1884, and one of its first goals was to promote the study of history in the public schools."[4] Historians argued that their discipline was the great repository of classical ideas and the ideals of humankind. This knowledge, defined by historians, was deemed essential for citizens to learn if they were to become effective and knowledgeable citizens. Learning the factual knowledge of history would "discipline" the mind.[5]

The decade of the 1920s marked the first time the term *social studies* was formally used. In 1921, the National Council for the Social Studies (NCSS) was founded by Earle Rugg as part of the American Historical Association (AHA). In 1935, Edgar B. Wesley broke the NCSS off from the AHA and coined what is perhaps the most well-known—yet most controversial and least agreed upon— definition of social studies to date: "The social studies are the social sciences simplified for pedagogical purposes."[6]

Stanley and Nelson[7] have described social studies as going through its most significant period of reform during the 1960s and 1970s. Many new materials and curriculum proposals were developed that attempted to integrate the social science disciplines into an interdisciplinary social studies education. These materials did not have history as their focus, but unfortunately they were not widely implemented by social studies teachers in the classroom. Most social studies teachers continued to rely on history-centered, chronologically oriented textbooks that were based on the fundamental principles of the 1916 NEA report.

During these times of reform, Stanley and Nelson report that eminent scholars such as Jerome Bruner were beginning to question the value of studying the structure of the disciplines (i.e., history) in the absence of the study of "pressing social issues."[8] Larry Cuban,[9] in a review of research regarding the history of teaching social studies, argued that during this period most changes, such as grouping strategies, interdisciplinary instruction, an emphasis on social issues, and a sensitivity to ethnic and diversity issues, were and have been still incremental rather than fundamental to how social studies is taught. Cuban concluded that what emerges out of social studies curriculum since the early 1900s are dominant patterns of teaching steeped in history-based, chronological textbook instruction with a smaller number of predominantly elementary school teachers who combine teacher-centered instruction with student discussion, debate, and role playing. Reinforcing Cuban's analysis, the Carnegie Forum on Education and the Economy issued a report that recommended that, "the focus of schooling [and social studies teaching] must shift from teaching to learning, from the passive acquisition of facts and routines to the active application of ideas to problems."[10]

A specific example is illustrative of Cuban's analysis. Jane Bernard-Powers[11] stated that gender issues have had minimal impact on the social studies curriculum. Bernard-Powers posits that there are profound "gendered issues" that belong in the social studies curriculum, such as teen pregnancy and death from gunshots among African-American males. But in spite of these pressing issues, the social studies curriculum has been slow to address issues of gender. Nel Noddings discusses the current state of affairs regarding feminism and gender in the social studies: "Feminism's initial effect on social studies changes the surface to some degree: more female faces and names now appear in standard texts. . . . Women have gained access to a world once exclusively maintained for men. On the negative side, social studies as a regular school subject has been flooded with trivia and is threatened by continuing fragmentation. Further . . . the women's genuine contributions have been glossed over because they do not fit the male model of achievement."[12]

At the turn of the twentieth century, the content of history classes included historical facts arranged in chronological order, incorporating lists of dates, names, and significant events related to political, diplomatic, and military history. Students were drilled to learn historical information through memorization, the goal being to provide students with the historical "facts" necessary to function as good citizens.

Significant elements of this early twentieth-century history-centered organization of the secondary social studies curriculum can still be found at the beginning of the twenty-first century. States such as California, Alabama, Virginia, Texas, and Massachusetts have created history-centered standards.[13] The curricula endorsed by these states have, as their primary focus, historical contents that are driven by fact-based, yearlong chronological survey courses that emphasize traditional. These twenty-first-century curricula still retain as their fundamental elements educational thinking that is over 100 years old.

In spite of research-based evidence to the contrary, contemporary critics of social studies education[14] have lamented the displacement of teacher-centered chronological history with social studies during the course of the twentieth century. These reformers believe that research supports the idea that expert problem solvers (effective citizens) are best defined "not in the skills they possess, but rather in their stores of available, relevant, previously acquired knowledge. . . . This store of historical and civic knowledge [facts, dates, names] has important consequences for the development of citizenship."[15] Diane Ravitch is even more direct: "Today's field of social studies is rife with confusion. Its open-ended nature, its very lack of definition, invites capture by ideologues and by those who seek to impose their views in the classroom. This too can happen in the teaching of history, but at least students may encounter contrasting versions of history from different teachers and textbooks, as well as programs on television. . . ."[16]

In other words, these "reformers" believe that history is getting short shrift in today's schools. More significant, this line of reasoning asserts that educators who do not center their instruction upon historical methods and facts from the leading ideas of Western culture are ideologues bent upon indoctrinating students into an antidemocratic, unpatriotic social studies curriculum. These and other like-minded social studies reformers are seemingly determined in sustaining and maintaining the history-centered, chronological, fact-based, teacher-centered curriculum constituted by and characterized in late nineteenth- and early twentieth-century educational thought. Despite Ravitch's argument that history has been displaced in the social studies, a close examination of the last 100 years of research in the socials studies by scholars such as Hullfish and Smith, Stake and Easley, Wiley, Shaver, Davis and Helburn, and Ross strongly indicates that history instruction is as popular as ever and is marked by a common pattern of teacher-centered instruction.[17]

Perhaps the most often heard and repeated criticism of social studies is that our students are "historically illiterate" and are losing their "civic memory." Critics of social studies have assailed the social studies curriculum for failing to teach students important facts. They claim that students just do not know important things, such as the date of our American independence, who our sixteenth president was, and so on. Richard Paxton, in an analysis of surveys of students' historical knowledge, found that the "bulk of evidence suggests that [American] students today know at least as much history as their parents and grandparents did—and probably more."[18] Even more interesting is that students' historical knowledge is at the same level as their knowledge of other disciplines. Students' scores on surveys of knowledge in literature and science were *lower* than social studies scores. Perhaps the problem is not with the students' knowledge as much as it is with the surveys themselves. These surveys spread the false notion that the biggest problem facing social studies students today is the retention of fragmented, decontextualized, historical facts. As for critics who want social studies to return to the "good old days" of teaching historical "facts," the research indicates that the "good old days" are simply and merely a myth.[19]

"SOCIAL STUDIES SUCKS" AND OTHER ENDURING PROBLEMS

At the beginning of the twenty-first century, it needs to be said, and to be said often, that many exemplary social studies programs exist and thousands of dedicated social studies educators are doing an outstanding job of teaching. If we were to listen solely to critics of education, be they conservative or liberal (often nearly indistinguishable), we might question whether social studies students are learning anything worthwhile at all and, as a result, if the foundations of our democratic society were about to go to wrack and ruin. My point is that it is not these hard-working social studies teachers but, rather, it is the antiquated curriculum of social studies as it exists in its broadest terms that is and should be our focus.

Students do not fondly remember the history-centered social studies curriculum. John Goodlad[20] asked students about the importance of social studies as compared with other traditional school subjects. Goodlad reported that social studies at the secondary level ranked below English, mathematics, and vocational education and was in a dead heat, in terms of importance, with science; junior high and senior high school students viewed social studies to be the least useful subject in their lives.

Students generally find history-centered social studies content uninteresting. I recently asked my university-based, preservice, social studies methods students to conduct an informal survey of middle and high school students about their attitudes toward social studies. The methods students were told to take care not to survey any students in their social studies classes. Of the more than 150 students interviewed across three middle schools and four high schools, not one student listed social studies as his or her favorite subject. Many students found social studies to be irrelevant to their lives, and many of their comments included the phrase "social studies sucks." Although these results are unquestionably unscientific, such candid comments are the cause of much concern among prospective social studies teachers.

In the past century, tens of millions of students have endured a history-centered social studies curriculum. In many states the school year is mandated to be 180 days long. School days last around seven hours, excluding lunch, beginning approximately eight in the morning and ending at three o'clock in the afternoon. If a student spends, conservatively speaking, 30 to 50 minutes each day in social studies classroom instruction and attends social studies class every day (subtracting two weeks for testing), the student will have logged roughly 90 to 125 hours immersed in a history-centered social studies curriculum each school year.

During this time, many of the activities that students face daily are with control, and not learning, in mind. Activities such as reading a chapter in a textbook and answering the questions at the end of the chapter is a time-worn, mind-numbing activity that can quickly extinguish the excitement for learning social studies in even the most motivated students. During many of the hours spent in history-centered social studies classes, students are learning less than ever, and the skills of interpreting graphs, charts, and tables are not being emphasized.

Goodlad described the elementary social studies curriculum as "amorphous." At the secondary level, most students sit in general, survey-oriented courses where world and American history are taught in one year. In the secondary social studies classroom, "topics of study become removed from their intrinsically human character, reduced to the dates and places readers will recall memorizing for tests."[21]

For the past 100 years, much of social studies instruction has been limited to using the standard textbook. Teachers use the textbook because it helps them neatly organize history into "bite-sized" teaching units for the classes they teach. However, textbooks are steeped in a fact-based, chronological presentation of history that is disconnected from and irrelevant to the lives of the students who use them. As many as two-thirds of all social studies teachers rely on a history or an American government textbook and use it as their dominant teaching resource. Unfortunately, most of us who have read a social studies textbook know it as anything but a "page-turning" experience. In fact, it is highly recommend as a cure for insomnia.

Learning history via a textbook is uninteresting at best and misleading at worst. James Loewen, in a comprehensive content analysis of American history textbooks, *Lies My Teacher Told Me*, has stated that textbooks give students no compelling reason to like or appreciate social studies.[22] Textbooks are generally unscholarly, political documents that attempt to inspire patriotism without encouraging students or teachers to ask questions about the historical issues between their covers. Loewen asserts that history textbooks provide a "rhetoric of certainty" that promotes historical "truth" and discourages critical analysis of the events, facts, and issues included in them. Loewen found that textbooks supply irrelevant, erroneous details and often omit pivotal facts about marginalized peoples. While supporters of textbooks argue that textbooks have improved dramatically in recent years, textbooks are failing now, more than ever, to connect a chronological, history-centered curriculum to the lives of students. The more we use history textbooks as the primary source of information in social studies classes, the more likely that students will receive a social studies education that is incomplete, incorrect, and uninspired.

Gary K. Hart, former secretary of education for the state of California, recently returned to the classroom teaching ninth-grade history. As secretary of education, he helped implement a history-based curriculum and wrote guidelines on what textbooks to use. As a social studies teacher, Hart has abandoned a chronological approach to teaching history and moved to a nonchronological, intense study of selected topics. Since his conversion from a history-centered curriculum, Hart believes that social studies teachers need more freedom to innovate in the classroom.[23]

With teachers focusing generally on history and government, and using textbooks as the main instructional vehicle, there is precious little interdisciplinary teaching being conducted and little focus on relevant social issues and themes. History is taught as though all students were destined to be historians. This should not be a surprise. University history departments are filled with professors who give lecture after lecture to their students. A walk past the classrooms of many professors of history will lead one to wonder whether historians have yet discovered that the chairs in which their students are sitting in neat rows listening to their lectures are no longer bolted to the floor.

After having been subjected to years of lectures, eager history majors enter the public school classrooms armed with their lecture notes and a history textbook, ready to teach in the style in which they have been taught. These prospective social studies teachers have themselves been students for twelve years in public schools and four or more years in the universities. They have been passive recipients of hour upon hour of history-based, teacher-centered instruction. Sixteen years of history-centered instruction is difficult for many, and often impossible for some, prospective teachers to "unlearn." More significant, images of the "great lecturer" who holds students spellbound for hours while spinning his or her historical yarns is a powerful and seductive educational icon. Even though most of us have seen very few, if any, of these icons in action, their aura is very alluring.

The fact is, in most public school and university history classrooms, virtually no attention is paid to the relationship between and among the social science disciplines. For over 100 years, history has been taught in our schools and universities without an interdisciplinary focus on the social sciences. Though the term *social studies* is used to describe the history-centered curriculum taught in elementary, middle, and high schools, the interdisciplinary focus that the term implies is, ironically, rarely taught. Perhaps Henry Ford meant to say: "History *without social studies* is bunk."

TEACHING TOWARD THE FUTURE

Teaching toward the future requires that we examine critically the values and those traditions of the past (e.g., small schools, community-centered lifestyles, communities of learners) that have been extinguished by the industrial age. These traditions could help us determine how we can build a democracy that supports and sustains the social, political, environmental, and economic well-being of *all* citizens on the planet. Concepts such as oppression, marginalization, exploitation, and violence must be studied in the social studies curriculum as a means by which to interrogate various interpretations of citizenship and citizenship education, as well as a mechanism through which we can uncover both oppressive and antioppressive possibilities—a point of view that signals the limits, and even obsolescence, of a twentieth-century Deweyan perspective toward citizenship and democracy.[24]

During the past 100 years, social studies has given a conceptual and moral legitimacy to the values and ideals born in and embodied by the Industrial Revolution. A social studies curriculum that teaches toward the future would seriously question the historical imperatives that so often have ignored and obliterated cultural traditions—ideas that once were essential to one's survival in the industrial age. Competition, which breeds a lack of trust among individuals, mixed with heavy doses of rugged individualism, have rendered extinct forms of knowledge and networks of support that can provide healthy and positive alternatives to our total reliance on capitalism.[25] If social studies educators are to avoid becoming irrelevant in the contemporary world, then they—we—must take efforts to move our curriculum from a history-centered focus to an interdisciplinary, social studies focus. This, of course, is easier said than done. It will not be easy to change 100 years of curricular practice, nor will such change necessarily be widely embraced.

In the following sections, I briefly outline four issues that social studies educators might address to help teach toward the future: (1) celebrating curricular diversity in the social studies; (2) questioning the purpose of being nonpartisan, or neutral, as a social studies educator; (3) challenging the existence of history-centered, chronologically based survey courses; and (4) widening the modes of assessment of the socials studies curriculum. While, overall, these are modest proposals, I hope that we, as social studies educators, will begin the debate as to how the social studies curriculum must change to deal with the challenges of the twenty-first century.

CURRICULAR DIVERSITY IN THE SOCIAL STUDIES: END THE DEBATE

Social studies educators need to spend the next decade discussing new approaches for the social studies curriculum that could be introduced into public school practice. If the turn of the twentieth century is any indication, the decisions we make for social studies may result in setting a curricular agenda for the remainder of the twenty-first century. But rather than trying to install a specific agenda as we did in the industrial age, perhaps an even more significant outcome from such a conversation is the idea that there may be many ways to conceptualize the social studies curriculum, rather than a singular set of state or national standards. Embracing true diversity regarding what and how we teach via social studies must be a core value. Rather than seeking the "best way" to teach social studies, we need to examine how what and how we teach are *different*, not simply (or inherently) better.

In our culture of debate, differences in and of opinion are largely adversarial, a conflict among opposing camps. Debate implies arguing a position, attacking the opposition's weak points. It promises a winner and a loser. Rather than debate, it is time to have an open dialogue that transforms, extends, and enriches the social studies curriculum. We need to learn from, and not be defeated by, our differences. Rather than positioning ourselves to preserve a particular vision of the social studies curriculum, we need to discuss things openly, to share and learn from our differences. It is time to embrace the diversity in our field that we believe (or at least frequently claim to believe) is essential to democratic society.

THE MYTH OF NEUTRALITY

For decades, there has been an underlying assumption that social studies teachers should be politically neutral in the classroom. At first glance, the assertion that teachers can and should remain neutral sounds reasonable, logical, and necessary. Unfortunately, the notion of a teacher's, or any person's, "neutrality" on a critical social issue is simply an impossible goal. Anyone who has spent any time at all in a classroom observing student behavior clearly understands that students are able to pinpoint a teacher's political and social beliefs in minutes—even when the teacher is striving to be "objective" or "neutral." Ask any student about his or her teacher's political beliefs and the student will recite them by chapter and verse. Political beliefs are, all too often, the "unspoken" but highly visible subtexts of a teacher's classroom. These political subtexts encourage students who are seeking to gain the teacher's attention, praise, and high grades to engage in a sophisticated "dance," in which they spend their time in the classroom figuring out what ideas the teacher wants to hear and how best to repeat and restate those ideas. Under the guise of being "neutral," a teacher's opinions are seldom, if ever, questioned or thoroughly discussed; when they are, they often are simply considered to be the source of last resort to be remembered and regurgitated on the next examination. To deny that this exists in today's classrooms is putting one's head into the sand.

An honest, open classroom discussion regarding controversial social issues should involve many divergent points of view, interrogating both the teacher's and the students' opinions. To cast issues simply as having only one or two simplistic perspectives—often belonging to the teacher—is to encourage students to engage in reductionist, fragmented judgments that discourage critical thinking. Students need to be challenged to question the teacher's and their own points of view. In order to do this effectively, the teacher needs to provide information that represents multiple points of view. More important, when students seem to be set on a specific point of view, the teacher needs to argue an opposing viewpoint—especially when the students' view supports a teacher's known political beliefs.

Teachers should never insist that students repeat or blindly adopt the ideas that they themselves believe; to do so would be to engage in antidemocratic teaching techniques that dangerously threaten personal liberty and our democratic way of life. Teachers must encourage their students to question ideas regardless of their origin. Simply stated, students who purport to think critically have a responsibility to become familiar with many points of view and be able to vigorously argue ideas they do not support as if they were their own.

It is essential to encourage discussion about "hot button" political issues if the curriculum is to have any relevance for students. Schools exist to promote and support thoughtful citizens who practice critical thinking. In our society, continuing the myth that teachers can, and should, remain neutral in the classroom does not support the noble and important goal of teaching for democracy.

SURVEY CLASSES: A MIND-NUMBING CURRICULUM

Much of the contemporary social studies curriculum is delivered in what are referred to as "survey classes." We have all experienced a world history or American history class that is taught over the duration of a semester or school year. Most would agree that it is difficult to teach the history of the world or of America in one semester or academic year. Survey classes are a very common way to organize the social studies curriculum. These classes are designed and taught using a teacher-centered, chronological, textbook-driven ordering of the curriculum. The dilemma with survey classes is that there is an impossible amount of information "to be covered" given the time period of the course. When taught using a chronological approach, much of the information at the end of the class—the time period that is most recent and is often closest to the learners—is not addressed or is quickly dismissed, further distancing the curriculum from the lives of the students.

From the point of view of learning theory, what commonly results in survey classes is a shallow, surface-feature approach to concept development. Experiences in these classes are devoid of a rich and deep set of experiences or sustained study likely to instill an interest in the topics being discussed, or a sense of moving from novice to experts as learners. These classes do not ensure understanding and appreciation of the topics on which they focus. More significant, survey courses tend to remove social studies topics from their intrinsically human character. There is a sameness to these courses and a detachment from real people. In-depth inquiry is obliterated by a tidal wave of mind-numbing facts, names, dates, and places.

Social studies curricula that are not based on this survey mentality could have as their focus an interdisciplinary approach. Classes that might move away from a survey-based structure would support decision making and form a unified, interdisciplinary social studies curriculum. Instead of building social studies on the discipline of history, imagine semester-long social studies courses titled *War through the Ages: Its Impact on Political and Social Thought*, or *From Greece to Gandhi: Democracy and Its Practice*, or *Race, Power, and American Society, Social Class, and Privilege*, or *Ideology, Government, and Economic Life*, or *Bombs and Borders: Nationalism and International Relations*, or *Philosophy and Ethics in Democratic Life*, or *Media and You: On Becoming a Critical Citizen*, or *Alternatives to Democracy: Utopian Visions or Competing Ideologies?*, or *Technology, Society, and the Environment*, or *The School: An Institution of Social Equality or an Instrument of Reproduction?* These classes provide (or could provide) an alternative to the *History of the United States 1865–2000*, or *History of the Ancient World* or *Western Civilization*.

A contemporary social studies curriculum that moves away from an industrial-age-survey approach structures knowledge as continuously recreated, recycled, and shared by teachers and students. This curriculum encourages students to view knowledge critically and helps them build on their social knowledge and skills. Survey classes are irrelevant in today's world. Students need a social studies curriculum that can help them make sense of, and provide connections with and to, their world. If students are to become citizens of the world, then we must provide opportunities in the social studies curriculum to question, make decisions about, and transform their societies.

TOO MANY TESTS

Social studies as a field of learning is conducive to the development of decision making and reasoning skills. Students learn such things as deriving concepts from related events, testing new hypotheses based upon another set of circumstances, exploring causal relationships, drawing conclusions from an array of data, addressing and analyzing a divergent set of perspectives related to an issue or issues, and asking questions about concerns of "fact." The assessments used in many social studies classrooms, however, reflect a quite different set of learning priorities. Assessments rarely require skills other than the recall and feedback of memorized information.

The preponderance of assessments in the social studies curriculum involve listening, reading textbooks, completing workbooks and worksheets, and taking written quizzes and examinations. Matching, multiple-choice, fill-in-the-blank, and true-or-false test items, mixed with the occasional essay or short-answer question, are the dominant forms of assessment. Repetition and forced memorization are the teacher's "coins of the realm" for social studies curriculum and instruction. In such a curriculum, there is little time available for sharing ideas or for teachers and students learning from one another. Tests here measure only a small sample of students' intellectual abilities. Creative and critical thinking is deemphasized or eliminated from the curriculum. Sitting for sometimes hours at a time while selecting recall-based answers to the ticking of the clock is an assessment mode that has been with us for hundreds of years. In this mode, students learn little about the content of the social studies curriculum, but they do learn other things.

These tests prepare students quite nicely for the world of work. By fixing a specific time to complete a test and by promoting a "do or die" mentality, tests in the social studies curriculum prepare students for the work situations they will encounter later in life. Such forms of testing require responses that have "correct" responses and are not open to question. More important, it is the teacher—the "final authority" on these tests—who is teaching students to assume that those in positions of authority know much more than they do simply because of their position as authoritarian figures.

Conventional tests are a recapitulation of behavioral objectives that actually grew out of the efficiency movement in education of the first third of the twentieth century; they are based on an industrial model of high productivity.[26] The lessons that students learn from these tests support an industria-age ethic of work and submission to authority. The dominant image for testing in social studies is based upon these timeworn industrial-age principles. Students passively listen to lectures, and they transfer facts from textbooks to worksheets. Students are methodically marched through time, chapter by chapter, test by test. One hundred years of these assessments demand that we look for alternatives.

Social studies assessments should serve to determine the success of a curriculum, provide information to students, and inform teachers and parents of children's learning and achievements. It is time to focus on assessments in social studies that

- are authentic in nature and designed to provide feedback that improves student learning;
- involve students, parents, teachers, and the community collaborating for improved student learning; and
- allow for a variety of measures that focus on individual student learning.

Assessments in the social studies should revolve around thematic questions that address how students apply information as well as the skills they have learned to integrate their work. This cannot be done solely through worksheets or multiple-choice or fill-in-the-blank or essay tests. Assessments can be created that allow students to *show* what they know. Teachers should make sure students understand the assessment in advance, as opposed to traditional testing where students know little about the evaluation process. Assessment should require students to think deeply about course content and use higher level thinking skills such as application, analysis, and synthesis. Such assessment encourages students to apply what they know through a project, performance, or product. More important, students should assess their own work in conjunction with the teacher's assessment. We can see how students are thinking and the knowledge they bring to a task by asking them to describe what they have learned, write about the strongest and weakest parts of their work, and choose criteria by which they will judge their work. If the social studies curriculum is to promote critical thinking and decision making, then the means of assessment we use must address critical thinking and problem solving among students.

THINKING OUTSIDE THE BOX

Similar to the beginning of the twentieth century, the advent of the twenty-first century is characterized by rapid change in our society and a call for serious educational reform. While many current social studies teachers certainly do a remarkable and commendable job, we must remember that the curriculum they work with was developed, essentially, over 100 years ago, an age very different from today. It is time for social studies educators to create a contemporary social studies curriculum that is relevant to our students, meets the needs of our rapidly changing society, and prepares citizens for their future involvement in democracy. Maintaining and sustaining a twentieth-century history-centered curriculum does not, and cannot, serve our students in the twenty-first century.

I hope that social studies educators spend the next decade discussing new approaches for the social studies curriculum that could be introduced into public school practice in the twenty-first century. What may emerge from such a dialogue are many different ways to conceptualize the social studies curriculum, rather than the singular set of state or national standards often imposed. That, indeed, would be thinking outside the box at the beginning of the twenty-first century.

— 3 —

Literacy Research and Education Reform: Sorting through the History and the Myths

MARTHA RAPP RUDDELL

Popular and some professional opinions today hold that (1) literacy achievement in the United States has suffered an ongoing downward spiral since a mythical golden period of high achievement, (2) the cause of this downward trend was (or is) the widespread and thoughtlessly careless use of instructional practice not supported by research, and (3) the current "research-based" instruction—of skills-first reading instruction with a heavy early emphasis on phonemic awareness and training—is somehow *new* and is the answer to all the literacy achievement "problems." Indeed, the latest federal education policy, the No Child Left Behind (NCLB) Act of 2001, not only endorses such instruction but also mandates yearly standardized testing of all children above second grade to "assure" that literacy skills have been learned. Contrary to this view is the actual history of American literacy instruction that is marked by periods in which new concerns about our children's literacy arose, followed by research efforts and instructional reforms (often fashioned in response to popular or political pressure) that were undertaken to counter these concerns, and resulting subsequent periods in which yet other questions surfaced. The questions asked in these cycles of periodic concern had direct influence on the research and instruction that followed. Further, the fact of the existence of this cyclical pattern of reform belies the notion that great waves of literacy instruction in this country were atheoretical or lacking a research base. The fact is, we have an unbroken history of well over 100 years of literacy research. That said, however, research results have always been subject to various interpretations and transformations into instructional practice. This chapter traces the development of research and reform in American literacy instruction and highlights the ways public and professional concern shaped research trends and instructional practices. It provides an analysis of current reforms and the research base for those reforms.

HOW DO WE READ?

Nila Banton Smith,[1] in her landmark history of American reading instruction, identifies 1894 as the beginning of American reading research. In that very earliest research, much attention was given to the question "How do we read?" with significant amounts of the research focused on the *physiology* of reading. Eye movement research between the late 1800s and continuing well into the twentieth and twenty-first centuries yielded information about eye-voice span, saccadic movement—the movement of the eyes as they scan across lines of print—reading rate, and differences in eye movement for skilled and not-so-skilled readers, and for silent and oral reading.

Much of the effect of the eye movement research was the instructional goal of fluency in both silent and oral reading, and a primary means for promoting and assessing fluency was an instructional practice called *round robin oral reading*. Round robin oral reading is the term used to identify the practice of having one child read orally while the others follow silently as that child reads. The "round robin" part comes from the common practice of students taking turns in oral reading around the room or around the reading group. Although this practice was not new to reading instruction in the United States during the early twentieth century, it nevertheless gained additional legitimacy as a means for developing oral reading fluency; it remains a common practice—sometimes called "popcorn reading"—to this day, not only in elementary reading groups but in secondary content classrooms as well.

Interestingly, as late as the 1940s and 1950s, researchers were still doing significant amounts of research on eye movement. In 1940, Luther Gilbert[2] studied skilled and less-skilled readers' eye movements as they read silently while another skilled or less-skilled reader read aloud in round robin oral reading fashion. What he found was that skilled readers appeared to be annoyed by the stops and starts of less-skilled readers and so simply read ahead or stopped reading altogether; less-skilled readers were unable to keep up with the flow of reading established by skilled readers and showed their frustration by discontinuing their attempts to read. In each case, the ultimate effect was what Harry Singer[3] called "eyes straying toward the window." Singer reported Gilbert's study as one that "should have made a difference [with respect to instructional practice] and didn't" because it had little effect on the continuing use of round robin oral reading in classrooms and schools.

WHEN IS THE BEST TIME FOR ONSET OF READING INSTRUCTION?

The 1920s and 1930s ushered in an interest in issues of reading readiness and the attending question "When is the best time for onset of formal reading instruction?" This was brought about by what Dolores Durkin identifies as "the new interest during the 1920s and 1930s in the 'scientific' measurement of children's behavior, including their achievement in school."[4] (We seem to be replicating this interest today with the current focus on standardized testing.) Durkin calls the interest in measurement "almost a craze to measure everything" stemming from the confluence of newly developed IQ and achievement tests and a prevailing belief that first graders were having difficulty learning to read because they were not "ready" when instruction began. Enter Mabel Morphett and Carleton Washburne.

In 1931, Morphett and Washburne[5] published the results of a study they conducted to answer the question "What is the appropriate age for the onset of formal reading instruction?" Conducted in Winnetka, Illinois, where Carleton Washburne was superintendent of schools and Mabel Morphett was a graduate student at the nearby University of Chicago, their study measured children's Mental Age (MA)—one of the constructs in the early years of intelligence measurement—at the beginning of first grade and then measured the children's reading achievement at the end of first grade and correlated the results. Their findings indicated that children reading successfully by the end of first grade entered first grade with a mental age of 6.5 years. In intelligence measurement, the chronological age most likely to be associated with an MA of 6.5 is 6.5; that is, most children have to be six-and-one-half years in age to reach an MA of 6.5. So, a 6.5 chronological age was generalized from the Winnetka study and became the standard age of entry into first grade throughout this country. Never mind that Winnetka, Illinois, was (and is) a community of generally high socioeconomic status, that the children being tested were the sons and daughters of University of Chicago professors, and that the school itself was using the "Winnetka Plan" for reading instruction—an instructional approach designed specifically for its children and not used anywhere else. The results of this study were nevertheless applied to all children in the United States and became the rationale and support for what Durkin calls the "doctrine of postponement" in which children's entry into first grade was delayed solely on the basis of age. This research and its resulting instructional reform satisfied the tenor of the times in which the public and policymakers alike demanded academic measures that were precise and "objective." Although rebutted and criticized by eminent researchers and many studies both contemporary to the 1930s and subsequent to that time, the standard of six-and-one-half years of age for the onset of formal reading instruction (i.e., entry into first grade) continued for generations in this country; thus, the Morphett and Washburne study has been described by some as "research that made a difference [in terms of instructional practice] and shouldn't have."

Interest in discovering the best time for the onset of formal reading instruction was but one part of the larger interest in *reading readiness*, that point in time at which a child is "ready" to begin reading (or for formal reading instruction to begin). One outgrowth of this interest was the widespread development of readiness tests and readiness programs intended to prepare children in kindergarten and early first grade for formal reading instruction. Designed ideally to meet the needs of individual children (as Carleton Washburne said, to make sure each child was "ripe" for instruction), reading readiness programs in actuality were used in a generally lock-step manner for all children in whatever period of late kindergarten or early first grade a school or district deemed appropriate. Reading readiness programs held heavy sway in early reading instruction for a long time (from the 1920s to the 1960s) in large part because of the equally stable adherence in this country, in both popular and professional opinion, to views of human growth and development that emphasized maturation (as opposed to social or other influences) as a major influence on cognitive growth and achievement.

WHY ARE OUR CHILDREN LEAVING SCHOOL UNABLE TO READ?

Early in the 1940s, we recruited soldiers into the armed forces in unprecedented numbers, as they became sitting ducks not only for the war experience ahead of them but also for American testing experts. And test them we did—we were not too choosy about human subjects review at that time. This led to the rediscovery that thousands of soldiers could not read well enough to do their work in the armed services (a discovery of earlier testing during World War I). This rediscovery, in turn, led to the research question "Why are our children leaving school unable to read?" This question coincided with earlier concerns about children in first and other grades who were not learning to read to a level of success and also with the focus on remedial reading that had begun in the 1930s; further, it served as a catalyst for interest in middle-level and secondary reading. Research dwindled during World War II, but the essential question of the 1940s segued into the 1950s as "Why can't our children read?" Rudolph Flesch had an answer: his widely known and much quoted book, *Why Johnny Can't Read*, published in 1955, in which he excoriated public education and called into question the then-current methods for beginning reading instruction—methods associated with basal readers (the old Dick and Jane books) in which children learned words in context first and later learned to analyze sound-symbol relationships.[6] Shortly afterward, in 1957, the Soviet Union launched *Sputnik,* which caused a national frenzy of criticism around the question of "Why can't our children read?" directed at American schools. The question really was "Why are we behind the Russians?" Although huge research studies did not immediately surface, federal money did, and from it came the question "What is the best method for beginning reading instruction?"

The National Defense Education Act (NDEA) of 1958 was passed in direct response to the combined events of the publication of *Why Johnny Can't Read* and the launching of *Sputnik*. This landmark legislation ushered federal funding (and attendant stipulations and controls) into local schools at a level never before seen in the United States. This landmark legislation established huge funds for development and implementation of Title I reading programs. In addition, it provided equally large funding for basic and applied reading research.

The United States Office of Education Cooperative Reading Studies,[7] more commonly called "the First Grade Studies," was launched in 1964, funded by NDEA, to answer the question of what is the best method for early reading instruction. These studies involved twenty-seven separate research centers across the United States and were coordinated by Guy Bond and Bob Dykstra at the University of Minnesota.

The goals of this research were twofold: first, to carry out a coordinated large-scale research program to examine early reading instruction under conditions that allowed the comparison of findings across multiple studies in a wide variety of classrooms and schools, and second, to discover once and for all the answer to the research question "What is the best method of beginning reading instruction?" The methods being compared included (1) basal reading, in which children first learned words in a meaning-based context and then analyzed those words to associate separate sound-symbol relationships (the Dick and Jane books); (2) phonetic emphasis, in which children learned and practiced sound-symbol associations and then blended sounds into meaningful words (phonics-first); (3) the Language Experience Approach, in which children read and reread their own dictated stories, and developed word analysis skills from manipulation and analysis of words in their dictated texts; (4) individualized reading, in which children self-selected books for reading instruction and teachers developed separate skill instruction as children's needs indicated; (5) linguistic emphasis, in which word families were taught for use in decoding linguistically consistent text, such as "Can Nan fan Dan?"; (6) the Initial Teaching Alphabet, or i/t/a, that used an altered English-language alphabet to achieve a one-to-one sound-symbol correspondence for beginning reading and then transitioned children into reading conventional written English after they became fluent reading i/t/a text (at about second or third grade); and (7) audio-visual Methods, including instruction called "Words in Color" that used a color-coding system to identify categories of words and to signal certain pronunciation consistencies.

The approach of these coordinated studies was to identify and study classrooms in which one of the different methods of instruction was being used—

thus, each classroom in the study was dedicated to a specific instructional method. All the studies were conducted in first-grade classrooms during the 1964–1965 school year. Each study lasted the entire year, and all studies used the same standardized tests to determine achievement at the end of the study year. Thirty-three thousand children and hundreds of teachers and schools participated in the First Grade Studies. Seven centers, each with studies involving multiple classrooms and schools, extended their research through the second and third grades in 1965–1966 and 1966–1967.

Many results came from these studies, and considerable opportunity for exploring nuance is available in them. The major findings related to the question "What's the best method for beginning reading instruction?" were as follows:

1. For every instructional method examined, many children were successful readers by the end of first grade. And for every method examined, some children were *not* successful readers at the end of first grade.
2. Those children in the synthetic phonics or phonics-first classes evidenced a slight achievement advantage over children in the basal reader and Language Experience Approach and other approaches at the end of first grade. This advantage was statistically significant but educationally small—an achievement difference of about one month.
3. By the end of the third grade, differences between methods washed out; the one-month "advantage" for phonics-first students had disappeared. The good readers in each method were reading on a similar level, and the struggling readers in each method were about the same distance behind.
4. Throughout the First Grade Studies, and even into the Second and Third Grades Studies, greater differences were found between *classrooms* than between *method*. That is, no matter what the method of instruction, children learned to read in some classrooms and did not fare as well in others.

One of the greatest influences of the First Grade Studies (and other research of this period as well as the social changes occurring in the 1960s) was expansion of the methods and materials for formal reading instruction. That is, the deemphasis on *method* and the corresponding emphasis on what is happening in the classroom as the defining characteristic of good instruction led to practice in which methods were combined or transformed; so, theoretically, teachers could use both heavy phonics drill and Language Experience stories in any given classroom. In reality, what happened was a great flurry of publication in which virtually every reading program in the country was rewritten, expanded to include many different kinds of instruction, and illustrated to reflect a changing society. Teacher guides in these new series were greatly expanded to give teachers many suggestions and teaching activities from which they were to choose in order to meet the needs of their own students. The goal was to make the guides "teacher-proof" so that no matter what choices the teacher made, she or he would be using high-quality reading instruction practice. In addition to the revisions of established basal reading series, many new series debuted during this time; in almost all cases, reading anthologies in the 1970s and beyond were expanded to include books for seventh and eighth grades to meet the needs of newly developed programs of reading instruction in middle and junior high schools.

What is significant but usually lost in discussions of the First Grade Studies is that the results of these studies were absolutely counter to Rudolph Flesch's theory and criticism in *Why Johnny Can't Read* that a specific method of reading instruction was the reason for poor reading achievement. Method proved *not* to be the differentiating factor in these studies, especially those that followed students' reading progress through the end of grade three. These research results did not, however, change prevailing popular belief.

HOW DO THE MANY ELEMENTS OF READING PROCESSES WORK TOGETHER?

The early 1970s saw a new research emphasis stimulated by the question "How do the many elements of the reading process work together?" This new question acknowledged the complexities of the reading process beyond the questions we asked over fifty years previously that focused on just eye movement and the like. Toward the end of the 1970s and in the early 1980s, due in large part to the work of the new Center for the Study of Reading headed by Richard Anderson at the University of Illinois, came the rise in prominence of the element of prior knowledge in the reading process and the subsequent generation of a wealth of research at the center and elsewhere on Schema Theory, a theory that changed virtually everyone's view of the reading process. Emerging also during this time was study in discourse analysis that parsed the elements of "story." Instructional reform did not grow immediately from these lines of research, but the end result was to break the hold that maturational theory had on our thinking about cognitive growth and development. From this work, we began to see the influence of prior knowledge, world knowledge, social interactions, and many other factors on humans' constructions of meaning and cognitive growth.

The early 1970s also saw the beginnings of national testing to measure progress in reading (and math and science) that continues today as the National Assessment of Educational Progress, or NAEP, reading tests. Interestingly, for over thirty years, the results of this testing have refuted charges of precipitous drops in reading ability in the United States (see Figure 3.1).[8]

In fact, the National Center for Educational Statistics (NCES) says of these results that nine-, thirteen-, and seventeen-year-olds' scores were higher in 1999 than in 1971. Although the differences are small, they are statistically significant. The most recent NAEP scores, 2002 and 2003 testing reading in urban schools, are remarkably similar to the 1999 averages.

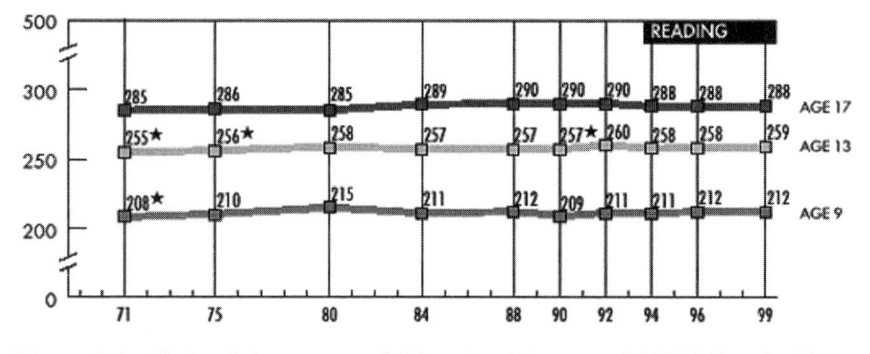

Figure 3.1 National Assessment of Educational Progress (NAEP) Trends, 1971–1999.

As with the results of the First Grade Studies, the results of this longitudinal research are rarely considered in the cyclical public cries of "The scores are falling! The scores are falling!" by editorial writers on a slow news day and by politicians looking for a headline. These are not hidden results; they are reported on the NCES website that is open for public access. The scores are *not* falling, and we have thirty years of evidence to confirm that.

HOW DO CHILDREN BECOME LITERATE?

In the 1980s, new questions emerged. In their longitudinal study that resulted in the book *Language Stories and Literacy Lessons*,[9] Jerry Harste, Virginia Woodward, and Carolyn Burke changed the old question of "When is the best time for the onset of formal reading instruction?" to "How do children become literate?" and "What do children's preliterate behaviors reveal about their literacy knowledge before the onset of reading instruction?" They found that what we used to call "scribbling" is preliterate writing, which children can read after they have written it, which is systematic and representative of the writing found in children's environments. They found that very young children know the difference between when they are creating art and when they are writing, and understand and use a variety of print functions in their environments. In other words, children produce different forms of writing based on function: lists look like lists, stories look like stories, and party invitations look like party invitations. In short, in Jerry Harste's words, they found that "Children know more than we ever dared imagine." Elizabeth Sulzby[10] asked a similar question in her seminal 1985 study of preschool children's oral reading of favorite storybooks and in her many subsequent follow-up studies. She discovered that very young children who have not yet been exposed to formal reading instruction develop a "linguistic repertoire" of things to do to manage text and to support their early oral reading experiences.

Anchored by the early Language Experience and Individualized Reading Approaches (recall the methods studied in the First Grade Studies), the Whole Language approach to reading instruction was the reform that grew from the understandings developed by observational research conducted in school and preschool settings over long periods of time in which children engaged individually and collectively in literate behaviors. The following understandings form the foundation of the Whole Language approach:

1. Children are active participants in their own language and literacy development; they build theories and test hypotheses as they construct meaning about their world.
2. Children's perceptions of print and their productions of oral and written language follow rule-governed, coherent behavior that reflects their current understanding of how print and language work.
3. Children enter school with a high degree of language competence; their reading and writing development progresses throughout the elementary grades in a parallel and interactive manner.
4. Children's reading and writing acquisition are influenced by their language and world knowledge, social interactions, and literacy environments, including available language models (family, teacher, peer group), language and literacy routines, and opportunities to use language in meaningful interactions.
5. Children's home and community language and literacy environments, interactions, and routines strongly influence their reading and writing development; close home-school linkage is important to their language and literacy growth.

Whole Language instruction was never considered a "method" of teaching; rather, it was and is built on classrooms in which "rich, authentic, developmentally appropriate school experiences"[11] are created by the teacher to extend students' literacy. The teacher is expected to have deep understandings of child and literacy development in order to be able to make decisions about the kinds of experiences that are appropriate for each child.

In many states, Whole Language instruction took the form of literature-based instruction in which educators moved away from using basal reader stories excerpted from books and taught with the actual literature itself. Unfortunately, along with new policies (in some cases, state policies) that focused on Whole Language or literature-based instruction came little if any professional development resources to assist teachers in changing their practice. In the end, many teachers and schools simply basalized the literature; for example, they taught *The Lion, the Witch, and the Wardrobe* using the same instructional strategies they had used when teaching Dick and Jane readers. On the other hand, many other teachers and schools created rich, vibrant literacy learning environments and opportunities for young children, in which children thrived.

Whole Language instruction was not, and is not, a fad. It is an approach to literacy instruction that capitalizes on children's natural affinity for language and literacy learning. And it is supported by a substantial body of research in which researchers spent days and weeks and years in classrooms and schools observing, recording, and analyzing young children's development toward fluent literacy (as opposed to running into the room, administering a test, and running back out again). The NAEP data attest to the fact that the great "drop" in reading scores attributed to Whole Language instruction in the 1980s and 1990s simply did not occur.

HOW DO LITERACY PROCESSES WORK?

In the early 1990s, our attention turned from the individual processing of text and "reading" *per se* to look at group and social negotiations of text, and the broadening of our lens to "literacy" research. Our question became "What is the nature of the interactions and transactions that compose literacy processes?" Further, interest in such constructs as intertext, transmediation, and activity theory guided much of our research, as well as renewed interest in the learning process for second language learners. As Patricia Alexander states:

> Interest shifted from describing the knowledge of the *one* to the shared understanding of the *many* and from discerning the fundamental laws of learning to capture the unique "ways of knowing" for particular social, cultural, and educational groups. . . . Thus, the predominant metaphor of the [1990s] became one of literacy as a sociocultural, collaborative experience. This metaphor was mirrored in the widespread popularity of such concepts as cognitive apprenticeship, shared cognition, and social constructivism.[12]

This sea change in our research agenda that evolved over many years was characterized in 1994 by David Pearson and Diane Stephens:

> [W]hat we know about reading, how we think about reading, even what we call "reading" has changed considerably over the last thirty years. Reading, once the sole domain of educators, has become transdisciplinary. The knowledge base that has grown out of the once separate fields of psychology, sociology, linguistics, and literary theory has been created by and/or shared with educators. Indeed, many individuals now identify themselves as educators *and* as cognitive psychologists, psycholinguists, sociolinguists, literary theorists, and even sociopsycholinguists.[13]

As the research has expanded to include many perspectives and voices, so too has instruction. Constructivist thought and teaching have grown directly from this base; in addition, Whole Language instruction has strengthened.

WHAT CONSTITUTES GOOD LITERACY RESEARCH?

In the late 1990s, and continuing today, external forces—policymakers, politicians, and state and federal departments of education—began exerting new pressures on the literacy research community. The question they imposed was "What constitutes good literacy research?" Laws were passed defining "acceptable" research as typified in California by Assembly Bill 1086, which declared only the narrowly defined "confirmed research" to be acceptable for informing educational practice (a definition that has now been incorporated into federal educational policy). A certain few studies were used as the sole basis for the revised California reading and language arts instructional framework, some of which raise questions regarding validity, reliability, and generalizability not unlike the questions raised—but never resolved—regarding the Morphett and Washburne study. The National Reading Panel (NRP)[14]—commissioned by the National Institute of Child Health and Development with members selected to represent a bias toward experimental research—conducted its review of literacy research for purposes which I described[15] four years ago as "judging certain research to be good or bad, worthy or unworthy; certain theoretical stances and research methodologies to be acceptable or unacceptable; and certain research studies to be representative of all that we know about literacy learning and instruction." The panel's choice of studies to include in their review was narrow indeed, limited to the analysis of experimental and quasi-experimental reading research conducted since 1990 and seemingly uninformed by studies that reflect the realities of classroom life or studies conducted any time in the almost 100 years of reading research before 1990. Not surprisingly, all observational studies, such as the Harste, Woodward, and Burke seven-year observation of young children developing toward literacy and Elizabeth Sulzby's many replications of her original research on emergent literacy, were not considered. Nor were the First Grade Studies. Nevertheless, the NRP report was widely disseminated and discussed, and in some instances considered to be The Final Answer. The report's primary finding was that effective reading instruction begins with systematic phonics instruction. As one might expect, reactions to the report were (and are) many and today are generally critical of the narrow scope of the research reviewed by the panel to arrive at policy conclusions. Jim Cunningham's review in *Reading Research Quarterly*[16] was particularly detailed. As Cunningham states:

> Most readers of the *NRP Report* will probably find themselves agreeing with at least one of the findings. Perhaps a majority of readers will agree with a majority of the findings. However, the test of quality for scientific research is whether knowledgeable and fair-minded *skeptics* find it persuasive. All research is persuasive to those who already agree with it. No research is persuasive to the person with a closed mind on a subject. The best science has the power to change the thinking of those who previously disagreed with its conclusions but

> who are fair-minded enough to admit they were wrong once the case has been made. Who is a fair-minded skeptic? Anyone who can point to several important issues in the past on which she or he has changed her or his mind because of research results. . . . How likely is that to happen? I predict that the knowledgeable and fair-minded skeptics who change their minds based on the NRP's findings will be few and far between. Too much professional and historical knowledge about teaching reading is ignored, too little common sense is brought to bear, and too little reading research is considered worthy of consultation.

The instructional reform growing from the NRP report was immediate and direct. Once again, reading series were rewritten on a wholesale scale, this time for the purpose of narrowing teacher options for beginning reading instruction simply to early, heavy, systematic instruction in phonemic analysis and phonics that leads to the beginning reading of "predictable text." The "predictable text" of these new instructional materials, however, is not the predictable text of the Whole Language classroom that encourages children to chant along with patterned text, like Bill Martin's *Brown Bear, Brown Bear* ("Brown Bear, Brown Bear, what do you see? I see a red bird looking at me. Red Bird, Red Bird, what do you see?"); rather, it is the predictable text of the old linguistic readers ("Dad had a sad lad."). All of this early instruction is heavily scripted so that teachers read verbatim from the Instructor's Manual and children respond to the scripted prompts. Local, state, and national policymakers accepted the NRP findings and began mandating use of the new instructional materials.

And now, in a reanalysis of the exact studies examined by the NRP, Gregory Camilli, Sadako Vargas, and Michele Yurecko[17] of the National Institute for Early Education Research have found that the conclusion arrived at by the NRP of early systematic phonics instruction is not supported by the data in those studies. Instead, in their reanalysis, they found that the NRP ignored the fact that in the studies they cited to support systematic phonics, over 30 percent included language activities as well, so "the NRP analysts missed the language effect for one simple reason: they didn't look for it."[18] They conclude that "Systematic phonics instruction when combined with language activities and individual tutoring may *triple* the effect of phonics alone."[19] They continue, "If the NRP results are taken to mean that effective instruction in reading should focus on phonics to the exclusion of other curricular activities, instructional policies are likely to be misdirected."[20] And misdirected they are. In many classrooms and schools today, the heavy emphasis on scripted phonics instruction and drill leaves little if any time for language activities and the reading of authentic text. This point was made poignantly clear to me in an e-mail conversation with a young fourth-grade teacher I had taught. She e-mailed me about her excitement over the Vocabulary Self-Collection Strategy (VSS)[21] I had taught her for increasing children's vocabulary knowledge. She wrote:

> The resulting program was an even greater success than I could have ever dreamed! I called my program W.O.W—Words on Wednesdays—and the students and parents absolutely fell in love with it. The words that became regular parts of the students' speaking and writing vocabulary were astonishing!
>
> We did 10 words each week (everyone submitted, me included, and then we eliminated down to 10) and ended up with over 200 words. The students averaged A's each week on quizzes and even at the end of the year, on a cumulative test of about 100 words, I had MOST of the students get 100 percent. The words had become that much a part of their working vocabulary. I could go on and on.
>
> I just wanted to thank you for introducing me to VSS and let you know how successful it made my students and me feel.

I answered her e-mail and said how pleased I was that VSS had been so successful and accepted her offer to share the data with me. She responded,

> I only have information from last year, as I haven't been able to do WOW this year (we have a district mandate to do the [Name] reading program and I haven't had the freedom to do WOW).

WHERE ARE WE NOW?

And so, the historical journey ends, and at its end, the question is: "Where are we now?" Overall, the results are mixed. On the one hand, most notably because so many politicians and policymakers are unaware of our research history, we are reliving our past without even knowing it. The insistence by some, both within and outside the educational community, that instructional *method* determines the quality of reading instruction ignores the lesson learned in the First Grade Studies, and that lesson is that the question "What is the best method of beginning reading instruction?" is not a useful one to ask. The unfortunate result is that attention to method ultimately draws attention away from the variables that did (and still do) affect reading achievement in the First Grade Studies: classrooms and teachers and schools. In 1967, Guy Bond and Bob Dykstra stated emphatically:

> Future research should center on teacher and *learning situation characteristics* rather than method and materials. The tremendous range of classrooms within any given method points out the importance of elements in the learning situation over and above the materials employed. [Emphasis mine][22]

Additionally, to the extent that the NRP report reduces our conversation to a method-against-method debate, we leave out of the conversation what we have learned from the locus of research since the 1970s: Literacy is a complex cognitive process and we cannot consider "reading" without also considering issues of schema development, transactions between reader and text, and the myriad social elements of literacy development and learning. Further, by selectively ignoring the full range of our research knowledge, policymakers, on the basis of a single test's results, are postponing children's entry into school, retaining children in K–1 classes, or creating half-grades to postpone entry into the next grade level because of low reading (or readiness) scores. Thus, they reenact the practices of the 1920s and 1930s that were ultimately abandoned due to the lack of evidence attesting to their effectiveness culled from either research *or* practice. In fact, the evidence we have about retention in school is overwhelmingly clear: Retention rarely, if ever, is effective in increasing students' reading, or any other, achievement in school.

And finally, by eliminating from our consideration research that is observational and qualitative, proponents of the "scientific" or "confirmed" research bias systematically reduce the knowledge gleaned from close observation and long-term study of children's literate behavior, and reduce further our ability to learn from children what they tell us everyday about their individual and collective literacy development. It is time to move from a position of narrow positivism to one of critical inquiry and analysis of both the ongoing scholarly research of many research traditions and the daily events in classrooms and schools—all of which must be leavened by our knowledge of the historical context of research and practice.

We need to examine closely the reforms we implement in the name of research. Far too many reforms are based on faulty assumptions or are hastily imposed "new" methods that recapitulate old practices or that are contrary to the research evidence we have. The evidence we have is that reading achievement has held steady for nine-, thirteen-, and seventeen-year-old students in this country for well over thirty years; great, sweeping "reforms" have had little effect. It appears that our children are resilient indeed; no matter what we do to them in the name of beginning reading instruction, they continue to learn to read. (I am not ignoring here the many children who do not learn to read successfully and spend all their years in school struggling; they are there and they are there in greater numbers than any of us want. The fact is, however, that in a world that is vastly more complex than it was thirty years ago, and in which classrooms and schools are vastly more diverse than they were thirty years ago, reading scores, on average, are slightly higher than they were thirty years ago.) The evidence we have also is that no one method of reading instruction works for all children; it is critical that policy mandates, not confines teachers to one "right" way to teach reading. Just as we should assume a stance of critical inquiry and analysis of research, so should we assume such a stance in developing instructional reform.

On the other hand, there is hope. For, in the end, today's schools are filled with dedicated and hardworking teachers, often performing astoundingly well under more than trying circumstances. We have learned an enormous amount about language and literacy in the past 100 years, and in the past twenty years, much of that knowledge is in the area of second language learning and literacy; we have achieved a rich understanding of the complex processes and transactions that compose literate acts. And while we have not always translated our research knowledge into perfect educational practice, we continue to try. In sorting through the history and the myths, then, what we can say is that (1) literacy achievement in the United States has not suffered an ongoing downward spiral since some mythical golden period of high achievement; (2) considerable and substantive research has been generated over the past 100 years to inform literacy instruction; and (3) research has not always been understood or attended to by policymakers and those who determine state and national educational law. The current tensions between opposing views of what constitutes good research and practice are pushing us all to think deeply and continue our efforts to ask new questions and to seek answers in many and varied ways.

— 4 —

The Mathematics Curriculum: Prosecution, Defense, Verdict

CYNTHIA O. ANHALT, ROBIN A. WARD, AND KEVIN D. VINSON

With the possible exception of reading and language arts, no subject area enjoys as much, and as widespread, approval for inclusion in the school curriculum as does mathematics. Whether viewed as one of "the basics" (i.e., one of the "3 Rs"), problem solving, skill acquisition, intellectual/applied process, or the learning of specific content knowledge, mathematics maintains support from across the pedagogical and ideological spectrum—from essentialists to progressives, from traditionalists to radical educational critics. And yet, simultaneously, it is a discipline that faces frequent, sustained, and extensive challenges, both warranted and unwarranted. In this chapter, we raise and pursue the following questions: Historically, what have been the places and purposes of mathematics education? What is the current "state of the field" (e.g., best practice, standards, competing dominant views)? To what extent, and on what basis, is mathematics education currently under attack? What is exemplary about contemporary mathematics education? Where do we go from here? We conclude by reconsidering both the positive and negative aspects of contemporary mathematics education, coming down, in the end, on the side that says that what we—mathematics educators, generally—do is good and deserves to be defended vis-à-vis the often underrated status, standing, position, and development of the school curriculum and, more broadly, of American public education.

THE STATE OF CONTEMPORARY MATHEMATICS EDUCATION

Mathematics has always played a significant role in the curriculum of American schools. From the beginning, its status as one of the 3Rs—"reading, 'riting, and 'rithmetic"—has largely gone unchallenged, and rightly so. In the beginning, of course, the greatest emphasis was on simple "figuring"—memorizing math facts, calculating, and so on—especially given that most students did not come close to high school graduation, let alone seek postsecondary graduation or employment in the technical or scientific professions (e.g., navigation, engineering).[1] In short, the early mathematics curriculum prepared workers to become farmers, shopkeepers, and factory workers. Today's workplace necessitates that the mathematics curriculum exceed proficiency with basic computational skills.

The mathematics curriculum pendulum is in constant motion. The beginning of the reform movement in mathematics education occurred during the first two decades of the 1900s, as pressures to provide an education for all students mounted due to the growth in school enrollments as well as the emerging research in theories of learning. Prior to this, nineteenth-century mathematics was characterized by long practice, often with involved problems. Educators and mathematicians were now advocating an integration of content and a shift to newer methods using concrete, developmental, and intuitive approaches.[2] Arithmetic, once a college and secondary school subject, was moved into the elementary school. The *Report of the Committee of Fifteen on Elementary Education* dictated that grades two through six focus on basic arithmetic; in grades seven and eight, the notion of number would continue and some algebra would be introduced.[3] At the secondary level, *The Reorganization of Mathematics in Secondary Education* called for a reduction in elaborate manipulations in algebra and less memorization of theorems and proofs in geometry.[4] This document also advocated a general mathematics program that included topics from arithmetic, algebra, intuitive geometry, numerical trigonometry, graphs, and descriptive statistics.[5]

From the 1920s through the 1940s the number and percentage of students attending school continued to increase dramatically and, consequently, the role of mathematics and how to teach it effectively were heavily scrutinized. Drill techniques, justified by such psychologists as Edward L. Thorndike, were utilized heavily in the elementary schools to teach arithmetic and algebra. Later in this period, however, two new theories of arithmetic instruction strongly influenced mathematics teaching and textbooks, namely, William Brownell's meaning theory and the readiness theory, attributed to the work of Gessell and other child development psychologists.[6] The impact of these theories on the mathematics curriculum resulted in the 1945 publication of the *Second Report of the Commission on Post-War Plans,* in which the National Council of Teachers of Mathematics (NCTM) suggested, among other things, that drill and repetitive practices be administered much more wisely and that more emphasis and careful attention be paid to the development of meanings as well as students' readiness for learning mathematical ideas.[7]

During the 1950s, the launching of *Sputnik* by the Soviets served as a catalyst for the United States to rethink and revise the current mathematics curriculum yet again. Another catalyst was the developing awareness of inequities, both gender and racial, in mathematics classrooms. "New math" was born in 1951, and one of the most influential of the new math projects was the School Mathematics Study Group (SMSG). Public controversy surrounding this curriculum began almost immediately, with critics claiming it was too abstract, disconnected from the real world, and used language unfamiliar even to mathematicians.[8] Most significant in this new math era, however, was the birth of numerous institutes deigned to improve the preparation of teachers of mathematics.

During the 1960s, which is sometimes referred to as the "modern math era," the mathematics curriculum reverted to more traditional, pedagogical approaches, as mathematicians espoused that rigor and precision would result in deeper mathematical understanding.[9] By the late 1960s the math curriculum, which was once characterized by the rote learning of facts and algorithms, transitioned into one with a more conceptual, hands-on approach to learning.

"Laboratory mathematics" marked the beginning of the 1970s as manipulatives and other hands-on materials were introduced into the teaching and learning of mathematics.[10] At the close of the 1970s, however, a back-to-basics approach resurfaced. It was during this time that the debate over what topics and skills should be taught as part of the mathematics curriculum became widespread and rather fevered. Most educators agreed that not only was equal access by all citizens in the United States to mathematics a critical issue that needed addressing, but it was evident that society's technological advances were rendering some basic mathematics skills obsolete.

In the early 1980s the publication *An Agenda for Action* advocated that problem solving take the forefront in the mathematics curriculum.[11] This document propelled the birth of other publications, including *Everybody Counts* and *Curriculum and Evaluation Standards for School Mathematics*, which specified the "essential" ingredients of the K–12 mathematics curriculum and also explored how students learn mathematics.[12] Thus, the late 1980s became known as the "era of realization."[13]

In the mid-1990s it became evident that members of the education community misinterpreted the spirit of NCTM Standards, thinking that the majority of traditional, basic mathematical skills be eliminated from the curriculum and that schools focus solely on problem solving and developing higher order thinking skills. Thus, members of the NCTM convened and revised a new set of consolidated standards, namely the *Principles and Standards for School Mathematics*.[14] These updated standards provided a clearer vision of the essential ingredients of today's mathematics curriculum, clarifying NCTM's position on the need for both traditional, basic skills as well as higher order thinking skills, while also identifying the importance of equity, technology, and assessment in mathematics.

One trend that has gained momentum since the last decade of the twentieth century is the movement by state and local communities to adopt their own standards. Although most of these efforts were largely influenced by the NCTM Standards, one unfortunate consequence has been that some states publish their guidelines only months before decisions are made in the textbook adoption process. Consequently, textbooks may be selected for classroom use that superficially meet state guidelines but lack field testing and innovation.[15]

Clearly, over the last century, mathematics education has undergone substantial changes, but at times the arguments and practices of today echo those of the past. Slow but noticeable progress has been made toward greater equity, national standards, and higher expectations of teachers and students while some changes, in particular those relative to technology, have been abrupt but continue to evolve.[16] Undoubtedly, mathematics and conceptions of and aims for mathematics education are infinitely more complex and varied today than during the early history of American schooling. Our goal in this section is to articulate the current status of pre K–12 mathematics education in the United States.

Here, we follow primarily the work of the National Research Council (NRC). In *Adding It Up: Helping Children Learn Mathematics,* the NRC focuses on several critical indicators, most importantly "learning goals," "instructional programs and materials," "assessments," "teaching," and "achievement."[17] The NRC offers the following conclusions:

- *With respect to learning goals:* "We see the efforts made since 1989 to develop standards for teaching and learning mathematics as worthwhile. Many schools have been led to rethink their mathematics programs, and many teachers to reflect on their practice. Nonetheless, the fragmentation of these standards, their multiple sources, and the limited conceptual frameworks on which they rest have not resulted in a coherent, well-articulated, widely accepted set of learning goals for U.S. school mathematics that would detail what students at each grade should know and be able to do."[18]
- *With respect to instructional programs and materials:* "The methods used in the United States in the twentieth century for producing school mathematics textbooks and for choosing which textbooks and other materials to use are not sufficient for the goals of the twenty-first century. The nation must develop a greater capacity for producing high-quality materials and for using effectively those that are produced."[19]

- *With respect to assessments:* "The current national focus on standards-based testing is a definite improvement on the past focus on comparison testing. But standards-based assessment needs to be accompanied by a clear set of grade-level goals so that teachers, parents, and the whole community can work together to help all children in a school achieve these goals. . . . Continuing informal assessments throughout the year can help teachers adjust their teaching and identify students who need additional help. More such help might be available if money formerly spent on comparison testing were reallocated to help children learn."[20]
- *With respect to teaching:* "There is a growing body of evidence suggesting that states and local districts 'interested in improving student achievement may be well-advised to attend, at least in part, to the preparation and qualifications of the teachers they hire and retain in the profession. . . .' [The] NAEP identified the percentage of teachers with full certification and a major in the field they teach as a strong and consistent predictor of student achievement in mathematics, considerably stronger than such factors as class sizes, pupil-teacher ratios, state per-pupil spending, or teachers' salaries. This link between teacher qualification and student achievement raises the question of how good that achievement is."[21]
- *With respect to achievement:* "[M]any U.S. students are not being given the educational opportunities they need to achieve at high levels."[22]

What *Adding It Up* suggests is a state of affairs in which mathematics education is both good and bad, positive and negative. Although some things are working well, others need improvement. Significantly, the NRC contends that the causes in both directions are multiple—purpose, content, method, assessment, money, policy, and so on. The NRC shares the wealth and spreads the blame, a position with which we agree and with which we totally concur. For instance, we accept that mathematics education should be goal-driven—that purpose ought to influence (at least) classroom life, especially via the curriculum—but question, to some extent, that standards-based teaching should, finally, predominate.

THE CRITICISM

Criticism of contemporary mathematics education in the United States tends toward a few principal and repetitive points. Overall, it emphasizes certain beliefs organized around and stemming from the notion that, in one way or another, American students (1) do not *know* enough and (2) cannot *do* enough. As with other modes of recent school criticism, much of this effort builds on concerns initially expressed in *A Nation at Risk,* and draws upon conservative commentators (e.g., E. D. Hirsch, Jr.), professional academics (e.g., mathematics professors), and a range of corporate and government leaders.[23]

The possibility that students in the United States neither know nor can do enough mathematics generally originates via one of two dominant perspectives. Some critics insist that the problem involves too little focus on traditional fact-based content (e.g., memorizing multiplication tables) and the memorization of algorithmic procedures and formulas (e.g., the "old-fashioned" steps "inherent" in long division). Stills others make the claim of ineffectiveness based upon either (1) national achievement studies (e.g., the National Assessment of Educational Progress [NAEP]—"the nation's report card") or (2) international comparison tests (e.g., the Third International Mathematics and Science Study [TIMSS]). Still others, though, insist that math-based curriculum and instruction is *too* traditional. In many cases, from our own viewpoint, these criticisms represent a too cozy relationship among academic content, elitist notions of economic competition, and cultural conservatism, each of which, we maintain, threatens innovation and improvement in mathematics education as well as current goals associated with "deep understanding" and individual and cultural diversity. In that these have been recently unduly influential, we address No Child Left Behind (NCLB) and standards-based educational reform (SBER) in the following section.[24]

NCLB AND SBER

The NCLB Act of 2001 implies that, left to their own devices, teachers and students (as well as those involved with helping and working with them) will mess up—that is, by themselves, they cannot be counted on to implement effectively a significant and rigorous system of curriculum and instruction. Moreover, according to the national government—especially the White House of President George W. Bush and the Department of Education under Secretary Rod Paige—not even states and local districts can be counted on to produce and actualize an appropriate system of public schooling. Thus, a particular, singular, and disciplinary system must be put into place and enforced. The idea, apparently, is that good education requires distrusting teachers and students.

As such, the major principles of NCLB are:

- Increased accountability;
- More choices for parents and students;
- Greater flexibility for states, school districts, and schools; and
- Putting reading first (though, of course, there are other provisions as well).[25]

What these components imply is that teachers and students will not—or cannot—be relied on to do quality work unless made to by some higher and overriding authority. The understanding seems to hold some high-stakes consequence—being left back in grade, firing, withholding funds, and so on—over teachers and students, or they will not teach and learn "real" and "important" mathematics.

More specifically, the government recently has expanded upon NCLB to explicate how it can "help" to improve mathematics achievement.[26] As the administration suggests:

> *The Challenge:* America's schools are not producing the math excellence required for global economic leadership and homeland security in the twenty-first century.
> *The Solution:* Ensure schools use scientifically based methods with long-term records of success to teach math and measure student progress. Establish partnerships with universities to ensure that knowledgeable teachers deliver the best instruction in their field.[27]

The assumptions here are remarkable. The first, of course, is that teachers, students, and schools seek—amazingly—to use something less than the best methods of mathematics education. The second is that the purposes of preK–Ph.D. mathematics education are "global economic leadership" and "homeland security." Perhaps our students should be learning and understanding mathematics for other reasons, too?

Overall, what NCLB (and, to some extent, more contextualized modes of SBER) signifies is that the federal government apparently knows more about math education than do professional math educators. Perhaps. But, in terms of defending public schools, we continue to put our faith in educators and math professionals ahead of our faith in the federal government.

More specifically, and perhaps not unexpectedly, the administration argues that NCLB distinctly improves—as long as math teachers conform—mathematics education. As the White House (and its policy advisors) ask, "How can [and why should] No Child Left Behind *help* improve math achievement?" The answer?

- Math is a critical skill in the information age. We must improve achievement to maintain our economic leadership;
- Math achievement is improving slightly, but much more work must be done to ensure that our children receive a sound background in mathematics;
- No Child Left Behind creates Math and Science Partnerships to rally every sector of society to work with schools to increase math and science excellence;
- The president has called for increasing the ranks and pay of teachers of math and science; [and]
- Our nation must research the best way to teach math and science and measure students' progress in math.[28]

On the other hand, there is no clear indication that this means math education improves (or will improve—or even *can* improve) under NCLB. Still, if nothing else, at least the national government takes (or claims to take) mathematics education seriously.

Even more precisely, the administration claims the following statements (both hopeful *and* critical) to be true:

- While technology advances with lightning speed, stagnant math performance in schools shortchanges our students' future and endangers our prosperity and our nation's security;
- According to the 2000 National Assessment of Educational Progress (NAEP), the average math scores of fourth, eighth, and twelfth graders have improved only slightly;
- . . . [O]nly a quarter of our fourth and eighth graders are performing at or above proficient levels in math. Twelfth-grade math scores have not improved since 1996, and a closer look at those scores reveals that the biggest drop occurred at the lowest levels of achievement. These are the students who most need our help and who can least afford to lose any more ground;
- The National Science Foundation and the U.S. Department of Education will provide an estimated $1 billion over five years for results-oriented partnerships between local districts and universities to bring urgency, tested methods, and high-level expertise to rebuilding math excellence;
- Partnerships [between schools and universities] will invite businesses, science centers, museums, and community organizations to unite with schools to improve achievement;
- The program rewards states for increasing participation of students in advanced courses in math and science and passing advanced placement exams;
- To ensure accountability, the partnerships must report annually to the U.S. Secretary of Education on progress in meeting their set objectives, aligned to state standards;
- No Child Left Behind requires states to fill the nation's classrooms with teachers who are knowledgeable and experienced in math and science by 2005. The president supports paying math and science teachers more to help attract experience and excellence;
- No Child Left Behind requires that federal funding go only to those programs that are backed by evidence;
- Over the last decade, researchers have scientifically proved the best ways to teach reading. We must do the same in math. That means using only research-based teaching methods and rejecting unproven fads; [and]
- The new law also requires states to measure students' progress in math annually in grades 3 to 8 beginning in 2005.[29]

Arguably, all of this reflects both traditional criticism and the presumption that (1) contemporary American mathematics education is failing and (2) teachers must be monitored more exactly and severely than ever before. Yet we are not entirely convinced of the validity of some of the points cited by the administration and upon which, in part, NCLB is based. There are, of course, dangers, especially with respect to the annual testing provision and the concomitant demand for curriculum standards and standardization. For as we have maintained previously, in addition to curriculum and instruction per se, the imperatives of democracy, antioppression, authenticity, and the collective good must be kept in mind.[30]

TIMSS

The criticisms implied in NCLB and other models of SBER frequently draw on various kinds of formal and comparative testing data. Much of this criticism chastises American schools, teachers, and children for underperforming with respect to and against those in other "industrialized" countries. Most specifically, TIMSS asks:

- How does student knowledge of mathematics . . . in the United States compare with that of students in other nations?
- How do . . . mathematics curricula and expectations for student learning in the United States compare with those of other nations?
- How does classroom instruction in the United States compare with that of other nations?
- Do U.S. teachers receive as much support in their efforts to teach as do their counterparts in other nations?
- Are U.S. students as focused on their studies as their international counterparts?[31]

TIMSS, perhaps, offers the most comprehensive comparison of international mathematics achievement in existence. But what does it really say? How badly, or how well, in other words, do American children perform?

TIMSS focuses mainly on the mathematical ability and achievement levels of fourth-, eighth-, and twelfth-grade students, and involves thirty-eight participating nations. The most recent and comprehensive data come from 1999 results and focus on fourth- and eighth-grade students. Specifically, TIMSS demonstrates that (for eighth-grade students, among other findings):

- In 1999, U.S. eighth graders exceeded the international average of the thirty-eight participating nations in mathematics and science;
- In mathematics, U.S. eighth-grade students outperformed their peers in seventeen nations, performed similarly to their peers in six nations, and performed lower than their peers in fourteen nations in 1999;
- Of the five mathematics content areas assessed in 1999, U.S. eighth graders performed higher than the international average in fractions and number sense; data representation, analysis, and probability; and algebra. They performed at the international average of the 38 TIMSS-R—with "R" defined as "repeat"— nations in measurement and geometry;
- In 1999, the United States was one of sixteen TIMSS-R nations in which eighth-grade boys and girls performed similarly in mathematics. In four nations, eighth-grade boys outperformed eighth-grade girls in mathematics.[32]

Additionally, TIMSS indicates that between 1995 and 1999 (with respect to the twenty-three nations that participated in both TIMSS and TIMSS-R):

- There was no change in eighth-grade mathematics . . . achievement in the United States;
- Across the five mathematics content areas in common between TIMSS and TIMSS-R, there was no change in achievement for eighth graders in the United States and most of the other twenty-two nations;
- U.S. eighth-grade black students showed an increase in their achievement in mathematics over the four years. . . . U.S. eighth-grade white and Hispanic students showed no change in their mathematics . . . achievement between 1995 and 1999; and
- There were no changes in mathematics . . . achievement for U.S. eighth-grade boys and girls between 1995 and 1999.[33]

Moreover, TIMSS compared the achievement of eighth-grade students in 1999 with their achievement in 1995 when they were fourth graders. It found that (among other discoveries), "the mathematics . . . performance of the United States relative to this group of nations was lower for eighth graders in 1999 that it was for fourth graders 4 years earlier, in 1995." Thus, students in the United States seemed to do better in mathematics in grade four than in grade eight.

Lastly, TIMSS commented on "Teaching and Curriculum in 1999," especially regarding "differences in teaching and curriculum between the United States and other TIMSS-R nations." Specifically:

- According to their teachers, U.S. eighth-grade students were less likely than their international peers to be taught mathematics by teachers with a major or main area of study in mathematics, but as likely as their international peers to be taught by teachers who majored in mathematics education . . . ;
- Ninety-four percent of U.S. eighth graders said that their mathematics teachers showed them how to do mathematics problems almost always or pretty often in 1999, which was higher than the international average of 86 percent;
- Eighty-six percent of U.S. eighth-grade students reported that they worked from worksheets or textbooks on their own almost always or pretty often during mathematics lessons in 1999, which was higher than the international average of 59 percent;
- A higher percentage of U.S. eighth graders reported using computers almost always or pretty often in mathematics classes (12 percent) . . . than their international peers in 1999 (5 percent);
- A higher percentage of U.S. eighth-grade students reported that they could almost always or pretty often begin their mathematics . . . homework during class (74 percent . . .) than their international peers (42 percent . . .).[34]

Overall, and in the end, with respect to the findings of TIMSS and TIMSS-R, math education in the United States seems at least adequate. While not perfect, in our view and even in that of TIMSS, many positive and productive processes ultimately take place.

NAEP

NAEP serves well as a source of criticism for those opposed to the contemporary workings of American mathematics education. Yet NAEP, like TIMSS, shows that in many ways students are doing fairly well (surprisingly or not). In fact, the major findings for fourth and eighth graders, the same subset of students measured by TIMMS, are that:

- The percentages of fourth graders performing at or above *Basic,* at or above *Proficient,* and at *Advanced* were all higher in 2003 than in all previous assessment years since 1990 [*Basic, Proficient,* and *Advanced* are terms employed by NAEP to represent levels of student achievement];
- The percentages of eighth graders performing at or above *Basic* and at or above *Proficient* were both higher in 2003 than in all previous years since 1990; [and]
- The percentage of eighth graders performing at *Advanced* was higher in 2003 than in 1990.[35]

Like TIMSS, what NAEP demonstrates, contrary to the views of many contemporary critics of mathematics education in the United States, is that students do—and are doing—a pretty reasonable job. In other words, fourth and eighth graders know more—and are being taught more by their teachers—than perhaps many Americans suspect.

NCTM: PRINCIPLES AND STANDARDS

The NCTM has long sought to improve and strengthen preK–12 mathematics curricula through the creation of rigorous and substantive standards documents, including those related to teaching, content, and assessment (as well as others). Perhaps today, the most significant is its *Principles and Standards for School Mathematics,* published in 2000. Together with the curriculum standards developed in the various states and local districts, *Principles and Standards* presents a powerful guide to, and influence upon, contemporary mathematics education.

Principles and Standards initially builds from its foundational "six principles for school mathematics." These are:

- *Equity:* Excellence in mathematics education requires equity—high expectations and strong support for all students.
- *Curriculum:* A curriculum is more than a collection of activities; it must be coherent, focused on important mathematics, and well articulated across the grades.
- *Teaching:* Effective mathematics teaching requires understanding what students know and need to learn and then challenging and supporting them to learn it well.

- *Learning:* Students must learn mathematics with understanding, actively building new knowledge from experience and previous knowledge.
- *Assessment:* Assessment should support the learning of important mathematics and furnish useful information to both teachers and students.
- *Technology:* Technology is essential in teaching and learning mathematics; it influences the mathematics that is taught and enhances students' learning.[36]

Of course, for this chapter, the curriculum principle is most important. As the NCTM states:

> In a coherent curriculum, mathematical ideas are linked to and build on one another so that students' understanding and knowledge deepen and their ability to apply mathematics expands. An effective mathematics curriculum focuses on important mathematics that will prepare students for continued study and for solving problems in a variety of school, home, and work settings. A well-articulated curriculum challenges students to learn increasingly more sophisticated mathematical ideas as they continue their studies.[37]

In addition, *Principles and Standards* includes five "content standards" and five "process standards." The content standards emphasize both *interdisciplinary* topics—"number and operations," "measurement," "data analysis and probability"—and *disciplinary* topics—"algebra," "geometry." The process standards embody skills and understandings pertinent not only just to mathematics, but to other subject matter areas and domains as well. They encompass "problem solving," "reasoning and proof," "communication," "connections" (i.e., content integration), and "representations" (i.e., the depiction of mathematical ideas in the forms of "pictures, concrete materials, tables, graphs . . . symbols, spreadsheet displays, and so on").[38]

Although some of the orientations and specifics of the NCTM's work might be controversial, as is the case with any other system of curriculum standards, the organization does succeed in melding teaching and learning; purpose, curriculum, instruction, and assessment; disciplinarity and interdisciplinarity; fact and skill; content and process; traditionalism and change; and criticism and praise. All things considered, the NCTM has outdone the work of many other professional educational organizations.

PROFICIENCY

Regardless of particular, personal opinions, albeit most optimistically, everyone interested in mathematics education desires and advocates "mathematical proficiency." That is, no matter what ideology or educational philosophy we hold, we all want students to know and to be able to do and understand math as well as possible.

But what is mathematical proficiency? Certainly, it can mean different things to different people. NCTM posits that their ambitious Standards are required to develop societal members who have the capability to think and reason mathematically and who possess a useful base of knowledge and skills; that is, a mathematically proficient society, regardless of what it *might* mean. We (1) follow the National Research Council (NRC) and (2) ground proficiency in the "nature" and hermeneutics of the curriculum.

According to the NRC in *Adding It Up,* mathematical proficiency incorporates five interrelated or "intertwined strands" of comprehension, namely:

- *conceptual understanding*—comprehension of mathematical concepts, operations, and relations;
- *procedural fluency*—skill in carrying out procedures flexibly, accurately, efficiently, and appropriately;
- *strategic competence*—ability to formulate, represent, and solve mathematical problems;
- *adaptive reasoning*—capacity for logical thought, reflection, explanation, and justification;
- *productive disposition*—habitual inclination to see mathematics as sensible, useful, and worthwhile, coupled with a belief in diligence and one's own efficacy.[39]

Moreover:

> *the five strands are interwoven and interdependent in the development of proficiency in mathematics.* . . . [Thus, m]athematical proficiency is not a one-dimensional trait, and it cannot be achieved by focusing on just one or two of these strands. . . . That proficiency should enable [children/students] to cope with the mathematical challenges of daily life and enable them to continue their study of mathematics in high school and beyond. . . . The five strands provide [in the end] a framework for discussing the knowledge, skills, abilities, and beliefs that constitute mathematical proficiency.[40]

As critical as we can be, and have sometimes been in the past, we recognize that NCTM, TIMSS, NAEP, and the variety of both supporters and critics of contemporary mathematics education all hope for some level of mathematical proficiency, and that fundamentally mathematical proficiency, whatever its nature, is imperative with respect to a high quality mathematical education.

CONCLUSIONS: PROSECUTION, DEFENSE, VERDICT

No one can argue that the world is becoming more mathematical. Unfortunately, decision makers do not think mathematically at times and, thus, decisions are often made that could have benefited from mathematical insights drawn from teachers and mathematics educators. While, clearly, not all that occurs relative to mathematics education is perfect, certainly a lot of good does transpire. There are, of course, various differences of opinion.

Nonetheless, we believe that whatever good occurs can be attributed to teachers and students (and, no doubt, others) as they strive to do their very best under often difficult circumstances (frequently imposed upon schools by the various powers that be). Our verdict? Mathematics education is strong and ever evolving (though interested readers might see the recent special issue of *Educational Leadership*[41] for more details), though, indeed, it is not all that it can be.

The authors advocate that mathematics be taught using engaging, collaborative, and pedagogically sound strategies and that authentic investigations be effectively integrated such that learners of mathematics realize that mathematics is a natural, integral, and necessary part of their lives. By experiencing the natural connections between the mathematics curriculum and their everyday lives while using appropriate tools and technology, students will come to view mathematics as an enjoyable part of their environment. Regardless, mathematics in our schools must remain a key point of concern. If, and only if, we take mathematics education seriously, can we even *begin* to claim that we are doing all the positive things that we can do to meet the needs of twenty-first-century learners.

— 5 —

Science in Public Schools: What Is It and Who Is It For?

BRUCE JOHNSON AND ELISABETH ROBERTS

Science literacy for all is the hallmark of science education reform in public schools today. It is an appealing idea, one that seems at first glance to be rather straightforward. In practice, it has been anything but that.

Take a moment and think about the meanings of two interwoven aspects of science literacy for all. First, what is it? What does it mean to be scientifically literate? Second, who is it for? Are we talking about what is important and relevant for all students, or are we talking about exposing all students to science in the hope that more will master its rigors and become our next generation of scientists?

In this chapter, we explore these two important aspects of science in the public schools. Rather than artificially separate the discussion into the "what" and the "who," we talk about them together. They are truly two sides of the same issue, and it seems to us to make sense to deal with them in that way. First, we look at how we got where we are in science education today. Next, we explore the current major emphases, issues, and realities. Finally, we contrast where we are with where we might be in relation to science literacy for all.

HOW WE GOT HERE

For over 100 years, what constitutes science in public schools in the United States has swung between an emphasis on content and an emphasis on process. These shifts have been closely related to changes in perceptions of the purposes of public schools. For science, the debate has been between preparing future scientists and helping all people understand science and its applications in and to their lives. The place of science in the public school system became established in the late 1800s through the influence of those in higher education, such as the Committee of Ten, who essentially determined the curriculum of the new public schools by setting college entrance requirements. Science began to take its place in education as both a subject and a method of instruction.

During the early part of the twentieth century, the rapid spread of public education beyond K–8 led to calls for a common curriculum for high schools. The common science subjects that are almost universally found in high schools date back to the 1920s. Biology, chemistry, and physics became the standard set of courses, while other areas of science were either set aside or subsumed into these courses. For instance, specific courses in botany, zoology, or anatomy were merged, at least to some extent, into biology. Other sciences such as geology and astronomy were, for the most part, left out. At the same time, school science became firmly founded on the disciplines of science—in other words, the disciplines themselves determined what knowledge, models, and examples within a field must be mastered in order for students to be deemed scientifically literate. In the public school curriculum, science remained a "classic" discipline, meant for those students intending to continue on to college. As scientific knowledge grew and became more specialized during the first half of the twentieth century, so to did the accompanying textbooks and curricula.

In contrast to the increased focus on specialized curricula, the progressive education movement issued repeated calls for an examination of the purposes of schooling. John Dewey and others called for reform in order to make schools more relevant to students and more focused on the needs of society. In science, this meant such things as concentrating on broad ideas and principles, providing opportunities for students to develop critical thinking skills, using "real" problems, and emphasizing the practical applications of science.

Through the late 1940s and the 1950s, there was a gradual movement away from the concern about social and personal relevance in education that had been a focus of the progressive education movement. A shortage of scientists in World War II was one of the factors that led to a rejection of progressive education. With the Soviet Union's launch of *Sputnik* in 1957, the gradual shift became an overnight crusade to change science education in order to produce more and better scientists. The crisis of *Sputnik* and the Cold War with the USSR led the United States government to launch its own massive effort in curriculum reform in general and in science education in particular. There was an unprecedented level of support and funding from the federal government, much of it through the government's National Science Foundation. Jerome Bruner and Joseph Schwab provided the theoretical basis for the curriculum reform movement of the 1960s. Bruner emphasized teaching the structure and organized content or knowledge of science, while Schwab focused on the processes of inquiry used by scientists. Scientists became increasingly involved, coming up with the "big ideas" of their disciplines for which courses could be designed. The aims of science education included both knowledge and processes in the pursuit of the end result of more scientists and engineers. There was little emphasis on how science relates to social problems or to the lives of the learners. Practicality was out and experiential learning was sent to the domain of vocational education, often meant for those who "couldn't handle" the "rigors" of a more academic program.

Elementary education, long grounded in the child-centered philosophy of Froebel and others (including Maria Montessori), had not until now considered science in the curriculum. Building on the field of developmental or age-based psychology vis-à-vis the work of Jean Piaget, Bruner developed a theory of the curriculum as a "spiral"—that one could teach any subject at any age, provided the content was represented in a way that was accessible to the developing mind of the learner. For example, Piaget argued that children develop an understanding of function, or of how a change in one variable leads to a change in another, when they squish clay on a surface with their hand and discover that the harder they squish, the flatter the clay becomes.

Such research and emerging theories on the nature of learning led to the first stage of science education reform in the early 1960s, when the instructional strategy of "hands-on" learning was first introduced. The 1960s and 1970s brought a wide range of educational reforms, including everything from classrooms without walls to "discovery-based" science programs such as Elementary Science Study (ESS). The curriculum reform movement produced a great number of science curricula and texts, including the Biological Sciences Curriculum Study's texts for secondary biology classes, CHEM Study for secondary chemistry, and Science—A Process Approach (SAPA) and Science Curriculum Improvement Study (SCIS) for elementary science. The baby boom generation was the first educational cohort to be exposed to this type of science curriculum: playing with pulleys and levers, mixing mystery powders, or building models of cellular osmosis using hard-boiled eggs, vinegar, and iodine.

Despite its power to engage learners, this first wave of elementary science reform failed to last. Research on the nature of social change and diffusion of innovations in schools uncovered several reasons. School administrators, trained according to models of efficiency that arose from the Industrial Revolution and behaviorist theory, believed that implementation meant delivering the kits to classrooms. Teachers were provided few opportunities to learn either the content on which the kits were based or the underlying model for learning. Systems for restocking the consumable materials were rarely established. After several years, the remains of most elementary science kits wound up interred in the back of the school storage closet.

Even as the elementary reform faltered, the cultural liberalism of the 1960s and 1970s, the success of the United States space program, and the growing awareness of Earth as an ecosystem gave rise to the Science-Technology-Society (STS) movement. STS educators emphasized the practical and personal aspects of science, the role of technology in science, and social and cultural perspectives on science. Yet even as STS emerged, disillusionment with the social liberalism of the 1960s and 1970s in general and with many of its related educational reforms in particular led to the federal government's 1983 report, *A Nation at Risk*. The findings in the report, such as that students failed to demonstrate basic understandings in core content on standardized tests, drove fears of the "dumbing down" of education and the loss of a competitive intellectual and economic edge in the international arena. Science rose to the status of literacy and mathematics as key to national interests. Federal funding again poured into science education reform with the goal of not only producing future scientists but also educating all citizens to become better decision makers in a complex, scientific world.

WHERE WE ARE

It was in this context that the current reform efforts were born. While concerns about a lack of well-prepared scientists were (and are still) frequently heard, changes in our understandings about the nature of science and of learning in science have led to a new vision for science education, that of "inquiry." Inquiry as a unifying theme in science education aims to provide coherence across our philosophies of what knowledge in science is most important, our beliefs about how people learn and use science, and recommendations about science teaching and assessment. As such, inquiry is necessarily a fuzzy notion, not unlike democracy, and represents many interests. Although most educators and scientists agree on the general ideas of inquiry, fundamental differences in belief about science education remain. In fact, not one but two sets of "national" guidelines for science education emerged: *Benchmarks for Science Literacy,* produced by the American Association for the Advancement of Science (AAAS) in 1993, and the *National Science Education Standards,* produced by the National Research Council (NRC) in 1996. A brief explanation of the origins and distinguishing features of each document is critical to understanding the challenges of science education that public schools now face.

In 1989, the AAAS published a slim book, *Science for All Americans.* The result of three years of research and negotiation among scientists, mathematicians, educators, philosophers, and historians, the book judged the present science curriculum to be "overstuffed and undernourished" and argued for "a common core of learning . . . limited to the ideas and skills having the greatest scientific and educational significance for scientific literacy."[1] *Science for All Americans* defines the scientifically literate person as:

> one who is aware that science, mathematics, and technology are interdependent human enterprises with strengths and limitations; understands key concepts and principles of science; is familiar with the natural world and recognizes both its diversity and unity; and uses scientific knowledge and scientific ways of thinking for individual and social purposes.

This was a radically new conception of both science as a discipline and the purposes of science education. Science is now characterized as a human pursuit inextricable from cultural values, economics, and politics; dependent on mathematics as a language of reasoning; and integrally tied to technology design and development.

Three years after *Science for All Americans,* AAAS published *Benchmarks for Science Literacy*, the first comprehensive "map" to essential understandings, or "benchmarks," in science. The metaphor of benchmarks is embedded in a newer psychology of human cognition that views "understanding" as a complex web of interdependent concepts that develop both from concrete experiences and our reflections on those experiences. It is key to understand that benchmarks are neither "facts" nor "outcomes" in the traditional sense of educational objectives but rather landmarks of cognitive knowledge that are necessary for a literate person in order to understand science concepts, reason scientifically, and comprehend the nature of scientific inquiry and how scientific knowledge has been constructed throughout history. The authors of *Benchmarks* deemphasized the use of scientific vocabulary, traditionally a large proportion of instruction and testing in science, arguing that few adults will remember or need to know the differences between revolve and rotate, nimbus and cumulus clouds, or meiosis and mitosis. They also consciously chose not to use the technical language of educational objectives but instead to phrase the goals in language that children at different levels of cognitive development would use. Thus, for example, a typical benchmark from grades six to eight, The Living Environment, reads: "By the end of 8th grade, students should know that individual organisms with certain traits are more likely than others to survive and have offspring. Changes in environmental conditions can affect the survival of individual organisms and entire species."[2] Likewise, *Benchmarks* identifies abilities to do science and understandings of the nature of science: "Scientists differ greatly in what phenomena they study and how they go about their work. Although there is no fixed set of steps that all scientists follow, scientific investigations usually involve the collection of relevant evidence, the use of logical reasoning, and the application of imagination in devising hypotheses and explanations to make sense of the collective evidence."[3]

The authors of *Benchmarks* describe its development as "truly a grass-roots effort" involving hundreds of teachers, administrators, engineers, mathematicians, and scientists who met in an iterative process over three years and across almost all fifty states. The Benchmarks discuss in detail issues of language and thinking about learning that the development group grappled with during their process. They describe the research base and specific findings with which they worked and carefully acknowledge their stumbling blocks, pitfalls, and the reasons behind their choices of metaphors, such as benchmark, and regarding their views relative to the division of grade levels and underlying theories of human development, learning, and teaching. Their intent, as described in the preface, was to meet the challenges of education in the context of exploding types and quantities of scientific knowledge and an increasingly diverse society, "not by offering a standard curriculum to be adopted locally but by providing educators in every state and school district with a powerful tool to use in fashioning their own curricula."

If these samples of the Benchmarks signify that this is not the science of yesteryear or the science that most Americans think children should learn in public school, then most people probably agree—that is, such a view probably dominates. Two fundamental decisions—to deemphasize both technical vocabulary and phrasing in terms of measurable objectives—represent a definite shift in beliefs away from science as authority toward all people having an understanding of, and a voice in, the conduct of science. This shift follows in the footsteps of modern philosophers, such as Thomas Kuhn, and the emergence of postmodernist sociological research into the actual practices of scientists. Educators now propose that the traditional "correct" scientific method, that of testing hypotheses, is but one process embedded in a larger system of inquiry into the natural world that is not necessarily "objective" per se but rather and inherently one that emerges from human culture and communications practices. For those coming from traditional scientific training or educational systems, this represents nothing less than a new worldview, a new paradigm. And as Kuhn pointed out in *The Structure of Scientific Revolutions*, new paradigms are neither obvious nor easily accepted by those trained within the conceptual "box" of the old. School and curriculum practices arise out of a continuous negotiation among diverse cultural and political beliefs. As such, in the case of science education, many critical issues have not yet been reconciled.

Although *Project 2061* and the development of *Benchmarks* had been underway at AAAS for nearly eight years, a second group of educators and scientists convened under the auspices of the National Academy of Sciences and the National Research Council with a federal mandate to develop a set of national standards in science. This group published its version as the *National Science Education Standards* (NSES) in 1996. In contrast to the Benchmarks, the NSES grew out of *A Nation at Risk* and a resulting movement for national education standards first put forth by the National Governors Association (headed by then Governor of Arkansas Bill Clinton) in 1989. While acknowledging *Benchmarks* and *Science for All Americans* as "precursors," the NSES are presented as the "official" guideline document for science education and differ in several essential respects from its predecessors.

A brief comparison of the tables of contents (see Table 5.1) demonstrates the differences in underlying beliefs about the nature of science and what should concern science education, particularly in the realm of what content knowledge is deemed important and how that content is to be organized. Note that the NSES eliminate mathematics and retain the original physical-life-earth science structure of the early high school curriculum as well as traditional disciplines of study. The nature of science is presented as Inquiry-with-a-capital-I, whereas the history and nature of science are presented as secondary to knowledge in the disciplines. (One could argue, in the light of modern thinking, that both documents err by attempting to separate out "the nature of science" from a discussion of knowledge.) One strength of the NSES as a document is that it presents the "content understandings" of science within the context of the larger systemic factors that must be in place to support true educational reform, including teacher professional development, assessment, program design, and community supports. In this, the NRC upstaged AAAS, who had designed its overall project with these elements and was working on several publications in support of the Benchmarks.[4]

There are ongoing debates and concerns about both of these guides, as well as the state and district standards that have emerged in their wake. In

Table 5.1
Comparison of Table of Contents in Science Content Areas

Benchmarks for Science Literacy	NSES
The Nature of Science	Unifying Concepts and Processes
The Nature of Mathematics	Science as Inquiry
The Nature of Technology	Physical Science
The Physical Setting	Life Science
The Living Environment	Earth and Space Science
The Human Organism	Science and Technology
Human Society	Science in Personal and Historical Perspectives
The Designed World	History and Nature of Science
The Mathematical World	
Historical Perspectives	
Common Themes	
Habits of Mind	

particular, many ask: Who determines what is of "greatest scientific and educational significance"? This is a valid question in a pluralistic democracy, one that is acknowledged by the authors of SFAA and *Benchmarks* but not by the NSES. While some of the members of AAAS sat on the advisory board and team that directed NSES, each document arose from different purposes, and each has philosophical roots in early and ongoing conversations about the purposes of public schooling. In theory, the emergence of two sets of standards in science could be heralded as giving more options to districts, schools, teachers, and curriculum developers—Apple or IBM. In practice, the NSES as "official" public policy has become the more widely promoted and cited document. We suspect this is due to its being more reflective of the traditional "structure of the disciplines" model of science. The Standards align more readily with existing college entrance examination requirements, standardized tests, and the multibillion dollar educational materials industry. Regardless of one's political leanings, however, both documents raise particular challenges that have been left to the users to solve. Our discussion now examines some of these.

CHALLENGES

As always in education, one overarching question is how best to turn theory into practice. While the vision of "inquiry" is grounded in research on cognition and learning, we are still far from certain exactly how to design learning experiences that will result in students' achievement of understanding of all the 200-plus Benchmarks or Standards by the end of grade twelve. We also must grapple with the traditional power structures and models of schooling that hold to a "one-size-fits-most" view of learning and teaching and must negotiate a consumer-driven, sound-bite-oriented culture. For example, research across disciplines indicates that learning is a continual process of making sense of our experiences through hands-on investigation and reflection, communication, and negotiation within a community or culture. Novices become experts through an iterative process of encountering and solving problems, one by which they construct some understanding of both deep content knowledge and problem-solving strategies. Expertise is a multifaceted phenomenon that includes the ability to focus attention, sustain motivation, recognize patterns, recall prior experiences with similar problems, and to see "under" the surface features of a problem through to the big ideas. We know that expertise in physics, for example, is the ability to see under the concrete features of a ball and a ramp to recognize that the problem is really about forces. A scientist has the ability to interpret data in the light of theory, to weigh evidence and construct arguments that will illuminate or challenge existing explanations. Still, scientists and science learners are cognitively very different. In science education, we know a lot more about how to describe the characteristics of "experts" than we do about how to develop them. Scientists conduct inquiry with and from a deep knowledge base and an apprenticeship in research methods. In contrast, science students encounter content knowledge understandings *at the same time* they are learning methods of inquiry. Students' discourse in a community of learners, framed within traditional school structures such as forty-five-minute class periods, has very different processes and rules than discourse in a community of scientists. Science in the last fifty years has become increasingly distributed across a network of people, laboratories, and countries who coordinate their work in order to address data-intensive questions such as the nature of matter or the sequence of the human genome. Yet students are still being instructed and evaluated primarily as individuals in classrooms that have little connection to the outside world beyond the realm of the commercial Internet. Finally, we know that students interpret experiences from their senses, which can lead them to "naïve conceptions" or "misconceptions." Overcoming misconceptions requires multiple experiences, careful reasoning, and time for students' brains to develop the ability to reason abstractly and logically. The Benchmarks and the Standards have presented science educators with a paradox: construct learning experiences that engage and empower all learners that nevertheless result in their achieving an understanding of over 200 specific items. How does a school system with standards, regulations, standardized tests, and college admissions concerns reconcile itself to such a stochastic outcome, to these disparities between the nature of science and of education?

Given the advances in our understanding of how people learn, and that learning is an active process of sense-making, we can no longer speak of science as a body of accumulated facts without equally considering how those facts are developed and understood by students. We know from four decades of research that people learn through an active, experiential process, filter their experiences through prior knowledge and beliefs, and develop both communication and reasoning skills through extended practice with language, discourse, and symbol systems or representations (such as mathematics). Yet the specifics of what inquiry is, what it looks like in action, and other practical matters have been left to today's generation of teachers and educators to create. Needless to say, this has caused a few bumps in the road to science literacy for all.

As an example of some of the promises and challenges of implementing the vision of inquiry in public schools, we offer a story from our own experience. Beginning in the 1970s, a group of researchers in cognitive psychology began to focus on children's understandings of particular science concepts. This research revealed that while students often could "demonstrate" knowledge by selecting the correct answer on a test, they retained fundamental misunderstandings that were masked by their ability to memorize vocabulary. In physics, students could define "heat" and "temperature" without being able to explain how one related to the other, or why it was important to calibrate a thermometer in an experiment. Students clung to ideas based on daily life, such as the idea that different objects at room temperature are warmer or cooler because they feel so to the touch—when in fact the objects are at the same ambient temperature (it is the different transfer rates of heat from our hands to the object that creates the sensation of different temperatures).[5]

Some of these researchers then went on to exploit the powers of a new tool, the microcomputer, to allow students to collect temperature data through electronic probes and instantly view that data as a graph of temperature change over time on the computer screen. These "microcomputer-based laboratories" (commonly known as MBL or CBL) promised to "revolutionize science education" with the power of real-time experiments and graphic representations. In fact, several researchers[6] did find that, under certain conditions, middle and high school students were able to develop a depth of conceptual understanding of the difference between heat and temperature as well as an ability to interpret correctly graphical displays of data (one of the most persistent problems in science and mathematics education today).

Over the past twenty years, the development and availability of these and other technology "tools for learning" has exploded, especially in science and mathematics. Technology supplies powerful tools to support inquiry. The features of real-time data collection and display, video, animation, and other multimedia presentations all have been shown to help students develop conceptual understandings of important underlying phenomena in science, especially those that are highly abstract (such as heat and temperature), exist at scales we are otherwise unable to observe (macroscopic and microscopic, extremely long or short periods of time), or conflict with everyday experience (such as Newton's laws of motion in a world without friction).[7] Scientists, in fact, created the Internet as a tool for exchanging large amounts of geographically dispersed data.

Why then do we not see these tools in every science classroom, at appropriate grade levels? On one hand, initially, there were practical realities. Most of the money in technology budgets for education went into wiring schools for the Internet, managing networks, and purchasing hardware and software. Additionally, there was either a lack of vision or a daunting degree of resistance to change. Few resources were invested in developing or communicating a vision of technology or providing teacher professional development to ensure equitable distribution and curriculum integration. As Seymour Papert described, schools reacted to technology innovations by "inoculating" against the innovation—isolating technology from daily school activity by setting it aside in laboratories reserved for a few. Moreover, we would argue further that an innovation such as collecting and analyzing real-world data with microcomputers went against our culture's deeply held beliefs about what science education "ought to be."

Lastly, we raise a philosophical question. Even if the MBL is a tool that helps students overcome misunderstandings about heat and temperature, how important is that understanding for all students to achieve by the time they graduate from high school? Is it more important than understanding where the energy comes from to heat or cool our homes and schools? From a curriculum perspective, how important is this concept relative to other scientific understandings needed by all Americans? To physicists (it was primarily physicists who began this educational research), this idea is key to a body of knowledge in energy and thermodynamics and, therefore, of pressing importance to research, technology design, and educational reform. From an educator's perspective, perhaps there are two big ideas to get to by twelfth grade: All matter is composed of atoms, and all matter exists in different states depending on the amount of energy atoms can absorb and transfer. To most educators, neither of these ideas is useful or appropriate to children whose brains have not developed to the point where they can reason abstractly about invisible phenomena. But from the perspective of daily life, perhaps the most important thing to understand is that one doesn't want to lick a metal pole when the temperature is below freezing.

Thus has science reform emerged in practice. As in many large-scale reform efforts of the last fifty years, social and political pressures for immediate solutions propelled science educators to recommend and roll out full-scale implementation of curriculum, assessment, and teacher professional development even before the NSES went to press. As a predictable result, schools and teachers have struggled with developing practical solutions in a high-stakes, high-expectations environment over the last ten years. To some degree, avoiding a definition of inquiry was a legitimate choice for educators who hold constructivist beliefs, as a central tenet of constructivist teaching and learning is that there is no "one right way" to "do" inquiry. But in the traditional system of public schooling, such uncertainty is difficult to accept. Though neither the Benchmarks nor the Standards are intended to be guides to either curriculum or instruction, they often are interpreted as such. An entire industry of "standards-based" textbooks, instructional materials, teacher professional development programs, assessments, and research has grown in their wake. Most new textbooks now include a table at the front that purports to align the content in the text with specific benchmarks or standards. District and state adoption committees pressed for time and resources often rely on these tables, rather than the content or instructional methods within, to select new materials for their schools. The result is a general misconception among the public and educators that a standard can be "taught" in one or two classroom activities. Thus, for science curriculum today, most people embrace a fuzzy notion of inquiry as "hands-on and minds-on," while they lack an appreciation of the complexity of orchestrating such a process for all learners.

Despite these problems, the past ten years have demonstrated that inquiry is more than just a vision when it is implemented and supported systemically. We have learned from our earlier reforms. This time, educators and policymakers were aware that a philosophical commitment to a vision of "inquiry" would require a host of practical and structural considerations. Both AAAS and NSES followed their standards documents with others[8] that articulated the various parts and interactions among them that are needed to create organic and long-term change. A second wave of large-scale federal curriculum development grants, mirroring those of the early 1960s, generated a new generation of "inquiry-based" curriculum programs, such as Full Option Science System (FOSS), INSIGHTS, and STC. Soon after came a wave of large-scale reform programs funded by the National Science Foundation to provide intensive and sustained teacher professional development in order to ensure the curriculum materials would be fully implemented in classrooms.

Research from these efforts, some in the form of program evaluations, highlights the central importance of considering curriculum as a system that extends beyond the physical materials to include vision and leadership, professional development, assessment, and the larger range of resources, such as parents, communities, and businesses.[9] In the emergence of the ecological and narrative research traditions, action research, and partnerships between researchers and teachers in real-world schools, we begin to build understanding of the ways in which diverse learners can engage in science. When communities put these integrated pieces into place over five to ten years, children can develop a sense of science and the natural world that is conceptually rich, embodies the nature of science and scientific habits of mind, involves more learners (not only the select few), and affects student achievement not only in science but also in so-called core areas, such as language arts and mathematics.[10] In these communities, local leadership, especially that of the principal, has been critical to developing and sustaining the vision, management, financial resources, and political will necessary to make long- and large-scale science education reform happen.

There are, however, still too many cases where one or more of these systemic pieces is missing or is not aligned with a (if not *the*) vision of inquiry. As in our above example of the MBL, a gap exists between the vision of the standards and the realities of available time, resources, and beliefs. Assessments in the form of high-stakes testing are not aligned with the teaching and learning promoted in science education reform efforts. Curriculum selection and time allotted to subject areas are driven by standardized tests. It is not atypical for an elementary teacher to be told that he or she must give up instructional time for science to these other areas or to practice test-taking skills. Middle school science teachers are told to prepare their students for the rigors of mostly traditional (content coverage) high school classes, which in turn are rigidly defined by standardized achievement tests and college entrance requirements. Despite educators' overall adoption of the vision of inquiry or constructivism, and despite twenty years of reform efforts, our beliefs, habits, and social and cultural systems continue to frame science as a discipline separate from, and now competing with, other content areas.

WHERE WE MIGHT BE

One would be hard-pressed these days to find a science educator at any level who would disagree with the goals of science literacy for all. It is clear that the dual focus on content and process, on what science tells us and on the nature of science, must be included in the "science" part of that goal. What should be included in the "literacy for all" part of it? Because science literacy for all is a broad concept, we have opportunities to be creative in developing the next generation of curriculum. To return to an earlier metaphor, having Benchmarks as well as the Standards keeps the "market" open for alternative approaches to both inquiry and curriculum. In fact, we would argue that it is both possible and necessary to frame a more radical perspective to science literacy for all.

For instance, let's look again at an example from physics, understanding heat and temperature. Energy is a fundamental concern of science, and a great deal of effort has gone into trying to find out what students know about heat and temperature, what their common misconceptions are, and how they are best addressed. These ideas have an important place in standards documents, and students across the country are taught these ideas. How important are these ideas in everyday life? If students better understand these ideas, what is the result? Certainly, one would hope that those going on to study physics would understand these ideas well enough to be successful. It may even be important for scientists studying other areas. But it is difficult to imagine how the ideas are crucial for the rest of us.

On the other hand, there are some critical ideas about energy that are vitally important in our daily lives. For example, each of us gets and uses energy every day. We get our personal energy to live from the food we eat. We also use a great deal of energy to do all kinds of things—from driving cars to working on computers. Where does that energy come from? Much of it comes from burning fossil fuels, in the gasoline or diesel fuel in our vehicle and in the form of coal or natural gas used to generate electricity in our power plants. Why is that important? First, fossil fuels exist in a limited supply. While there is disagreement about how fast we are using up the supplies, no one would argue that we have an unlimited amount. They will someday be gone. Second, burning fossil fuels has harsh consequences, including air pollution, acid rain, and releasing greenhouse gases into the atmosphere. This is an idea with implications, important implications.

Do people understand this? Hardly. Ask anyone you know where his or her electricity comes from. What is the source of the energy used to generate the electricity where you live? We have been asking people this question, and hardly anyone can answer it well. Ask a related question. Is it important to save electricity by doing things like turning out the lights when leaving a room? If so, why? Once again, most people say it is important, but few are able to say much beyond the ideas that wasting is bad and that saving electricity saves money. Hardly anyone understands the connection between his or her hands on the light switch and the consequences of burning fossil fuels.

Surely these energy ideas are of at least equal importance to an understanding of heat and temperature. We would argue that they are of much greater importance. Every one of us makes decisions about our use of electricity every day. These decisions will become even more important in the future as fossil fuels become scarcer and the environmental consequences of depending on them increase. They do not, though, even get equal time in the science curriculum. Why not?

It seems that science literacy for all has meant more of the same science, simply getting it to more students and focusing on helping more students succeed at it rather than making the science being taught more meaningful and important for all. The focus has been on teaching the science better rather than on teaching better (more important) science.

There is currently a renewed focus on the big ideas of science content areas and on understanding how science works rather than on the details and minutiae, the facts and figures. But how have these big ideas been identified? Asking scientists to tell us what are the most important things for students to understand about their discipline is an interesting way of going about selecting what is important. It is based on the belief that we all need to understand a scientific discipline the way a scientist working in it does. Is that really the best way to figure out what is important?

Taking a look at what people need to know in their everyday lives is a different approach, one that hearkens back to John Dewey a century ago. It brings us back to the fundamental questions about the purposes of public schools. Are they meant to prepare people for life or to prepare them for jobs?

Surely, public school science should help students understand how science works—what counts as scientific evidence, what is science and what isn't science, and science as a way of knowing. These ideas are more evident in the standards than they are most classrooms, but the ideas are certainly a part of current reform efforts. A central argument in inquiry, though, is that people learn best when they engage in active experiences that are important and meaningful to them and connected to their daily lives and experiences. So we would ask, then, given that we cannot teach everything in science, especially by grade twelve, which is more important to understand: the mechanisms by which heat is transferred or stored in physical matter, or where the heat energy we use in our daily lives comes from and the implications of that energy production for human and environmental survival? Ideally, we all would have the time and resources needed to understand both. Realistically, we need to choose. Public school science should be both relevant and important. That is where current efforts still fall short in the pursuit of science literacy for all.

— 6 —

Character Education: Coming Full Circle

FOUR ARROWS (DON TRENT JACOBS)

> How can they expect a harvest of thought from those who have not had the seedtime of character.
>
> —Henry David Thoreau

> From the animals, the stars and the sun and the moon, man should learn.
>
> —Chief Letakots-Lesa (Pawnee)

The history of Western character education can generally be categorized into two philosophical orientations. One views character education (C.E.) as a socialization process that inculcates "a collective moral code from the community to the individual through direct instruction, consistent modeling and external incentives."[1] This long-standing approach, which I will refer to as the "Conservative Model," continues to dominate most C.E. programs in public schools today.

The second approach stems from the progressive movement in education. It focuses on developing the students' ability to reason according to ethical and moral principles or universal virtues. In contrast to the Conservative Model, it encourages "open-mindedness, holistic moral development, interactive learning, allowing children to develop naturally and the cultivation of children's ability to make moral judgments through social experiences."[2] I will refer to this as the "Liberal Model."

Both these models contrast with a third approach to character education that is seldom discussed in C.E. literature because it emerges largely from perspectives common to many non-Western indigenous cultures. This view regards C.E. as a spiritual process hallmarked by "a sacred awareness that we are all related and that all things in the seen and unseen universe are interconnected."[3] This "Spiritual Model" offers a possibility not usually conceived in Western C.E., that is, the idea that moral relationships extend beyond anthropocentricism into the visible and invisible aspects of the natural world.

In using these models as a way to explore and understand character education in public schools, I focus more on ideology than on statistical data about the "success" of C.E. programs. Schooling is a socialization process that finds direction through the ideologies of those in charge. Thus, ideological explorations seem vital to analyzing program goals as well as to analyzing how people define and measure C.E. objectives. Framing this chapter with comparisons among these three models expands the ideological debate and offers a unique way to reflect on which aspects of modern C.E. have appropriate value for the future and which do not.

I want to state at the outset that I am not neutral about such choices, and my support goes largely to the Spiritual Model. My observations have led me to conclude that the Conservative Model is more about compliance to authority and to the status quo than about authentic character. The Liberal Model offers important reasons for C.E. but may foster only two aspects of character, those that relate to critical thinking and to awareness of global issues. Although these are crucial dimensions of C.E., reflection and awareness alone are not sufficient to meet the most authentic universal goals of C.E. The Spiritual Model emphasizes being at peace with oneself and one's relationship to the world in ways that involve feeling connected with all life forms—ideas, again, that are largely absent from both the Conservative and the Liberal Models.

A number of Western educators have acknowledged the importance of indigenous perspectives in education. For example, Patrick Slattery says in his text on the subject, "Curriculum development in the postmodern era should give attention to the wisdom embedded in native American spirituality, for it is in the very sacred land of the native people that American education now finds its home."[4] Similarly, Larry Brendtro, a foremost expert in "at-risk" education states:

> Native American philosophies of child management represent what is perhaps the most effective system of positive discipline ever developed. These approaches emerged from cultures where the central purpose of life was the education and empowerment of children. Modern child development research is only now reaching the point where this holistic approach can be understood, validated and replicated.[5]

My endorsement of selected aspects of the indigenous worldview for effective C.E. does not mean that I believe it is privileged in the sense that it is the only absolute truth. Rather, I concur with J. Baird Callicott, who says,

> The indigenous worldviews around the globe can contribute a fund of symbols, images, metaphors, similes, analogies, stories and myths to advance the process of articulating the new postmodern worldview. Thus the contemporary custodians of traditional and indigenous non-Western systems of ideas can be co-creators of a new master narrative for the rainbow race of the global village. They have a vital role to play. . . . We may anticipate a global intellectual dialogue, synthesis, and amalgamation to emerge, rather than an era of Western philosophical hegemony.[6]

With this quote in mind, I submit that public schools may be able to reclaim an authentic role in helping to develop those student dispositions that are vital to educational outcomes by better understanding all three models.

GROUNDING THE MODELS

Both the Conservative Model and the Liberal Model of C.E. emerge from the history of Western education in general. Although such history is too vast a territory to cover in this chapter, a good way to understand the nature of a tree is to study its roots, and the roots of Eurocentric C.E. may well be in Aristotle's book *The Nicomachean Ethics*, arguably the first C.E. text, written in 350 B.C.E.[7]

Aristotle is clear that we are not made good or bad by nature but by habit and training. Virtues, he says, are not found in the passions or faculties of humans but, rather, express themselves through human "states of character" that must be developed through training and hard work. He describes states of character as relating to intellectual or moral virtues, the former requiring teaching, experience, and time, the latter coming about as a result of habit. In both cases, he trusts not nature but rational thinking and teaching as the vehicles for attaining states of character. He uses Olympic athletes as an example of how character can be developed.

Ultimately, he claims, virtues are tied to the happiness of self and of one's friends. Such happiness may be thought of as either a gift from God or a gift to God. To cultivate such happiness, however, takes time and experience within the domain of men (again, specifically not of nature). According to Aristotle, neither animals nor children are capable of being truly happy any more than they are capable of being virtuous.

If we continued to study Aristotle's treatise on virtues and C.E., we would see the essence of ideas that would later influence the philosophies of such thinkers as Nietzsche, James, Heidegger, Piaget, Vygotsky, and Dewey, as well as many others whose writings addressed morality, character, child development, curriculum, and pedagogy. Here, I summarize some assumptions about C.E. that these and more contemporary character educators may have inherited from *The Nicomachean Ethics.*

1. Attitude, effort, and talent are essential for developing character over time.
2. Teachers possess the expertise with which to cultivate character in students.
3. Children are essentially a blank slate when it comes to character development (C.D.). (Here Aristotle disagrees somewhat with his teacher, Plato.)
4. Nature is not a model for C.D. Only in "cities" do the tools exist for C.D.
5. Human passions and faculties can be unhealthy in the absence of C.D.
6. C.E. has both an intellectual and a moral dimension, and both require training.
7. Rational thinking is a basic requirement for C.D.
8. The source of good character comes from the human desire for happiness, both for oneself and for other people in one's society.
9. Happiness through C.D. may be thought of as either a gift from God or a gift to God.
10. Time, teaching, and social experiences are all required for C.D.
11. The training of Olympic athletes is a model for C.D.

Both the Conservative and the Liberal Models seem to incorporate some of these assumptions of Aristotle, in contrast to the Spiritual Model, which seldom relates well to Aristotle's views. I will attempt to illustrate this by presenting Aristotle's basic assertions (in italics), followed by a brief explanation of how each of the three models might relate or might not relate.

Attitude, Effort, and Talent Are Essential for Developing Character over Time

Conservative C.E. tends to see those who do not "pick themselves up by their bootstraps," as per William Bennett's message in the selection of stories for his *Book of Virtues*,[8] as being less than virtuous. Bennett and others of this model prefer attitude, effort, and talent to intellectualizing and reflecting on social experience.[9] These traits, which too often have more to do with class and income than character, are well demonstrated in the achievement of concrete objectives and are exemplified in those who have achieved financial success, thus serving Conservative economic agendas with assumptions that those who have not "succeeded" simply did not have the character to do so.

In the Liberal Model, C.E. also tends to honor these requirements, though in a different way. It is about prosocial dispositions that require a caring attitude, consistent effort at reflecting on social experience, and intellectual talent that is developed over time. Accordingly, the task of a C.E. teacher is to facilitate democratic experiences that promote moral deliberation.[10]

The Spiritual Model for C.E. assumes a worldview that sees *harmonious relationship* as a fundamental prerequisite for a good life. It believes this is more important for character development than effort, attitude, talent, or academic reflection. With such a worldview, generosity is not a goal that one attains via conformity or intellectualism. Rather, it is the vital condition of existence that is obvious in the symbiotic relationships in nature. C.E. in this model is more about developing the courage to manifest this reality than a process of authority-driven schooling that "teaches" moral dispositions.

Teachers Possess the Expertise with Which to Cultivate Character in Students

Conservative C.E. sees this expertise in terms of what is often referred to, following Paulo Freire, as "the banking system of education," that is, teachers must use their expertise to inculcate, or "deposit," character into students based on their expert knowledge about character. It tends to believe that a "pervasive relativism and an ultraliberal view of morals, a belief in the absolute right and freedom of the individual to choose his or her own lifestyle, have eroded the best of what a more traditional view of ethics and morality once provided."[11] Therefore, a counter to such relativism is the expert authority's ability and will to inculcate absolute values and dispositions that have "proved" themselves in the examples of historical role models.

The Liberal Model and its emphasis on social justice and critical pedagogy also relies on the "expertise" needed by a teacher to facilitate reflection and to guide students toward democratic practices and moral dispositions but also encourages students to create meaning from experience. Many of the Liberal Model's assumptions about social justice awareness appear to be based on Lawrence Kohlberg's theories of moral development that emphasize a sense of justice as the highest moral concept.[12] The connection to Aristotle is that Kohlberg's stages of moral development clearly parallel Aristotle's levels of ethical development. Both emphasize sequential increments of habitualized training that ultimately might lead toward the highest levels of ethical conduct. Nel Noddings, a leader in the Liberal Model of moral education, also refers to the importance of habit, suggesting that expertise can be attained through habitualized activities that presumably can translate into the authority to teach character (or "caring," in Nodding's case).[13]

In the Spiritual Model, there are no "experts." Children develop character by valuing those traits in themselves that help them to be of value to others. Adults tell stories, conduct ceremonies, offer feedback, and serve as role models to maintain community welfare as an intrinsic cultural goal, but once in place, it is natural for children to develop those virtues that lead toward this goal. Children come directly from the spiritual world and already possess the seeds for producing the highest degree of morality. It is up to teachers to help them *not* forget this inherent wisdom. Nature and animals serve as much as community members for "teaching" that which safeguards this memory.

Indigenous thinking rejects the idea of the expert for the same reasons it honors the sacred wisdom inherent in all life-forms. Giving too much significance to a single entity risks taking significance away from another. Meaning-making is more important than absolute truth seeking because meaning-making gives significance to things and events. The significance comes from a sacred realization that the microcosm is a mirror of the macrocosm and that symbolism, ritual, historical perspectives, and a process-oriented language are all reflections of a great but *mysterious* truth. To recognize this significance calls for the character traits of patience, respect, humility, fortitude, courage, and generosity.[14]

Children Are Essentially a Blank Slate When It Comes to Developing Character

Conservative C.E. is true to Aristotle's assertion (and later John Locke's philosophy) about the blank slate metaphor. It has little faith in the existence of any innate propensities toward virtue in children (let alone the recognition of the sacred wisdom discussed above that is assumed in the Spiritual Model.) Wynne and Ryan, for example, call for teachers to "Develop written rules of behavior for the classroom and/or the whole school which prohibit all reasonably foreseeable forms of disruption and/or specify the behaviors required."[15] Similarly, Nash believes that "pervasive relativism and an ultraliberal view of morals, a belief in the absolute right and freedom of the individual to choose his or her own lifestyle, have eroded the best of what a more traditional view of ethics and morality once provided."[16]

The Liberal Model does not abide by the concept of the blank slate per se, emphasizing that "facts" are always subject to interpretation of some sort. Unlike most leaders of the Conservative Model, liberal educators do not tend to follow the ideas of Emile Durkheim, who said, "All education is a continuous effort to impose on the child ways of seeing, feeling, and acting which he could not have arrived at spontaneously."[17] However, as described in the next section, liberal character educators do often adopt Aristotle's "rational thinking" imperative, which indirectly assumes that an understanding of virtue is not innate but must be developed through critical analysis.

As we have already seen, the Spiritual Model as exemplified in the indigenous worldview sees children not as blank slates but as beings whose sacred knowledge is great owing to their proximity to the spirit world from which they came.[18] In practice, C.E. programs in public schools that embrace this idea look for and find "teachable moments" in every activity and for every aspect of the curriculum so that these sacred connections are not lost.

Rational Thinking Is a Basic Requirement for C.E.

The Conservative Model, in being critical of overintellectualizing character and favoring instead a more didactic approach, would seem to be against Aristotle's idea of rational thinking. Yet, in assuming the wisdom of the authority that intends to inculcate character traits, conservative character educators would likely concur that the basis for their assumptions are indeed rational. For example, Lickona, another conservative pillar of the C.E. movement, maintains that there is a single, objective, universally valid notion of human character that is not based on mere subjective preferences but on *rationally* construed affirmations embraced by religious traditions around the world.[19] Conservatives claim that socialization is not mere indoctrination because their standards are rationalized.[20]

The Liberal Model places more importance on rational thinking than is exemplified by merely saying that it is behind traditional thinking. As Dewey states, "When our faith in the scientific method is made manifest in social works, the possibilities for the future will emerge to conquer human problems."[21] Lisman also acknowledges the vital need for rational thinking when he says, "Being able to critically analyze ethical issues and make effective ethical decisions is as important as the will to be moral."[22]

Challenging Dewey's confidence in science, the Spiritual Model is more distrusting of the hypothesis–test–new hypothesis method of Western science. Observation and experience are important in indigenous science, but verification relates more to a "big picture," to metaphysical perspectives, stories, people's histories, and to the wisdom of nature and animals. Intuitive resources and prayer are more important than analysis or rationalization. Communion in nature can remind one of what is already known just as well as critical thought can, sometimes even better. Spiritual power is also incomprehensible. To attempt to remove mystery in the pursuit of rational wisdom is to risk removing that which is sacred. Thus, in the Spiritual Model of C.E., education becomes "a vehicle for unfolding ever deeper levels of life's great mysteries and increasing degrees of respect for the significance of life's interconnections."[23]

Nature Is Not a Model for C.D.

Plato, Aristotle's teacher and the student of the father of Western philosophy, Socrates, quotes Socrates as saying, "I'm a lover of learning, and trees and open country won't teach me anything, whereas men in town do."[24] The Conservative Model is largely based on ideology that places man above nature and views virtues strictly in anthropocentric terms. (To be fair to Aristotle, he had some disagreement with Plato in this regard. Still, his study of nature was limited.)

The Liberal Model also sees humanity as superior to nature in its responsibility to be a steward of it. Although it embraces an environmental ethic, it would not comprehend the idea that nature is a model for C.D. Even though John Dewey did write about the problem of putting humans at the center of the world, there is nothing I could find in his writings to indicate that C.E. would not be a product of human interaction alone. Nel Noddings, in her book offering a caring curriculum as an alternative to the Conservative Model, does not mention nature or ecological concerns once.[25] That a liberal character educator can write an entire book about a caring curriculum and not expressly relate caring to our catastrophic situation or our intricate interdependence on the natural world is an example of the inability to see the natural world as a source and a focus for virtue awareness.

According to the Spiritual Model, both dominant forms of C.E. attempt the impossible—to bring wholeness to people who have separated from nature. The Spiritual Model assumes that "Humanity is harmoniously fused with the natural world through the ritualization of space."[26] Landscape is sacred, embodying a divinity that it shares with everything from trees and rocks to birds and animals. This symbiosis, so different from the conservative vision of controlling nature and the liberal vision of protecting it, is, in the indigenous view, the source of virtue. Even love itself may be lost without this sacred realization of our interconnections with nature:

> Oh what a catastrophe for man when he cut himself off from the rhythm of the year, from his unison with the sun and the earth. Oh what a catastrophe, what a maiming of love when it was made a personal, merely personal feeling, taken away from the rising and the setting of the sun, and cut off from the magic connection of the solstice and the equinox! This is what is the matter with us. We are bleeding at the roots, because we are cut off from the earth and sun and stars, and love is a grinning mockery, because, poor blossom, we plucked it from its stem on the tree of Life, and expected it to keep on blooming in our civilized vase on the table.[27]

Forster long ago identified the fundamental human problem as ecological rather than sociological. His solution was to be prepared to put aside technology and other modern conceptions that hinder connections between body and mind and between body and Earth.[28] This is the lesson that can still be taught in our public schools through the Spiritual Model.

The Source of Good Character Comes from the Human Desire for Happiness

Aristotle's view of happiness has probably been misappropriated by Western politics and economics, but it was not difficult to do. He believed that happiness requires external goods in order for a man to play a noble role in life, indirectly affirming the connection between character and the acquisition of private property. Thus, the defense of private property becomes a primary obligation of the civic official. Happiness, according to Aristotle, is related to reward and punishment and to reflection on a whole life. Like Augustine after him, he equates happiness with freedom but not the freedom of a child who cannot know happiness until a lifetime of good choices. It would not be difficult to make an association between these ideas and conservative views in and on contemporary American life nor with the historical emphasis on property rights, personal freedoms, and rewards and punishments that tend to define much of Western culture. It should not, therefore, be surprising if advocates of the Conservative Model of C.E. support didactic instruction that maintains the status quo.

The pursuit of happiness might also be embraced as a goal of C.E. in the Liberal Model because of its association with democratic ideals. Neither Aristotle nor John Dewey would see the idea of happiness in terms of self-seeking pleasure but rather in terms of those habits of life that are fulfilling to oneself and others. Dewey begins his "Theory of the Moral Life" by acknowledging his debt to Aristotle when he speaks about character in terms of voluntary habitualized actions and how emotional responses can be a failure of habit.[29] Dewey and other progressives behind the Liberal Model of C.E., in their appeal for democratic ideals and social justice, seem to accept Aristotle's ideas that happiness is strictly a phenomenon of one's actions in society, actions that must be trained by habit.

Those who would lean more toward the Spiritual Model would be critical of Dewey's position:

> The idealism of the Progressive Movement, especially as illustrated through the philosophy of John Dewey, appears to be one of the major causes for the lack of successful implementation of his ideas. . . . To an acute observer, corporate control of the economic base of a country would have to mean that all superstructures within that system must reflect the ideology of the controlling group. Yet Dewey's definition of democracy reflects a naïve interpretation of an evident reality. . . . Political, economic and social realities of that time as well as today cannot allow for educational goals or ideologies to be at variance with the ruling class goals or ideologies. . . . For the above reasons this writer has not been able to [find] in Dewey's philosophy of the practical classroom application of his techniques to the American Indian worldview.[30]

The Spiritual Model recognizes the realization of significance, rather than a pursuit of happiness, as a more important goal for C.E. From an indigenous perspective, spiritual education tends to mean significant, inviting reflection, and possessing power.[31] Spiritual power is also unconditionally benevolent. The "Great Mysterious" is generous not because of a need to fulfill a quest for happiness but because it is simply in the nature of creation to be generous. Spiritual manifestations of the powers that inform all living things also have these positive traits, so a good C.E. simply helps people become aware of them. Further, rather than freedom being the guiding principle, the concept of significance in the Other demands responsibility.

In their book *Reclaiming Youth at Risk,* Brendtro, Brokenleg, and Van Bockern state:

> Traditional Native American child-rearing philosophies provide a powerful alternative in education and youth development. These approaches challenge both the European cultural heritage of child pedagogy and the narrow perspectives of many current psychological theories. Refined over 15,000 years of civilization and preserved in oral traditions, this knowledge is little known outside the two hundred tribal languages that cradle the Native Indian cultures of North America.[32]

In spite of this, what good did Western assumptions about character and education do when Americans forced their notions of character on Indian people who survived their bloodier forms of conquest only to be taken from their families and forced into punishing boarding schools? Rather than the nurturance of a realization of significance and responsible action, or the cultivation of actions that come from the acceptance, attention, and affection of others, perhaps some notion of Aristotle's ideas about earning happiness at the end of life is behind what Block refers to as "social violence against children."[33] He refers to the kind of violence that comes from a postponement of "happiness" and a separation from nature.

Time, Teaching, and Social Experiences Are All Required for C.D.

It would be difficult to argue that time, teaching, and social experience do not somehow contribute to developing character. Certainly there would be no rebuttal from either the Conservative or the Liberal Model representatives. It would seem on the surface that even a spiritual perspective would benefit from these ingredients. From the Spiritual Model, however, comes a challenge to the emphases and interpretations of the three "requirements" that are used by the two other models. I have already mentioned that in the Spiritual Model the expertise of a teacher is less important than reflection on experience and the realization of significance of the Other. I have also argued that the Spiritual Model gives as much value to intuitive and environmental experience as it does to social experience. So, at this point, let us focus our attention on the issue of "time" as it relates to C.E.

Developmental theories emphasize the importance of stages (time-based) of and for moral development. Arguably, the most famous and most tested theory is that of Lawrence Kohlberg. Although Kohlberg himself would be placed in the Liberal Model, it would seem that both the Conservative and the Liberal Models assume his conclusions to be valid, namely that people pass through stages of avoiding punishment, seeking reward, gaining approval, caring interpersonally, respecting authority, having community welfare concerns, and, finally, acting according to principles of conscience, regardless of issues defined in the other stages. Most research seems to conclude that very few people make it to the last two stages, and this in itself may be telling. Yet the question is, Why not?

Is it possible that worldview is a more significant factor than time? Could children embrace the highest levels much earlier in life and with much greater frequency in the light of an alternative worldview, such as that offered by the Spiritual Model? Is it possible that few people ever reach Kohlberg's higher levels because of Western paradigms that do not meet our definition of spirituality?

Some studies have attempted to answer such questions and suggest that worldview may play a more important role than time.[34] Other studies show that typically Western approaches to C.E. would naturally stifle the attainment of authentic, non-self-serving generosity. For example, Fabes and colleagues have shown that chronic use of extrinsic rewards to motivate children actually reduces generous behavior.[35] Another potential problem with the emphasis on time, teaching, and social experience as prerequisites for successful C.E. is that it may limit thinking about other important concepts. For example, in her master's thesis on the relationships between First Nations Teachings and "Character Education," Yvonne Germaine Dufault discusses the importance of hope. She asks the question, "Is an underlying lack of hope spurring or hindering character education?" After significant research and a number of interviews of Native Elders, she concluded that hope is indeed an important aspect of character development.[36] Other concepts such as "beauty" might also be more important than time. Perhaps even timelessness should be considered.

The Training of Olympic Athletes Is a Model for C.E.

It would be unfair to judge Aristotle's use of the Olympic Games in terms of critical reflections on modern sports competition and the relative lack of character that is too often demonstrated in competitive sports. In Aristotle's day, the motto "It's not whether you win or lose but how you play the game" was most important and this is, frankly, the idea that Aristotle meant to convey. Nonetheless, the Olympics were competitive games and Aristotle's use of competitive athletes to illustrate character has proved problematic when considering that *both* conservative and liberal politicians refer to school reform in terms of being "more competitive in the global marketplace" and that much of the high-stakes testing movement is based on competitive scoring. The Conservative Model wants children to be socialized to conform to status quo authority and to employment market needs. The Liberal Model focuses on questions of power in reaction to the injustices that result from the dog-eat-dog ethic of capitalism but still tends to view the world as competitive in nature.

The Spiritual Model replaces the idea that our world is based on competition with one that sees relationships as essentially cooperative. In the indigenous view, relationships are neither tolerant of nor competitive with others. Rather, aboriginal people experience themselves as part of others and see in nature, even in the fiercest struggles, examples of symbiosis, not survival of the fittest. How this might affect an approach to C.E. in the public school classroom in contrast to the other two models should be obvious. For example, by minimizing competitive structures, intrinsic motivation to "do good" in such ways that individuals might be more likely to develop "good character" and act accordingly "when no one is looking" is imperative.

Happiness (the Reason for C.E.) Can Be Thought of as a Gift to or from God

Although this premise ties into the belief that lifelong happiness is the goal of C.E., I have saved it for last because of its relevance to religion. Because the connection between religion, spirituality, and C.E. is so pertinent to public schools, this seems a proper place to conclude the discussion of the three models.

Aristotle's reference to God is a foundational contribution to the mentality that has placed religious orthodoxy at the top of the hierarchy that governs morality. For most of America's history, for example, the Bible has been the ultimate sourcebook for character education. Throughout the nineteenth century and well into the twentieth century, Americans typically saw obedience to authority, including parental authority, as an expression of obeying and being reverent to God. *The McGuffy Reader* served during this period as our nation's C.E. textbook. No other book was more read, except for the King James Version of the Bible. Estimates of 50 to 100 million copies were sold prior to 1900, and it was used in some schools as late as the 1940s.[37] This book represented a heavy-handed approach to moral and religious instruction. Using an oppressively didactic approach, it touted only white, middle-class, Protestant values and beliefs.

How much of an effect does Christian religion have on C.E. in public schools today? As Gordon Vessels states:

> In spite of the fact that most religions over the centuries have linked morality and religious beliefs, few proponents of moral education in the pubic schools have acknowledged the important role that religions have played in the formulation and transmission of pro-social and pro-environmental values, and the powerful incentives for moral action that religious beliefs provide for many people.[38]

On this point I tend to disagree with my friend and colleague. Although educators might avoid making direct connections in official conversation owing to concerns about possible conflicts with multicultural attitudes or First Amendment law, it seems that religious authority continues to dominate C.E. programs.

Alfie Kohn, for example, criticizes the C.E. movement because of its Christian affiliations and assumptions. He goes so far as to say that most C.E. leaders today are Catholics. This is partly why he believes that changing the structures of education and society is a more vital target for C.E. than trying to build "character" in individuals, as long as the ideas about individual character are about socializing people into relatively dysfunctional institutions.[39]

In support of Kohn's arguments is the fact that in 1999, the U.S. House of Representatives voted 248 to 180 to post the Ten Commandments in public schools. This rider was attached to a juvenile justice crime bill. Its author convinced the legislators that only an improvement in youth morality could prevent young people from committing violent crimes, and that "biblical laws are the best source for such a task."[40] A number of states have passed laws either allowing or mandating that schools post the ten biblical mandates in all classrooms. Georgia's House Bill 1207 amended Georgia's Quality Basic Education Act to require local school systems to ensure that the Ten Commandments are displayed in every classroom within the school district "as a condition for receiving state funds."[41]

The connections between organized religion and C.E. have even reached beyond conservative or counterconservative ideology and into the military-industrial complex. This should not be surprising because the cross and the flag have gone hand in hand throughout history. A recent news item shows how this connection continues. General William G. Boykin, the new Deputy Undersecretary of Defense for Intelligence, recently made some controversial public comments that, surprisingly or not, have not been chastised by his superiors in any way. Discussing a battle against a Muslim warlord in Somalia, he told an audience, "I knew my God was bigger than his." Referring to the current occupation of Iraq he said, "We in the army of God have been raised for such a time as this." He even said on at least one occasion that President Bush is in the White House because God put him there.[42]

Blaming Aristotle for initiating the foundations of a worldview that has concretized religion into an "us versus them orthodoxy" may seem unfair.[43] Yet Aristotle did axiomize the Platonic rationale for Logos, which was characterized "not only as the ultimate good but also as masculine."[44] Aristotle's view that commonsense observations of things exist independently of our interpretations of them, combined with his realist, expert view of character education, made his reference to happiness and God a disruption of the holistic worldview of indigenous peoples who maintained the feminine and the mysterious in their concept of Creation. Power-based interpretations of

Aristotle have too often separated spirit from religion. Nature and the feminine have become things that must be controlled. Whitehead has referred to this problem we have inherited from Aristotle as a "fallacy of misplaced concreteness," or the error of mistaking abstract entities of thought for concrete factors of reality.[45] The spiritual quest for great questions has been replaced by a religious imperative for absolute answers.

Kevin Ryan and Edward Wynne, two of the foremost leaders in the C.E. field, support this didactic imperative for C.E. as well. They encourage teachers to develop written specific rules of behavior and emphasize obedience to authority and an honoring of traditional Christian orthodoxies. They, like Aristotle before them, believe in the requirement for adult autocracy in the development of character in children, and they oppose arguments for democratic classrooms in which the students participate more in the creation of their own character. They and other educators see the rise of humanism and psychological rationales for degenerate or unethical behavior as having pushed Christian doctrine to the side. According to authors like James Davison Hunter, whose book is endorsed by the Josephson Institute (founders of *Character Counts!*), character education is an opportunity to bring the Christian doctrine, with its "Good and Evil" language, back into our schools. Ryan and Wynne go so far as to say that our current dire moral condition results from the loss of virtues that transpired during the tumultuous sixties.[46]

The Liberal Model's view of religion tends to honor the many traditional religious ideas about morality but is critical of the didactic conveyance of them that inevitably creates competitive conflicts between and amidst ideologies and viewpoints. Its proponents favor situational understandings that reflect free market capitalism's contributions to poverty, economic inequity, and international conflicts and its responsibility for the loss of character, rather than the Conservative Model's emphasis on secularism or any such movement away from religious authority. In other words, it is bad institutions, not bad people, that result in the problems C.E. programs attempt to address. Religion may or may not be characterized by liberal educators as an example of a bad institution because, bluntly, this would simply be too unpopular a position to take.

Leming, however, would point out that both the didactic (Conservative) and the reflective (Liberal) approaches to C.E., in that both give attention to individual and community, would likely fail if they resorted to the kind of exhortations about virtues typically found in religious fundamentalism. Referring to the 1927 research project by May and Harshorne, showing how unsuccessful a didactic approach to C.E. can be, he concludes that this approach does less for making the world a better place than for creating positive school climates and service-oriented activities.[47]

The Spiritual Model, as mentioned earlier, is more concerned with the great mysteriousness of the cosmos, the sacredness of place, and the significance of Other than with either religious dogma or secular dogma in the form of psychological or sociological assumptions about service learning or school climate. When spiritual concerns are operational in a culture, reciprocity amidst interconnectedness makes harmony the ultimate C.E. principle. "In all spheres of Indian life, harmony was mandatory—a condition of nature itself, the resonance of a kind of sanity that predates psychology."[48]

Spirituality has no beginning or ending. It is not a rationalization for the linear conception of progress that undergirds Western beliefs about time and space. Rather, it "already exists in our consciousness at birth, even before we participate in life's various learning experiences. In American Indian cultures, this sacred aspect of the child is nurtured from birth so that the sense of interconnections colors all of the person's subsequent learning."[49] Such a belief about human nature runs counter to that inherited from European beliefs, which views people as mean, brutish, and selfish. It is also distinct from the liberal idea that psychological and social interventions are needed to protect children from social corruptions.

The Spiritual Model leads to a process of maintaining the balance between generosity and mastery, and between independence and belonging. This balancing work is on the path to *wolokokiapi*—a Lakota word for a profound sense of peace with all things. "Traditional native educational practices addressed these four bases of self esteem: (1) significance was nurtured in a cultural milieu that celebrated the universal need for belonging, (2) competence was insured by guaranteed opportunities for mastery, (3) power was fostered by encouraging the expression of independence, and (4) virtue was reflected in the pre-eminent value of generosity."[50]

CONCLUSIONS

In comparing and contrasting the three models of C.E., I have not intended to polarize them. No doubt there are obvious overlaps and similar intentions across and throughout each. I have, however, attempted to show a significant difference between the Western models in light of Aristotle's legacy and the non-Western, indigenous model, one very close to home (i.e., a synthesized theory about the spirituality of American Indian people). If we expand our anthropocentric view of C.E. in response to our discussion, perhaps we will learn that the future of C.E. in our public schools exists not only in human societies but also in our attention to the animal kingdom and in nature. Consider, for example, such exemplars of virtues as the snake, demonstrating the virtue of patience as it waits tirelessly for its prey; the generosity of the wolf raising the pups of an injured member of the pack; or the courage of the badger standing firm against a cougar. Study the journey of geese and imagine how we can learn to care for one another as they do. Watch the struggle of a salmon on its upstream journey and ponder its model for persistence. Find out about the many symbiotic relationships in nature and wonder why our institutions believe that competition rather than cooperation should prevail in the affairs of men and women. Watch the workings of nature in your backyard and reflect on the possibility that humans are not the only reasons for the universe and that gentleness and kindness spring from trees and plants as much or more than they do from humanity.

Sam Keen has written about the virtue of such wildness: "One way to define modernity is to trace the process by which nature has been desacralized and God has moved indoors." He continues,

> On an average day, if you stop, look and listen, you will discover phyla of angels bearing messages from the wild. . . . From any of these creatures you may learn the great spiritual lesson that you are not the center and sole reason for the existence of the universe. Any squirrel or English sparrow will testify by its *joie de vivre* that human ego-centrism and species chauvinism are both a mistake and a sin.[51]

Similarly, Chief Letakots-Lesa said,

> In the beginning of all things, wisdom and knowledge were with the animals, for Itirawa, the One Above, did not speak directly to man. He sent certain animals to tell men that he showed himself through the beasts and that from them, and from the stars and the sun and the moon, man should learn.[52]

If we can begin to understand what this really means in our world today, then perhaps we will have come full circle in understanding the true nature of C.E. and how we should be doing it in our contemporary public schools.

— 7 —

Not the Same Old Thing: Maria Montessori—A Nontraditional Approach to Public Schooling in an Age of Traditionalism and Standardization

Elizabeth Oberle and Kevin D. Vinson

The recent history of American public schooling is rife with efforts at reform. Especially post-1983's *A Nation at Risk*,[1] reformers have worked at an unprecedented pace and scale to create and implement change at a range of levels and according to a variety of perspectives and worldviews. Their aim? Ostensibly, the "improvement" of American public schools and classrooms. Although this indeed is a worthy goal, such labors have not been without their difficulties.

Attempts at reform have occurred at nearly all levels of schooling, curriculum, and instruction, from the national (the No Child Left Behind Act of 2001) to the state (charter schools, high-stakes testing) and district (total quality management); from schools (Robert Slavin's "success for all") to grade levels and content areas (the variety of curriculum standards). (Of course, these distinctions and their relevant reform movements often overlap.) If anything, what these various attempts share is their propensity to generate controversy, to attract both supporters and detractors from across the politicopedagogical spectrum.[2]

The purpose of this chapter is to explore one such reform attempt, namely, the inclusion of Montessori education within the context of public schools and classrooms. Moreover, we seek to explicate Montessori public education within the framework of "defending public schools," especially vis-à-vis curriculum and instruction. We begin by briefly overviewing Maria Montessori's biography and by summarizing the fundamental principles of her pedagogical approach. We conclude by considering the relationship between the Montessori methodology and the idea(l) of defending contemporary public schools (especially in terms of the curriculum).

WHAT IS MONTESSORI EDUCATION? AN INTRODUCTION/REVIEW

To the extent that the general public and most public school educators have even heard of Maria Montessori and Montessori education, what, in general, do they think? Why? For that matter, what do they think when they think of contemporary public schools and schooling more broadly?

Although relevant data are difficult to come by, most people who have heard of Montessori education probably assume that it represents principally an elite, private school movement—maybe even a movement connected primarily with small, wealthy, religious schools. Although this is not *necessarily* an unwarranted assertion, Montessori education involves, of course, far more than that, both in terms of its aims and commitments and its overall prevalence and pedagogical development.

Who Was Maria Montessori?

Maria Montessori was born in Chiaravalle, Italy, near Ancona, in 1870. Trained as a physician, a *scientist*—in fact, the first woman licensed to practice medicine in Italy (graduating from the University of Rome in 1896)—she pursued her lifelong interest in children and how they developed, learned, and "became human" in terms of constructing their unique personalities and identities according to her lifelong belief that children were actively engaged and intelligent beings. An empiricist, Montessori emphasized the significance of children's experiential interactions with their environments and the necessity of observation as a means of experimentally understanding teaching and learning and their importance relative to schooling and the evolution of humanity.[3]

Her work, as represented in such writings as *The Absorbent Mind, The Secret of Childhood,* and *The Discovery of the Child,* drew on her background in such fields as biology, psychiatry, anthropology, and mathematics.[4] Her unique (at least for the time) research methods emphasized the importance of empirical techniques (founded in part on the clinical observations she made as a physician) and strategies in understanding the relationships between the "general principles" of the development of the human child (across cultures) and the actualized and critical *individuality* of specifically existing human children in their own particular settings. Following her death in 1952 in Noordwijk, Holland, her life and work acquired international renown and celebrity, not only in terms of pedagogy per se (especially vis-à-vis instructional methodology, curriculum, and teacher education) but also in such fields as diplomacy, peace studies, politics, and the sciences.

Medical doctor, psychology researcher, early childhood educator, feminist pioneer, and social reformer, all are titles that can describe Montessori relative to the work she completed during her lifetime. Nearly 100 years later, her theories on the acquisition of knowledge are still being debated, implemented, and criticized by all sides.

Montessori was raised in a well-educated, conservative family in Italy during the Victorian era and given a "proper" education for a girl. She pushed, though, for more and went on to the university (with her father in tow as chaperone), initially to become an engineer, although she later changed her emphasis of study to biology, chemistry, and the fledgling field of psychology. Despite the protests of her own family, her professors and administrators, and her society at large, she completed the requirements to graduate with a doctorate and took a position at a clinic in Rome assessing potential patients for an insane asylum. It was during this time that she became familiar with the works of Jean Gaspard Itard, Antonio Seguin, Johann Heinrich Pestalozzi, and Jean-Jacques Rousseau. Friedrich Froebel was essentially a contemporary, and Sigmund Freud and his wife would later become close friends of hers. These progressive European men and their views on intelligence, the role of nature and the effects of the environment on learning, and the belief in all humans' abilities to engage their society had a profound effect on Montessori. She translated many of their works into Italian and studied their positions on "defectives." (This was a common term used for persons who were differently-abled. They were classified by their capabilities with equally humiliating words, such as "moron" and "idiot") True to her scientific training, she began a few experiments after observing young children housed at the insane asylum playing with crumbs and bugs on the floor of an otherwise barren room. By (at least partly) re-creating the experiments that Itard and Seguin had performed relative to teaching reading, writing, and basic arithmetic, she was able to help these more or less "forgotten" children to pass a standard examination for school. This, for all intents and purposes, set the world on its ear. Here were "cast-off" children who were in a lock-tight system and who had been able to enter the common society simply because Montessori had given them the gift of a suitable education to meet the demands of the day. This was all well and good, and the men of the institutions were pleasantly surprised if not startled by this "upstart" young woman. They challenged her to replicate the effects of her "little program" with other, so-called "regular" and "normal" children.

A suitable situation was found in Rome: A slumlord who ran a large tenement house was having difficulty with the children of working, single mothers vandalizing his property. As was the common sentiment, the order came down: "Do something with these children." Montessori welcomed the challenge, not necessarily to repeat the performance of the children from the asylum but as a chance to observe "normal" children in their play activities. She was a product of her learning, especially in her belief that these children would and could somehow be different and, therefore, would not necessarily need the same system of teaching but "merely" that it would be interesting to see what the children would be able to do from a scientific standpoint.

Much has been written by her exceedingly loyal followers, as well as her detractors, as to those early days in Rome (1905–1909), but clearly the children from the slums began using their chalk for writing appropriat words and stories, rather than graffiti, and began performing simple mathematical operations, rather than petty thievery.

When it was published that these children had also passed the standard tests for entrance into school, people began to take notice. Observers from many institutions and many countries arrived to observe for themselves what was happening. Montessori quickly became a major name in learned circles and was invited to speak both in Italy and abroad. In fact, her first lectures in America were just prior to World War I, and not only was she warmly received, but the first Montessori "societies" and schools were opened. The pressure for training lay people to teach by her methods was great, and thus she left the original school (*Casa dei Bambini,* or Children's House) in Rome, the others that had been opened nearby, and the daily operations of such schools to her followers so that she could begin the work of explaining her visions for early childhood education to the rest of the world.

Concentrated in the San Francisco area, the first American Montessori schools were a novelty, although the schools and training centers in Europe were well received (many have been in operation since opening in the mid-1920s). Montessori continued her lectures, her observations, and her writings, expanding her thoughts to include a stage theory platform of development. She, like other theorists (Piaget, the most notable) believed that humans acquired knowledge through certain developmental stages. Montessori called her stages "planes of development" and felt that there was a spiral pattern to the mastery of skills and concepts that was built upon sensory input and mental classification and categorization from previous planes of development.

Montessori Education: Principles, Philosophy, and Practice

The "Montessori Method" developed initially at the first *Casa dei Bambini* that Montessori established in 1906 in San Lorenzo in Rome. As with modern Montessori education, the basic principles were straightforward. First, Montessori believed that children were innate knowledge seekers and that they taught themselves. As she expressed it, young learners were "self-creating." Second, Montessori believed that, at each stage of development, education should include and evolve within "prepared environments," environments that enabled children to take on accountability for their own learning as they engaged the processes relevant to becoming able and actualized adults and citizens. More specifically, according to the American Montessori Society (AMS), Montessori's pedagogy stressed the following critical and structuring notions:

- The aim of Montessori education is to foster competent, responsible, adaptive citizens who are lifelong learners and problem solvers;
- Learning occurs in an inquiring, cooperative, nurturing atmosphere. Students increase their own knowledge through both self- and teacher-initiated experiences;
- Learning takes place through the senses. Students learn by manipulating materials and interacting with others. These meaningful experiences are precursors to the abstract understanding of ideas;
- The individual is considered as a whole. The physical, emotional, social, aesthetic, spiritual, and cognitive needs and interests are inseparable and equally important; [and]
- Respect and caring attitudes for oneself, others, the environment, and all life are necessary.[5]

Pedagogically, perhaps the most important, and most famous, emphases are Montessori's conceptualizations of the *prepared environment* and the *developmental plane.* According to the *Association Montessori Internationale* (AMI, founded by Montessori herself in 1929), the prepared environment of the Montessori classroom is one

> where children are free to respond to their natural tendency to work [and where their] innate passion[s] for learning [are] encouraged by giving them opportunities to engage in spontaneous, purposeful activities with the guidance of a trained adult. [Here, and t]hrough their work, the children develop concentration and joyful self-discipline.] Within a framework of order, [they] progress at their own pace and rhythm, according to their individual capabilities.[6]

These are environments that

> allow [children] to take responsibility for their own education, giving them the opportunity to become human beings able to function independently and hence interdependently.[7]

From this view, the prepared environment is one that "can be designed to facilitate maximum independent learning and exploration by the child," one in which "there is a variety of activity as well as a great deal of movement." In this situation, according to the Montessori approach, this "necessary preparedness" enables "children [to] work on activities of their own choice at their own pace." Further, "[t]hey [children] experience a blend of freedom and self-discipline in a place especially designed to meet their developmental needs."[8]

The notion of prepared environment is related, moreover, to the manipulation of learning materials and to the understanding of "normalization."

From the Montessorian view, materials are to be accessible (e.g., placed on appropriately high or low shelves) and available for individual student choice, interest, and use. They are, to a large extent, fully the responsibility of students—regardless of age (e.g., students obtain, return, and maintain them). More pedagogically precise, these materials aim at inducing activity, isolating a particular learning quality (e.g., comparison and contrast, size, color, shape, etc.), and inducing self-correctivity (i.e., students can perceive errors relative to their learning via the materials and correct them without [or with minimal] adult intervention) and interrelationality (i.e., that the various materials [should] build one upon the others).[9]

Normalization, for Montessori, meant not its typical (or "normal") definition of conformity and what "is normal" but, instead, a developmental process, one inextricably tied to the appropriate preparation of the pedagogical environment. Montessori observed that children do best in schools (and education more broadly) given maximal freedom in an environment designed to meet their unique growth and personal and social needs. Through continued work with materials that held their interest, selected independently from within the prepared environment, Montessori noted that children eventually acquired an increased sense of satisfaction, self, and inner fulfillment. The course through which this evolution occurred defined for her the nature and significance of normalization.

As she wrote in *The Absorbent Mind:*

> Only "normalized" children, aided by their environment, show in their subsequent development those wonderful powers that we describe: spontaneous discipline, continuous and happy work, social sentiments of help and sympathy for others. . . . An interesting piece of work, freely chosen, which has the virtue of inducing concentration rather than fatigue, adds to the child's energies and mental capacities, and leads him [or her] to self-mastery. . . . One is tempted to say that the children are performing spiritual exercises, having found the path of self-perfectionment and of ascent to the inner heights of the soul.[10]

As E. M. Standing, in *Maria Montessori: Her Life and Work,* defined the characteristics of normalization, they are:

- Love of order
- Love of work
- Spontaneous concentration
- Attachment to reality
- Love of silence and of working alone
- Sublimation of the possessive instinct
- [The p]ower to act from real choice
- Obedience
- Independence and initiative
- Spontaneous self-discipline
- Joy

As the North American Montessori Teachers' Association (NAMTA) says, "Montessori believed that these are the truly 'normal' characteristics of childhood, which emerge when children's developmental needs are met."[11]

The idea of developmental plane designates the transitions that occur during the birth through adulthood evolution of human beings. According to AMI, the specific planes are:

- Birth to age six: children are sensorial explorers, constructing their intellects by absorbing every aspect of their environment, their language[,] and their culture;
- Age six to age twelve: children become conceptual explorers[; they] develop their powers of abstraction and imagination, and apply their knowledge to discover and expand their worlds further;
- Age twelve to age eighteen: children become humanistic explorers, seeking to understand their place in society and their opportunity to contribute to it;
- Age eighteen to age twenty-four: as young adults, [individuals] become specialized explorers, seeking a niche from which to contribute to universal dialogue.[12]

More specifically, Montessori classrooms are divided into three-year groups, the purpose of which, according to Montessori's theories and observations, is to facilitate precisely and appropriately the continuum of growth and learning via human interaction and personal development and exploration, here both in terms of the individual and the social.[13] The multi-age divisions of the Montessori program are (1) parent-infant (ages 0–3), preschool (ages 3–6), lower and upper elementary (ages 6–9 and 9–12), and middle school (ages 12–14). Again, each presents its own precise purposes, materials, and activities and methodologies.[14]

And yet Montessorian curriculum and instruction can be both complex and multiple, formal as well as unpredictable and less than rigid. Consider the following applied example.

At the elementary level, the expectations of the learner and the appropriate pedagogical principles include:

1. Lesson repetition among students individually, that is after the initial presentation by the teacher, in order to concretize abstract concepts;
2. Cross-curriculum "webbing";
3. The view that ability is individual—adults and children work to the potential of each person, not to the average;
4. Ever-deepening interest on the part of the learner;
5. The perspective that respect, freedom, and responsibility are interdependent.

Our question, of course, is what these might mean in practice.

Lesson repetition implies recurrence and redundancy—not in a negative way but as individually developed experiences in an effort to habitualize, routinize, and conceptualize key (especially unfamiliar) ideas, such as, perhaps, counting and various other mathematical notions. Webbing suggests that each new idea leads to—and connects with—others, whether presented earlier or presented later. The individual nature of ability, as opposed to the "average level of students," indicates focusing on children moving forward according to their own singular lesson paces without unwarranted stigmatizations and without undue pressure to "track." The idea of ever-increasing interest insinuates learners follow their own natural curiosities and inclinations (a la Kilpatrick?), particularly vis-à-vis engaging the essential question of "why?" Lastly, regarding the case of the interconnectedness of ideas, such as respect, freedom, and responsibility, Montessori understandings suggest a relationship among values, culture, growth, success, and maturity, settings important, ultimately, to both liberal and conservative critics of contemporary American public schooling.

DEFENDING PUBLIC SCHOOLS AND MONTESSORI EDUCATION

According to NAMTA, well over 200 U.S. public schools are now Montessori-oriented, a number that continues to grow.[15] When viewed within the context of other contemporary public (though, granted, sometimes private as well) school reform trends (e.g., Waldorf education, charter schools, vouchers, public school choice), the commitment to Montessori public education seems to support at least two significant points. First, it represents, to some extent, the present dissatisfaction with "traditional" public schooling (or at least dominant images of it). Second, it supports the notion that *another way*—Montessori, Waldorf, and so on—might provide and prove to be a *better way* (especially within the contexts of the No Child Left Behind Act and standards-based educational reform).

Fundamentally, Montessori education offers but one alternative to the criticisms leveled at public schools from critics both of the political and pedagogical left and the political and pedagogical right. The "standard" right-wing critique centers on the beliefs that schools today are failing because they (1) have standards that are too low, (2) replicate the "worthless" theories and perspectives of the "liberal educational establishment," (3) maintain a monopoly, (4) focus on "self-esteem" (and the like) over content, (5) rely on "progressive methods" at the expense of "direct instruction," (6) have privileged "cultural relativism" over "traditional values" and "character," (7) have usurped the power and position of parents, and (8) misguidedly "throw more money" at schools even though this is neither (from this view) a solution to educational problems nor the answer to educational improvement.[16]

The standard left-wing critique is that schools fail students because they (1) stifle freedom and creativity in favor of conformity and discipline, (2) are dominated by noneducators (e.g., corporations, politicians, managers, test companies), (3) are too centrally controlled, (4) focus too much on fact-based, standardized content, (5) are too traditional in terms of assessment and instructional methods, (6) hyperemphasize homogeneity at the expense of diversity and difference, (7) neglect neighborhoods and local communities, and (8) are underfunded.[17]

Conceivably, of course, one could make a case in favor of the truth or utility of either or both of these critiques (although, indeed, we are more sympathetic to contemporary left-based criticisms). And, most likely, Montessori educators and other interested stakeholders probably possess and espouse a range of viewpoints relative to the overall effectiveness of traditional public schooling. Yet, what the Montessori approach does is connect with the concerns many (though not necessarily most) parents have (rightly or wrongly) that, at least broadly speaking, American public schools are failing or at least not up to snuff. While our own position is that this is not inevitably the case,[18] even so, Montessori education provides one appropriate and legitimate response to dominant modes of public schooling that can be consistent with a multitude of philosophical, pedagogical, political, and sociocultural goals.

In fact, arguably, Montessorianism takes seriously the apprehensions of the entire spectrum of educational criticism (relative to official schooling). It emphasizes, for example, freedom, mastery, diversity, scientific research and methodologies, formal curriculum, individuality, fairness, planning, and hard work (among others)—each of which to some extent can meet the demands of both conservatives and liberals (if not others). That is not to say, of course, that the Montessori system is perfect—obviously, it is not. Yet, it does favorably compare with many aspects of more established modes of public education.

According to NAMTA, the quintessential (and implicitly negative) characteristics of contemporary public school classrooms are their propensities toward:

- Textbooks, pencil and paper, worksheets and dittos
- Working and learning without emphasis on social development
- Narrow, unit-driven curriculum
- Individual subjects
- Block time, period lessons
- Single-graded classrooms
- Students [who are] passive, quiet, in desks
- Students [who] fit [the] mold of [their] school[s]
- Students [who] leave for special help
- Product-focused report cards[19]

Although, to some, this version of traditional education might seem to describe perfectly only the conservative agenda, increasingly it can be seen to characterize what we have previously called the liberal-conservative consensus and to indicate the current "will-to-standardize" or the "standardization imperative" of both the liberal and conservative "race" to the "middle of the road."[20]

In contrast, NAMTA characterizes the Montessori approach as favoring:

- Prepared kinesthetic materials with incorporated control of error [and] specially developed reference materials
- Working and learning matched to the social development of the child
- Unified, internationally developed curriculum
- Integrated subjects and learning based on developmental psychology
- Uninterrupted work cycles
- Multi-age classrooms
- [A setting in which students are] active [and] talking, with periods of spontaneous quiet [and] freedom to move
- [A setting in which] school[s] meet the needs of students
- [A setting in which special] help comes to students
- Process-focused assessment, skills checklists, [and] mastery benchmarks[21]

In effect, Montessori education provides parents and students an alternative option within the standard frameworks of public schooling. For those (generally liberal) critics who believe that traditional public education stifles freedom, individuality, and creativity, Montessori instruction offers spontaneity, choice, and creative student-centeredness. For those (generally conservative) critics who believe that public education has been "dumbed down," is "anti-knowledge," and is too "touchy-feely," Montessori instruction offers hard work, discipline (in the most positive sense), and an emphasis on fundamental skills.

CONCLUSIONS

Montessori education in the public schools raises a number of questions, yet it implies, as well, a number of productive and pedagogically sound principles and practices.

Some of the difficulties with the historical criticisms of the Montessori approach include such concerns as immutability versus evolution (i.e., the extent to which Montessori education changes or the extent to which it should or must change), "truth" or "universality" (i.e., the degree to which it implies a structure that can, or does, meet the needs of *all* individual students), and teacher education (i.e., the potential conflict between individual interpretation, creativity, and independence and individual teacher conformity and disciplinarity). At the extremes, these issues (rightly or wrongly, for good or bad) weigh heavily on the capacity of the Montessori approach to meet its educational agendas and its stated purposes.

On the other hand, Montessori education represents a little known alternative to more traditional modes of public schooling; most members of the citizenry have no idea that such a state of affairs even exists. When most people think of public schools—their own, their children's—they think of a homogeneous setting of traditionalism or of progressivism—either way, the same setup for everyone. Yet Montessori education demonstrates the diversity—often little understood, even *unknown*—that characterizes contemporary teaching and learning. This is most often, we think, quite a good thing. In any event, it presents the condition of "effective" methods regardless of one's political or pedagogical orientation—that is, whether one is conservative, liberal, reactionary, or radical. There is more going on, that is, than most people perceive. And, most profoundly, the Montessori effort—the movement—is on the ascendancy.

In the end, with respect to public education, the Montessori philosophy and its attendant methodologies imply something new, ironically new given the long and successful history of Maria Montessori's efforts and influences. If nothing else, it remains, after all this time, an option worth exploring and taking seriously. It is a viewpoint that should be reconsidered, reckoned with, and continuously and rigorously pursued. It is, that is, not the same old thing.

— II —

Critical Issues in Curriculum

— 8 —

The Military and Corporate Roots of State-Regulated Knowledge

STEPHEN C. FLEURY

INTRODUCTION

Over the past decade, many scholar-activists have spoken eloquently about the dangers and problems of the standards and testing movement that masquerades as "educational reform." Monty Neil, Alfie Kohn, Susan Ohanian, and other educators have helped bring national attention to the ill effects of high-stakes testing on everyday instructional and curricular practices, and to their deleterious social and learning consequences for students. Solid arguments against standardized testing include its negative pressure on effective instruction and learning, the mismatch of statewide examinations and standards, and the outright doctoring of test scores by teachers, administrators, and state bureaucrats.[1] Amidst the avalanche of attacks on public education throughout the 1980s and 1990s, Gerald Bracey annually reported data-based refutations of the charges in the professional school journal *Kappan*.[2] Similarly, Berliner and Biddle placed massive amounts of data within a comprehensive theoretical framework in *The Manufactured Crisis: Myths, Fraud, and the Attack on America's Public Schools*.[3] And Susan Ohanian's *One Size Fits Few: The Folly of Educational Standards* exemplifies the work of educators who have railed against the military-industrial-media complex.[4] Unfortunately, contemporary policymakers rarely take educators seriously in the public forum.

Measured against the full-press whirl and rhetoric of education "accountability," the tone and substance of most criticism appear weak and irrelevant.[5]

The premises of "standards" and "testing" seem successfully implanted in the consciousness of our nation's educators and parents. And, in an eerily Orwellian fashion, the phrase "equity and excellence" has been repeatedly chanted by policymakers and testing advocates, deliberately obfuscating the reactionary meanness of the reforms by couching them in progressive social rhetoric.[6] Similar to the way that rising inflation over time benefits debtors, the passing of time also benefits policymakers in their imposition of reforms. Each year, a new crop of teachers replaces a veteran cadre from the pre-standardized testing era, a historical process that eliminates potential pockets of resistance. In New York State, this demographic shift has been greatly assisted by hefty early-retirement incentive packages over the past half-dozen years. Eager to successfully meet expectations in their new position, neophyte teachers quickly absorb from their teaching and learning environment expectations that are ultimately defined by their students' performance on standardized exams. And in California, academic freedom has been tossed out the door as state law now requires university teacher educators to align the objectives of their courses and programs to state-defined goals.[7]

Within safe confines (i.e., my graduate curriculum class), many new teachers, some of whom are also parents, vocally espouse their antistandardized testing position; pragmatically, they accept what they believe to be the reality of testing and their responsibility to their students. Increasingly alarming, however, is that many of these prospective teachers consider themselves progressive in fully embracing reforms based on standards and testing. Unfettered by a pedagogical memory of inquiry, exploration, and divergent thinking, many new teachers express relief that state standards and objective tests guide them in knowing what to teach. Their point of view is simply practical. Despite sophisticated and well-articulated curricula, no document better identifies the curricular expectations of a school, state, or national educational system than those systems' examinations. Viewed negatively by opponents of testing, the fact that standardized examinations become the de facto curriculum is an intended outcome of those responsible for legislating their use.

It is dismaying to think that the enthusiastic response of new teachers results in a form of teaching and knowledge making that fosters in their students a pliable obedience to authority and imposition. How we think relates to how we live, and, considering that the current reform movement reinforces an authoritarian and hierarchical organization of knowledge, this relationship should evoke serious action by parents, educators, and anyone else concerned for the quality of life available for our students.

Arguments supporting standards and testing suffer from a presentism where accountability and standards are portrayed as an inevitable technical correction to a system that has academically and culturally deteriorated. A more careful historical reading would show that the testing and standards movement punctuates a larger cultural claim about social knowledge. Standards and testing are not the inevitable solution for improving education, but the corporate and military roots of curricular knowledge promulgate these Tayloristic techniques as the sensible response. The purpose of this chapter is to briefly outline this thinking, incomplete as it is, and explain some of its implications for students, teachers, and anyone else in society with an interest in the promotion of democratic thinking.

MILITARIZATION AND CORPORATIZATION DEFINED

The meaning of *militarization* and *corporatization* may vary from simply descriptive terms to highly charged "trigger words." Used here, militarization refers to the increasing acceptance of absolute authority (i.e., authoritarian), bound by the physical force of negative or positive consequences, as the basis of social decision making. Concepts legitimizing authoritarian relationships creep into our consciousness in many ways. For example, the imposition of standards and the use of standardized tests may be two such vehicles if neither the students nor the teachers have willingly collaborated, developed, or executed these social instruments.

Corporatization refers to the increasing abstraction of the locus of decision making over work and production, organized along authoritarian lines, and having a narrow, private, utilitarian purpose of increasing the capital of the "corp" through maximizing profit. In addition, the individuals who share in the profits and benefits of the corporation enjoy legal protection from most forms of public accountability (that is, "limited liability" from everyone outside of the corporate group), aside from whatever responsibility is due within the corporate structure. A crude analogy pointing out the civil absurdity of this concept might be the legal inability to hold someone responsible for taking another's life with a gun, the defense being that it was not the whole person (i.e., corp) who pulled the trigger, but rather, the errant behavior of a few of its members (the "arm" and "fingers").

Thus, since the late 1800s, this purely conceptual abstraction is not only treated as an empirical entity but enjoys the legal rights of a human being without most of the social responsibilities. Considering the nonempirical basis of a corporation (Have you ever seen, touched, felt, or heard a "corporation"?) and its powerful influence over people's behaviors, the idea of corporation may be the secular equivalent of other metaphysical constructs in the Western world wielding tremendous social influence, for example, "trinity," "soul," and "heaven," to name a few.[8]

THE MILITARY AND CORPORATE GENESIS OF EDUCATIONAL TESTING

In a short paper on *The Fascist Roots of the SAT Test*, Gibson provides a concise historical context of standardized testing that goes far beyond what most students learn in their education programs.[9] Alfred Binet's attempt to create a measurement of intelligence was used by the United States military in World War I. Proving efficient to sort and select officers and infantrymen, the IQ test was soon transformed into a more pervasive social instrument through a complicitous relationship among education psychologists, military advisors, and corporate investors. Lewis Terman and Robert Yerkes were instrumental in the military's original use of the exam, and, as prominent executives of the American Eugenics Society, continued to promote the idea, at home and abroad, that intelligence and race are genetically linked. The promotion of their "scientific" belief was so pervasive by 1929 that at least thirty states had passed sterilization laws; in California alone, over 6,000 "inferior" people had been sterilized.

The social damage does not end there, for in reviewing the scholarly works of Stefan Kühl[10] and Barry Mehler,[11] Gibson reports:

> There is a direct line from the IQ tests, to the American Eugenics Society, to forced sterilization, to Nazi extermination, a line that extends not only in theory, but also in History. . . . At their trials at Nuremberg, Nazi scientists not only pointed to U.S. research as a scientific basis for the death camps, but also rightly said that after the War, U.S. companies continued to try to recruit them.[12]

Carl C. Brigham, who assisted Yerkes on the military's IQ testing program, firmly believed that intelligence was biological and that mixing the races would diminish society's intelligence. Brigham's preventative contribution was the Scholastic Aptitude Test, a slight modification of the IQ test. Reviewing these researchers, Gibson reaches a compelling implication:

> The SAT became a deadly weapon. The rationale of racism, sexism, and class privilege built into the test necessarily means, at its end, not just sterilization, but death. The SAT was used to secure draft deferments during the Korean and Vietnam wars, ensuring the wars were fought by working class youth, especially black youth. . . . Nothing significant has changed about the results of the SAT scores, or the outlook of its authors since it was first written. Underlying the SAT is an equation of lies: Intelligence can be defined and measured, race is a biological-scientific, not social, construct, some people are simply better and deserve more, some lives are not worthy of life. There is nothing untoward about pointing at today's respectable test-promoters and saying: "Fascist."

Gibson's frustration with the complicitous misuse of testing as a social instrument, a misuse now visited upon young children, is understandable. But perhaps we should not make so much of the assumed connection between the historic effects of IQ and SAT testing and the as yet unforeseen social effects resulting from standardized testing in today's schools. Today's examinations may be more culturally and psychometrically sophisticated. And the standardized tests used in today's schooling measure academic achievement, not aptitude, as was the purpose of the IQ or SAT test.

Data showing whether today's examinations are more or less culturally and psychometrically valid than previously rarely appear in discussions about the current accountability movement. However, gender adjustments structured into the SAT and other standardized examinations, and the wholesale rescaling of the SAT a few years ago, may suggest that endemic test validity problems are being concealed. Furthermore, Robert Sternberg dispels the myth that examinations can be sorted into either "achievement" or "aptitude" tests. He reasons that any individual responds to test items on the basis of all previous experience, making it an indicator of what one has cognitively achieved.[13]

STANDARDIZING THE NATURE OF KNOWLEDGE

It is the nature of the content on standardized tests that belies the dangerous military and corporate roots of contemporary educational reforms. The rise of standardized testing, beginning with the IQ test and later the SAT, resulted from a confluence of efforts in the early twentieth century in which American corporations sought greater control over the organization and production of research knowledge, as well as of workers. With the assistance of the military and the co-opting of universities, corporation efforts transformed the very nature of knowledge, knowledge that ultimately establishes the standards for contemporary school subjects.

In the contemporary hierarchy of our social knowledge, math and science enjoy the highest status.[14] Typically the first subjects in K–12 or higher education to receive government or industry funding, they are certainly the ones for which students receive the most lucrative scholarships and grants. David Noble locates the rise in status of math and science in the early twentieth century with the research needs of industries. The major corporations—General Electric, Westinghouse, AT&T, DuPont, General Chemical, and others—collaborated on a number of fronts to gain control:

> First over the means of scientific industry through the establishment and enforcement of industrial and scientific standards; second over the products of scientific industry through the monopoly of patents and reform of the patent system itself; third over the process of scientific invention and discovery through the organization of industrial and university research; and finally fourth over the practitioners of industrial science through transformation of public schooling, technical and higher education.[15]

The emphasis on the control and monopolizing of standards, materials, and processes of knowledge making reflects the rationality of today's educational reforms. Noble explains that the transformation of all social institutions and the "habituation" of people for "new forms of productive activity" was a "monumental job."

> Gearing the society for new modes of production—capitalist, corporate, and scientific—entailed the creation of new forms of social life, individual identity, relations between people, patterns of work, leisure, consumption, definitions of human potential, education, knowledge, the good—in short, the production of society itself.[16]

Working through a variety of industry and university collaborations, the concerted effort on the part of corporations was to (1) shift the burden of scientific research production from their own private money to the public money of higher education; (2) influence the type of education workers receive to make them better prepared for the corporate environment (intelligent, but obedient); (3) utilize modern technologies of standardized testing for "efficiency" and for "'scientifically' fitting the man to the job."[17]

The standards and testing strategy of education reform was well honed at the corporate and university level decades before descending upon K–12 education. The Society for the Promotion of Engineering Education (SPEE) became the primary forum for changing higher education. Charles Mann, sponsored by SPEE, introduced testing into the schools in 1914 and advised industrial employers that not only were objective tests the most efficient in defining desired worker abilities and in selecting the actual workers, but that tests are "your most powerful means of controlling what is done in the school."[18]

Influence over university knowledge by the military was formalized during World War I under the auspices of the War Department Committee on Education and Special Training. The committee, including representatives from SPEE and from corporations such as Westinghouse and Western Electric, "all of whom donned uniforms for the duration," wielded broad authority to "introduce many of their educational innovations with relative ease while conditioning a good many educators to produce according to specifications, industrial as well as military."[19] The SPEE remained influential on the reform of higher education after the war, assisted now by the National Research Council and the American Council on Education (ACE). Special note should be taken of the ACE. Its membership "dominated from the outset by War Department Committee members" promoted the science of education; its testing program "coalesced eventually into the Educational Testing Service."[20]

The evidence is strong that corporate influence over scientific knowledge at the beginning of the twentieth century effectively changed our social epistemology—what questions are asked, how they are asked, and which ones will be investigated. Collaborating with the military, U.S. corporations gradually and deliberately transformed the purposes of universities and colleges into the production of knowledge and workers befitting a technocratized and corporatized society. Concurrently, a cultural form of militancy was fostered by instilling habits of worker efficiency and unquestioning loyalty toward corporate goals.

SEEKING PARSIMONY (OR "WE HAVE MET THE ENEMY AND IT IS US!")

The basis for evaluating theories involves, among its criteria, the degree to which a theory provides "parsimony," that is, the simplest, most verifiable, and sensible (empirical) explanation of the known information at hand. For example, aside from its implicitly threatening political implications, Copernicus's and Galileo's explanation of the solar system ultimately was accepted as superior to Ptolemaic theory because it provided a better and simpler account of all the involved phenomena.

The outcome of World War II includes alliances of NATO, SEATO, OAS, and the United Nations. For many citizens of the United States, another outcome is an American foreign policy that is often viewed as a tangle of incomplete doctrines, financial-aid assistance packages, humanitarian initiatives, economic trade agreements, and military agreements, often with countries in parts of the world that are unfamiliar until we are told that an "emergency intervention is necessary." William Blum, former State Department official and editor of the *Washington Free Press*, offers a parsimonious foreign policy theory. Spending years publishing exposés of the CIA and the government's involvement in various areas of the world, Blum documents over sixty-five interventions since World War II, with activities ranging from the destabilization of opposition parties to outright assassinations of political leaders. In Blum's words:

> It was all called national security. The American republic had been replaced after World War II by a national security state, answerable to no one, an extra-constitutional government, secret from the American people, exempt from congressional oversight, above the law.[21]

Blum's claims may sound absurd to most U.S. citizens, a reaction, perhaps, that demonstrates the successful indoctrination of our social studies education programs.[22] The enduring patriotic fervor of citizens suggests that even the least attentive students in school are likely to develop a firm belief that the United States benignly encourages the growth of democracy around the world.

In his farewell address fifteen years after World War II, President Eisenhower warned of the dangers for civil society from the military-industrial complex. Subsequently, reporting on this danger, Sydney Lens explains that after the war, a permanent war economy was *insisted upon*, maintaining a high level of production to meet the stockpiling needs of the military in their ever-constant vigilance to keep the world safe for—no, not democracy (although this claim is invoked when convenient), but—free enterprise![23]

Who was insisting? It may be possible to infer from Lens's analysis that a cabal of military leaders in influential political positions took it upon themselves to determine U.S. economic and foreign policy.

> [The root of concern for] Truman and the military men who ran his State Department was the issue of "free" versus "regimented" economies. The Soviet orbit's own economy was "regimented," and if the new nations—whose revolutions were supported by the Soviets—were to become similarly "regimented," *American free enterprise would find a large area of the world closed off to its trade and investment, as well as its needs in raw materials.* (Italics mine)[24]

The social studies curricula of U.S. schools typically frame the Cold War in terms of "totalitarian" versus "democratic" systems, a polarization that habituates alarm among students who learn to fear the impending loss of their individual, personal freedom. Yet, a closer examination of Cold War activities might suggest that the primary concern was for the freedom of U.S. industries to expand globally. Protecting the freedoms of U.S. citizens may have been a secondary benefit of Cold War policy, as was the freedom of citizens of other nations (ask a Vietnamese or Cuban).

Consistent with this parsimonious thinking, world domination may not be stretching the purpose and trajectory of U.S. foreign policy since World War II. Shortly after becoming president, Truman explained to a friend that "once the Russians are shown their place," the United States would run the world the way "the world ought to be run."[25] In a subsequent speech at Baylor University, which Lens feels should have been given more attention, Truman reflected the Cold War ideology of the United States:

> The enemy of free enterprises was "regimented economies," and "unless we act, and act decisively," said Truman, those regimented economies would become "the pattern of the next century." To guard against the danger he urged that "the whole world should adopt the American system." That system "could survive in American only if it became a world system."[26]

An adamant determination to procure and protect ever-expanding global markets and resources for our industries provides a parsimonious account of U.S. foreign policy. Regardless of variations in foreign policy emphases by different administrations and Congresses since World War II, the underlying premises guiding foreign policy emerged from the lessons of the Great Depression and World War II, keenly learned and persistently promoted by the industrial and military sector.

MAKING THE SCHOOLS SAFE FOR GLOBALIZATION

A highly esteemed colleague once remarked that "many conservative educational critics blame school failures on John Dewey and the Progressives, but Fredrick Taylor has had the most influence on the way schools are shaped."

Taylor's ideas about industrial organizational management, an authoritarian system of standards, efficiency, and accountability have trivialized most of the developmental and progressive educational ideas of the past century. Deeply engrained Tayloristic principles continue to provide a bulwark against the social meliorist effects of civil rights legislation. In the *Sputnik*-instigated Cold War educational crisis of the 1960s and 1970s, only reform principles consistent with entrenched Tayloristic behaviors endured. War Department and National Science Foundation funding supported subject matter experts (especially in the sciences and mathematics) who identified the most important concepts of their fields—a technocratic act that reified knowledge and trivialized the new pedagogy of student inquiry into a linear process for the "discovery" of preexisting knowledge. Evaluations of what came to be called the "new education" blame its failure on insufficient professional development, that is, inadequate resources devoted to resocializing how teachers think.[27] Further complicating the new education efforts were the changes brought upon the schools from civil rights legislation.

As Secretary of Education for Ronald Reagan in the 1980s, William Bennett called from the bully pulpit for an education founded on Character, Content, and Choice (The "Three Cs"), assuring cultural conservatives that educational reform would bring order to a chaotically changing social structure. It also signaled that Tayloristic principles for organizing and controlling teaching and learning would again dominate educational policies and practices.

The authoritarian tone and militant language *of A Nation at Risk* signaled that the purpose of education reform in the 1980s would be no less than preparation for globalized, industrialized, and, if necessary, military competition.[28] A forceful political strategy of deregulation followed, creating significant long-term changes in the direction of federal educational policy.[29] Three national education forums have been held since 1989 to continually enforce the corporate shape of education reform. These national reforms, including among their main cosponsors the Business Roundtable and the National Alliance of Business, continue to include a raft of cultural conservatives (e.g., Chester Finn is a regular) and increasingly involve more CEOs and highly selected educational politicians, but fewer governors.

The Third National Summit on Education was held at IBM headquarters in White Plains, behind locked gates and with restrictions on public access and the news media. According to Joy Wallace, one of the few reporters allowed to attend its proceedings, the urgent theme of the summit was that state governors and commissioners of education needed to improve achievement, or else! Wallace interpreted that "or else" to mean a turn to privatization, vouchers, and charter schools. And the only means implied to accomplish these demands was to "press forward" with standards and testing.[30]

The brazen tone of the Third Summit fortified many of the educational politicians in attendance. For example, having recently returned from the summit, New York State Commissioner Richard Mills warned a roomful of education deans and chairs of teacher preparation departments that, unlike the resistance and strikes in other states by parents, teachers, and educators, the standards and testing movement in New York State would involve "no nonsense!" In the mesmerizing voice of an evangelist and rhythmically tapping his fist on the podium, he proclaimed, "This—will—not—happen—here!" True belief? Bravado? Fear? One might wonder what creates such self-assured confidence, but for anyone present in the room, there was little doubt that Commissioner Mills was deeply committed to the themes of the Third National Education Summit.

For well over a century, New York State parents, teachers, students, and administrators have accepted—even embraced—standardized State Regents' examinations and regulations, so it is reasonable to think that the culture of New York State would be amenable to the increased intensity of high-stakes testing and standards. Yet, public resistance to high-stakes testing and standards arose rapidly in various quarters, and has evolved into effective legislative actions. Only a few months after Commissioner Mills denied the possibility of opposition, over two-thirds of eighth-grade students in the prosperous Scarsdale, New York district boycotted a state standardized test, as did students from Ithaca and Rochester. Around the same time, parents, teachers, administrators, and students "marched on the State Education Building in Albany and held a boisterous rally on the Capitol steps—the largest protest seen in the Capitol this year."[31] Resistance grew in the next two years as more parents and teachers became aware of the insidious and skewed effects of high-stakes testing.[32] The Rouge Forum,[33] Teachers Forum, The Coalition for Commonsense in Education,[34] the New York Performance Standards Consortium (representing twenty-eight districts), and Time Out from Testing[35] are but some of the groups of widely diverse members who sponsor resistance activities, testify at public hearings on the bias of testing, initiate and support legislative actions, maintain active websites, and consistently document the case against New York State's current regulation of knowledge.

STATE REGULATION OF KNOWLEDGE

Although I stop short of labeling the influence of the CEOs and politicians at the Third Education Summit a fascist conspiracy, it is important to note that federal and state education policies (policies that critics argue are racist, arrogant, and overly nationalistic) were formed in a mostly closed meeting between corporate leaders and the selected politicians who would most likely heed their requests.

The apparent change in nature between the First National Education Summit in the 1980s and the Third National Education Summit in 1999 exemplifies that the state regulation of knowledge is not a static formulation or a fixed authoritarian force. The First Summit involved a great deal of discussion among forty-nine state governors, and what emerged were recommendations for some far-reaching goals about literacy and student knowledge by the year 2000. The Third Summit involved about half as many governors, but the threatening stridency of its theme, the preponderance of CEO attendees, and the confidence of its leaders in demanding that their recommendations be put into effect indicate the hegemonic influence corporate America developed over educational policy in a little over a decade.

This is not a time for progressive-minded citizens to be discouraged. Michael Apple reminds us that the "state" is neither fixed nor simple, but has a constantly changing role as different interest groups struggle for influence.[36] Understanding the hegemonic nature of testing and standards policies, and recognizing that hegemony is a process in which power has to be constantly built and rebuilt, enables educators and other citizens to ask questions and become a counterhegemonic force.

A ROLE FOR EDUCATORS

Apple writes that "education is thoroughly political" and that "in order to defend the more democratic gains that committed educators and activists have won in many nations over the years, we need to act collectively."[37] Indeed, we need the work of Ohanian, Berliner, Biddle, and others to continue, even when the odds of directly influencing public policy seem overwhelming. Susan Ohanian advises that we might best "fight city hall" by talking and by getting our students to talk—and by influencing them to keep their students talking. Over the past twenty years, policymakers have conspicuously ignored and avoided the inclusion of educators in their quest for reforms via standards and testing. It is also glaringly apparent that these same policymakers are seriously concerned about what educators teach in the classroom.[38] Perhaps they are concerned for good reason, because educators, especially those of us in higher education, are in the "belly of the beast." We work in institutions that are instrumental for the production and reproduction of capital and capitalism—one reason why corporations and the military have attempted to control them since the early twentieth century. But while colleges and universities share responsibility with other social institutions in creating wide disparities between the haves and the have-nots, higher-educators are also in the position to promote social justice and are ultimately responsible for providing an education that is personally liberating and socially progressive. College graduates are likely to assume positions of power, and their knowledge and social disposition will greatly affect our children's movement toward or away from democratic living. An uplifting view is that educators can redefine the direction of educational reform and can develop citizens and teachers of citizens who are able to rise above the constraints of corporatized and militarized thinking.

Toward this noble end, it is important to encourage students toward a better understanding and disposition of knowledge. *What* one understands about knowledge and *how one learns to be disposed* to knowledge is a foundational area for liberating the thinking of teachers, students, and, ultimately, citizens for a democratic society. This is not a proposal for yet another technocratic form of critical thinking but rather a serious reminder that the liberating aspect of teaching and learning is not a matter of testing and standards but, instead, involves coming to the realization that what people think they know is, at best, contingent and ever-changing, value-laden, and inextricably related to how they live in the world.

— 9 —

Extreme Takeover: Corporate Control of the Curriculum, with Special Attention to the Case of Reading

STEVEN L. STRAUSS

INTRODUCTION: CORPORATE AMERICA'S INTEREST IN CURRICULUM

The last decade or so of education reform has been primarily about the transition from corporate *influence* over classroom curriculum to corporate *control*. This is especially true in the field of reading, where the question of corporate influence has never really been in doubt but where teachers, students, and parents are just now beginning to grapple with the consequences of control.

Corporate influence over the reading curriculum is easy to detect each time a child sounds out a letter from a decodable primer, writes in a phonics workbook, or takes a quantitative reading assessment examination. The phonics industry showcases these wares at teacher and educator conferences, as if such conferences were mere trade shows. The materials are colorfully packaged and slickly marketed, the better to attract the eye of the one who comes bearing a school district's blank check.

A new era of outside control over the reading curriculum can now be detected, quite easily in fact, with the unprecedented legal requirement that teachers drill children in intensive phonics, whether they need it or not and whether teachers believe in intensive phonics or not, using only approved materials, under the threat of sanctions against both teachers and students for failing to make "adequate yearly progress." These measures are codified in President George W. Bush's No Child Left Behind Act of 2001, the successor to Clinton's Reading Excellence Act. The latter mandated only phonics, without yet imposing high-stakes testing and accountability punishments, whereas Bush's bill simply tightens the screws already set in place by his predecessor.

The chief architect of the new pedagogy is corporate America, which has united around an education policy articulated primarily by the Business Roundtable, a coalition of CEOs of the country's leading corporations. Over the past fifteen years or so, the Business Roundtable has agitated successfully in favor of standardizing the school curriculum nationwide and imposing high-stakes testing and punitive accountability. Its goal has been "not just to improve individual schools but to reform the entire system of public education."[1] It is well on its way to achieving its goal.

To corporate America, the era of mere influence over curriculum, as opposed to complete control over it, has become unacceptable. This is because classroom curriculum holds the key to something that corporate America now feels is indispensable to its very survival as a global hegemonic class. When properly engineered, classroom curriculum can create workers with world-class skills in information technology and digital literacy. According to the Business Roundtable, "investment in workforce training and skills upgrading is an urgent priority for U.S. competitiveness. In the integrated global economy, workforce quality drives national competitiveness. . . . The structural transformation of the American economy demands a substantial improvement in the training and development of the U.S. workforce."[2]

It is precisely the skills of digital, electronic literacy, to be drilled into the emerging U.S. domestic labor force of the twenty-first century, that the Business Roundtable is counting on to maintain the global competitive edge of its corporations. For its part, and in intimate collaboration with corporate America, government scientists have offered up intensive phonics as the key to setting future workers on the path to digital literacy.

Indeed, the politicoeconomic driving force behind the government's reading research was stated quite succinctly by Duane Alexander, director of the National Institute of Child Health and Human Development (NICHD). On presenting the report of the NICHD's National Reading Panel to Congress, Alexander declared, "the significance of these findings for the well-being of our children and their families and teachers, and the implications for the future literacy of this nation and for the economic prosperity and global competitiveness of our people is enormous."[3] And to complete the circuit of coercive pedagogy in the service of corporate America, Reid Lyon, director of the NICHD's reading research branch, testified before Congress in favor of tying the NRP's intensive phonics recommendations to high-stakes testing and accountability.[4]

It is interesting that Lyon has repeatedly defended intensive phonics on the basis of its alleged scientific support. But he provided not a single piece of evidence that high-stakes testing and punitive accountability improve educational performance or that they do so without undue harm to children. His testimony, therefore, was politically inspired and antiscientific.

Corporate America sees its strongest and most worrisome competition coming from corporate Europe and corporate Asia. According to Norman Augustine, "We are concerned that the graduates of America's schools are not prepared to meet the challenges posed by global economic competition."[5] Augustine is the former CEO of Lockheed Martin, former chairman of the Education Task Force of the Business Roundtable, and education advisor to President Bush.

In order to beat back the challenge, corporate America has concluded that it must train and maintain a domestic workforce with the world's most advanced level of labor productivity. In the age of the technological revolution in electronics, this translates into creating workers who possess the most advanced levels of fluency in reading and writing the literature of software and hardware, a labor skill that can be called e-fluency.

Various corporate-friendly research and policy organizations have looked into the prerequisite, component skills of e-fluency. In its 2000 report, the Congressional Twenty-first Century Workforce Commission, set up by President Clinton, identified reading and mathematics as foundational to e-fluency.[6] The commission's director, Clinton-appointee Hans Meeder, encouraged schools to implement the intensive phonics curriculum recommended and promoted by the NICHD in its NRP Report. Meeder had previously worked for the U.S. House of Representatives Committee on Education and the Workforce. He is currently an assistant Secretary of Education under Rod Paige and President Bush. Meeder has no academic background in education.

The Business Roundtable has taken on the job of promoting corporate America's education reform scheme to manufacture a workforce drenched in twenty-first century literacy. In order to make certain that schools would implement the "tough academic standards" demanded by corporate America, the Business Roundtable urged lawmakers to write legislation mandating regular testing in reading and mathematics, and in order to make certain that teachers and students would take the tests seriously, lawmakers were further urged to tie the test scores to "rewards for success and consequences for failure."[7]

To ensure popular support for this extreme takeover, a new pedagogical language had to be circulated and popularized. Reading and mathematics have been incessantly referred to as the new "standards," as if there were something substandard about art, music, and physical education. Measurable growth in the acquisition of knowledge labor skills is called "adequate yearly progress." Opponents of the scheme are cynically accused of harboring "the soft racism of low expectations."

The language of corporate coercion is supplemented, of course, with material coercion. The prospect of a high-paying job in the digital economy is held out as bait for a student who does well in the new curriculum, but, as usual, this is nowhere guaranteed. Negative incentives include the threats of retention and withholding of diplomas, and in some states, the local business community has announced that it will routinely look at a job applicant's high school transcripts.[8]

Though corporate America describes the new twenty-first century digital literacy as a labor skill that goes beyond the skills needed in the era of the twentieth-century industrial worker, its model of the educational organization needed to create the next generations of knowledge workers is just the same old industrial assembly line. It has been quite explicit about this.

For example, corporate America has justified its right to decide on matters of education and curriculum on the grounds that it is "the principal customer of the products of the education pipeline."[9] Indeed, it refers to schools as "a workforce development system that will serve its principal customers," where high school graduates are merely the final, finished products to be purchased as commodities on the labor market.[10]

The manufacture of this commodity proceeds via a sequence of steps called "curriculum," beginning, as does any manufacturing process, with raw materials and the machines to process them. In the workforce development system, these are fresh young minds and dutiful, compliant teachers, respectively. The teachers, living tools in the assembly line process, sculpt and mold the children, the living raw material, beginning with the inculcation of elementary skills, proceeding to successively more complex skills.

As with any assembly line process, quality control mechanisms must be in place to weed out products of poor quality. This is one of the functions of high-stakes testing and accountability. Its other function, of course, is to let products of acceptable quality proceed to the next stage in the manufacturing process, that is, to be promoted and to graduate.

In assembly line manufacturing, products of poor quality, along with waste products of the manufacturing process, undergo two possible fates. They are either discarded or alternative uses are found for them. One of the chief educational landfills where flawed products can be discarded is prison, whose construction is on the rise and whose residents typically include students who don't make it, as the National Institute of Child Health and Human Development has acknowledged. A major alternative use for flawed products is anticipated in the No Child Left Behind Act. The bill includes a little publicized section that permits the Pentagon greater access to student names and addresses, for recruitment purposes, of course, an alternative use of partially educated material but one that is particularly crucial in the current era of "endless war."

The sheer size of the new workforce corporate America wants, as well as the anticipation that it will be needed for decades to come, defies corporate America's willingness to take full responsibility for its own perceived needs.

From its selfish perspective, it is much more efficient, and less damaging to profit margins, if the public schools do the job training as a matter of official curriculum. In return, corporate America offers nothing to young people and their parents other than the *possibility* of getting a good job. Thus, this entire project represents the kidnapping of public schools and the looting of public coffers by corporate America for its own ends.

A bipartisan Congress has all along been a willing accomplice in this grand theft. Its contribution has been No Child Left Behind, the legal basis for corporate America's invasion of the classroom, analogous to providing a president with a declaration of war. Sadly, this is not just metaphor. As Norman Augustine explained, "Competition in the international marketplace is, in reality, a battle for the classroom."[11]

Thus, children are not only raw material to be molded by a workforce-development system into knowledge workers, they are also cannon fodder in a global war for control of markets. No Child Left Behind is, fundamentally, a law whose function is to conscript the entire educational system, including its administrators, teachers, and students, and transform it into factories for the war effort. Those students who succeed will fight on the domestic front, while those who are picked off by the Pentagon will fight in foreign countries, all part of the same war.

The media have done their part as well. They have popularized the unfounded notion that we are living in the midst of a literacy crisis, one that requires an urgent solution, or else—or else what? They have covered up the fact that the supposed literacy crisis is corporate America's own problem, that it needs a certain *type* of literacy among its workforce to maintain a hegemonic lead in labor productivity. They have never seriously publicized the fact that private schools for children of wealthy corporate CEOs will *not* be subject to No Child Left Behind, so they will be free to offer an educationally rich curriculum that does not shortchange the arts, music, and physical education. Clearly, these schools develop the nation's future rulers, while the public schools, under the guise of educational standards, develop the nation's future workers.

The scientific community has furnished the "objective" cover for No Child Left Behind. For example, the report of the National Reading Panel presented the findings of a meta-analysis of selected instructional techniques in reading, but the section on phonics looked at a scant thirty-eight articles, all that the National Reading Panel could find from the entire worldwide English-language database on phonics intervention spanning a period of nearly three decades. One of the "technical advisors" to the National Reading Panel, Barbara Foorman, was herself an author of more than 10 percent of the articles in the phonics section, so in this capacity, the National Reading Panel violated the crucial anonymity condition of any legitimate meta-analysis. Protecting itself from conflict of interest was hardly taken seriously anyway. The mass-distributed summary report of the NRP was prepared with the assistance of Widmeyer-Baker, a public relations firm contracted to McGraw-Hill, a major manufacturer of phonics materials.

Barbara Foorman has acknowledged that any reader of the summary report who does not also read the lengthy full report will be "misinformed," but this warning appears nowhere in the report itself.[12] The most striking piece of misinformation is the assertion of the summary report that the benefits of phonics instruction persist through all the elementary school grades, while the full report asserts that there is no evidence of any benefit beyond first grade.[13] Of course, it is the lightweight, thirty-five page summary report that is the primary promotional tool for "research-based" reading instruction.

The scandal of the National Reading Panel report has drawn no objection from corporate America. Apparently, it trusts the panel's motives and is willing to let intensive phonics be the method of choice to initiate children into workforce development. Indeed, corporate America has backed off on recommending any particular instructional method, especially in reading, stating that the field is too complex, and is content, for the time being, to leave the details to its paid experts.[14]

But intensive phonics will fail, since it is a demonstrably defective paradigm for understanding reading development, instruction, and assessment. Nearly forty years of research on how children construct meaning in their interaction with print has clearly shown that letter-sound relationships are just one of a number of cognitive resources the reader uses and that it is no more privileged in this role than knowledge of syntactic structures, semantic systems, and background knowledge and beliefs.[15]

Thus, we can anticipate a sharpening conflict between corporate America and the scientific community in the years to come. However the details of this conflict work themselves out, one thing is absolutely certain: corporate America will demand the same control over publicly funded scientific research that it now demands over publicly funded classrooms.

The battle for the classroom is only just beginning.

THE ROLE OF PHONICS IN THE "BATTLE FOR THE CLASSROOM"

Phonics focuses on very little things, like letters of the alphabet and the phonemes to which they allegedly correspond. Globalization and economic hegemony focus on very big things, like the world's markets, oil, and the World Trade Organization. As expressed through this rather banal and jejune contrast, the two seem to have absolutely nothing to do with one another. However, their bedroom intimacy has already been noted, and further elements of their tabloid relationship need to be examined.

Wherever the Business Roundtable and the National Institute of Child Health and Human Development first met, they now hang out together in Bush's Education Advisory Committee. Members of this committee include Ed Rust, Jr., CEO of State Farm Insurance Companies, and former head of the Education Task Force of the Business Roundtable; Norman Augustine, already identified as former CEO of Lockheed Martin and former head of the Education Task Force of the Business Roundtable; and Reid Lyon, director of reading research at the National Institute of Child Health and Human Development and one of the chief architects of No Child Left Behind. Rust and Augustine have bought Lyon's intensive phonics, and Lyon, the erstwhile stumper for "trustworthy" science, has bought Rust's and Augustine's demand for high-stakes testing and accountability (for which absolutely no supportive scientific evidence exists whatsoever) that it will improve educational achievement without unacceptable side effects.

Obviously, this is far from the first time that scientists have colluded with those in power. We often think of such collusion as characteristic of totalitarian societies. Medical doctors did "research" for the Nazis, and biologists in Germany twisted Mendelian genetics to buttress racial superiority "theories," taking their cue, in fact, from the U.S. eugenics movement. Stalin outlawed Mendelian genetics as a "fascist" and "Trotskyite" aberration, and gave state approval, including funding and research facilities, to the idiotic agricultural theory of Trofim Lysenko, whose antigenetics vernalization theory was a snake-oil promise to bring the Soviet Union out of its famine. Lysenkoism eventually was repudiated, in part due to the courageous work of Soviet dissident scientists.

It is relatively easy to understand why some scientists would acquiesce to the state. It is simply not possible for most scientists to pursue their work without substantial, independent funding. They are, indeed, dependent in this respect on outside sources of material support. Their love for their work, and perhaps even a strong dose of denial, can overcome otherwise objectionable government policy. Some, of course, support the political goals of the state.

But the question of why phonics would resonate with the corporate business community is a different matter. Mere respect for science itself does not explain the Business Roundtable's acceptance of intensive phonics, since there are other scientific conceptions of reading and reading instruction that could also have competed for the ears of Rust and Augustine. The answer must lie in the perceived capacity of intensive phonics to achieve corporate America's goals. In this, intensive phonics is practically ideal.

Corporate America's ultimate goal for education is to turn it into a workforce development system to construct a labor force that has facility with digital technology, electronic databases, fiber optics, and, more generally, with the whole field of information processing. Viewed conceptually, phonics can be thought of as the most elementary form of information processing of written symbols. Each letter is the smallest functioning unit on a printed page. Decoding the letter to discover the sound it is connected to is a form of data manipulation. Joining successive sounds together into a word is a higher level of data manipulation. Joining words together into phrases and sentences leads ultimately to the construction of meaning itself.

Intensive phonics is couched in a theory of reading that regards word identification as the crucial, fundamental psychological operation. This is achieved via identification of the word's component sounds, themselves identified by using phonics rules to connect the word's letters to their corresponding pronunciations. The measures of word identification that supposedly characterize a proficient reader are *speed* and *accuracy*. These are *quantifiable* measures and, therefore, lend themselves readily to quantitative testing and serial monitoring. In turn, these measures can enter into the calculations that decide whether a school has made "adequate yearly progress."

In all these respects, intensive phonics is an appealing pedagogy to corporate America, because it promises to create well-trained data manipulators and can be monitored quantitatively. Thus, it ideally ties together a plan for manufacturing an e-literate workforce with high-stakes testing and accountability.

In all these areas, intensive phonics is diametrically at odds with meaning-centered reading, or whole language. According to advocates of the latter reading paradigm, several decades of scientific research on how readers construct meaning have clearly demonstrated that letter-sound relationships play a distinctly ancillary and subordinate role when compared with the role of syntax, semantics, world knowledge, and belief systems. In reading the sentence "Chopin played the piano," knowledge that Chopin was a piano player and that "the" is syntactically followed by a noun already narrows down the possibilities for the identification of the last word. It is much more efficient to *predict* that the final word is "piano," perhaps even scanning just the first letter "p" for some additional confirmation (without necessarily sounding it out), than to sound out each individual letter, put them all together, and then suddenly realize that the word is "piano." Whole language researchers have been able to show, in fact, that proficient readers process written text on the basis of such predictions, using a variety of resources to narrow down the possibilities, and to improve their chances of being semantically right. It is precisely the efficiency of good predictions that makes good readers read fast and the laboriousness of sounding out letters that makes poor readers read slowly.

Thus, whole language is interested in meaning construction rather than data manipulation. It emphasizes the open-endedness of interpretations rather than the accurate and speedy identification of words and, therefore, assesses reading *qualitatively*, not *quantitatively*. It is not an intrinsically appealing approach to reading instruction for advocates of the workforce-development system.

Unfortunately for such advocates, however, whole language has won the support of vast numbers of teachers over the past several decades because of its sturdy scientific foundations and because teachers have been able to see for themselves that real readers, both proficient and nonproficient, really do what whole language theorists claim. Good readers use a variety of "cuing systems" to construct meaning, while poor readers overemphasize letter-sound relationships.

Of course, many teachers support the use of phonics and do not agree with whole language. But this is precisely what should be expected among professionals, where it is recognized that judging the needs of an individual child is based, in part, on a teacher's expertise. Therefore, it is not just advocates of whole language who will find themselves on the enemies list of the corporate agenda but also those democratic-minded phonics advocates who believe that using phonics should be a matter of individual choice, based on expert assessment of a child's needs, ideally in collaboration with the child and the child's parents.

Interestingly, it is the most enlightened proponents of whole language who advocate for democratic classrooms and for freedom of choice on the part of professional teachers. This is because whole language recognizes the individuality of interpretation, the crucial role that critical thinking plays in nurturing this, and the necessity for classrooms to be democratic if critical thinking is to be promoted.

Leaders of the National Council of Teachers of English (NCTE), an organization of 70,000 teachers and educators, are among these enlightened thinkers. NCTE has published two relevant position papers on these matters.[16] In its *Position Statement On Reading*, NCTE describes reading as the process of constructing meaning from print, using the full complement of psychological resources available to the reader, including syntax, semantics, world knowledge, belief systems, *and* letter-sound relationships. In the other statement, it opposes the government issuing any "official" definition of reading or science, such as that which appears in Clinton's Reading Excellence Act and Bush's No Child Left Behind Act.

Therefore, in order for corporate America's agenda to become a reality, a battle must be waged against sizable forces of resistance, among whom are whole language teachers and phonics teachers who believe in democracy in the classroom. This is Augustine's "battle for the classroom."

Intensive phonics identifies for corporate America one of its main enemies in this battle, namely, the paradigm of meaning-centered whole language to which it is counterposed, while high-stakes testing and accountability provide the means to eradicate the enemy from the classroom. The appeal of intensive phonics to advocates of the workforce development system is that it can attack whole language at the micro level, decrying its "unscientific" sloppiness in allowing young readers to merely predict words rather than getting them right every time. But this attack is a decoy for the real goal, which is to eliminate what whole language champions at a macro level, namely, democratic classrooms and critical thinking. Clearly, if classrooms are democratic, someone might propose that curriculum should be more than just vocational training.

So, over the past decade, the government has enabled scientists associated with the NICHD to point intellectual turrets at the microcharacteristics of whole language. As opposed to the principles of whole language, these scientists claim that letter-sound decoding is the fundamental element of reading. They claim, incredibly, that readers do not use context when reading. They boast scientific evidence from a major medical-model meta-analysis of instructional techniques. They show pictures taken with high-tech functional magnetic resonance imaging cameras that identify where in the brain phonological decoding occurs. The message that phonological decoding is supported by the most trustworthy science has been played over and over again in the print and broadcast media, so much so that phonics has become a household term.

But in targeting the micro aspects of whole language, and in building support for its elimination from the classroom, the macro aspects of whole language are displaced as well. Of course, the media has not played up this aspect of the attack. But in creating an educational refugee out of whole language, outside control moves in.

An ideology of control greases the skids for high-stakes testing and accountability. It promotes the notion of "standards" without public debate, thus allowing the most powerful social groups to define what constitutes standards. In the end, these will be whatever is thought to promote their own self-serving interests.

Therefore, even if intensive phonics proves to be a big bust, and even if corporate America does not see digital literacy advancing at a pace it feels comfortable with, the present focus on intensive phonics will still have achieved one crucial goal: The government has been allowed into the classroom, and coercive pedagogy has been legally sanctioned. Teachers and students will be told what to do and what standards they need to follow. Whether it is phonics that the government uses to promote mastery of corporate-defined standards or some other pseudoscience, the command and control center has been established.

But phonics will fail as surely as every other snake oil fails, as surely, for example, as the pseudoscience of Lysenkoist vernalization failed when Stalin and his cronies demanded that scientists come up with a cure for their agricultural crisis. The dynamics of this certain failure can play out in a number of ways. Government agents whose job it is to carry out the reading agenda may find ways to revise their own "scientific" curriculum, perhaps even to the point of incorporating elements of whole language, without of course acknowledging this publicly. The most hardened phonics advocates may demand even *more* phonics in the classroom and try to deal final blows to art, music, and physical education on the grounds that they are taking precious time away from "reading." Already, naptime is being eliminated in some kindergarten classes so that children have more time for test preparation.

Some may claim that the problem lies with teacher training at the college level and pressure for new, state-approved certification requirements, that is, for "standards" in colleges of education, a clear violation of academic freedom. Extremists with this point of view may even advocate terrorist tactics, as was actually the case with Bush's chief phonics advisor, Reid Lyon, who publicly, and very soberly, announced his desire to "blow up colleges of education" (November 18, 2002), that is, to start teacher training from a new ground zero.[17] Finally, corporate America itself may step in from behind the scenes and demand the removal of the current science generals, including Reid Lyon himself, and their replacement by others whose snake oil sounds more credible.

Every one of these, or other, machinations will further expose the undemocratic nature of corporate control of the curriculum. They will therefore create opportunities for those who believe in teacher professionalism, children's rights, and democratic classrooms to make their case before more and more people.

CRACKS IN THE SYSTEM AND OPPORTUNITIES FOR RESISTANCE

There is no more well-armed force on earth than corporate America. It controls the skies and the broadcast airwaves in them. It controls the seas and all the water and life it has polluted there. It looks upward and dreams of controlling space. And now it casts its vision right here at home, eager to control the classrooms of children of working people.

But ordinary working people are also armed, with a desire for peace and justice, with democratic ideals, and even with truths about education and childhood that can instill the desires and ideals with practical power. This power can be applied to all the opportunities that currently exist and that will open up in the future to expose corporate America's plans to destroy childhood in the name of profits.

These opportunities can be found in numerous places. At the level of science, the intensive phonics program can be exposed for the scandalous pseudoscience it really is. Purportedly based on a "medical" model of research, the National Reading Panel report never once asked the full panoply of questions that are routinely asked when medical interventions are examined, questions that deal not only with benefits but also with side effects and toxicities.

There is no question that intensive phonics has adverse consequences, because it takes time away from real reading, turns many children off to reading as a result of its boring laboriousness, and can directly harm children who enjoy books by telling them, incorrectly, that they are nonreaders, when this is based solely on an ill-conceived test score.

Furthermore, no medical model of intervention has the added stipulation that a patient has no right to refuse treatment or to opt for a treatment that is considered less likely to succeed. No medical model of intervention forces a physician to prescribe a certain drug or perform a certain operation against his or her better judgment. No physician with any self-respect would ever tell a patient that a drug or surgical intervention is being recommended because "that's what the law is forcing me to do."

At the level of democratic rights, the program of intensive phonics also fails. With No Child Left Behind, the government has actually established a state definition of science. Science must be experimental in design, even though other scientific methodologies are widely employed, including descriptive methodologies for phenomena that are difficult to quantify, such as cultural rituals, animal behavior, and interpretation of written language.

As a corollary, No Child Left Behind legislates a government definition of reading. Its provisions for high-stakes testing and accountability are elements of a coercive pedagogy, designed to force teachers to act according to government prescription.

In a democracy, the curriculum of public schools should be a matter of public discussion. While some may feel that vocational training is the central mission of curriculum, others may feel that childhood itself should be the mission, à la John Dewey, and that specialized training should be left for a later time. Thus, the battle for the classroom is, in a sense, a battle for the curriculum, with the future worker and the present child representing its two poles. In an important sense, therefore, opponents of curriculum for a workforce-development system are, at the same time, opponents of abusive child labor, or to put it more accurately, of abusive child labor training.

Clearly, the struggle around democratic rights carries over into the struggle around issues of pedagogy itself. And it is at the level of pedagogy that the corporate agenda is probably most vulnerable, because there is already movement throughout the country, and increasingly vociferous, against the implementation of high-stakes testing. Indeed, the Business Roundtable has posted a document on its website on how business leaders can monitor and counteract the growing "testing backlash." It notes, quite interestingly, that the opponents of testing are more likely to include mothers than fathers. Without searching for explanation, it regards the men as allies and the women as potential troublemakers. Clearly, this finding, if accurate, reflects the historically determined cultural and emotional distancing of fathers from their children, as compared with mothers. One has to wonder if the Business Roundtable is proud of this finding.

Teachers object to high-stakes testing on many grounds. Arbitrary numbers decide funding and promotion. The serious consequences of the test scores compel teachers to "teach to the test," thus eliminating creativity from the profession and ultimately turning it into mere test preparation. And the notion of standards itself is clearly one-sided, with the one-dimensional emphasis on vocational training creating refugees out of other far more standard elements of the human experience, such as music, art, and physical education.

In struggling to maintain their professionalism in the classroom, and to resist corporate America's extreme takeover of curriculum, teachers will discover a variety of allies. These will include those parents and students who have already organized local anti-high-stakes testing groups, themselves motivated by a desire to preserve quality curriculum and avoid turning assessment into punishment. Teachers will find allies in the children's rights movement and among women, traditional opponents of any form of child exploitation. It will find allies among African-Americans and other minorities, whose children traditionally do not do as well as white children on culturally biased standardized tests. It will find allies among antiwar activists who object to an education bill that gives the Pentagon freer access to children's names and addresses. And since the bureaucracy of the American Federation of Teachers has gone on a public campaign in support of the corporate-government scheme, teachers will find allies among coworkers who have long sought democratic changes in the union, and a leadership accountable to its members and to parents and students rather than to the needs of corporate America.

Though it may be a difficult one, it can truly be said that the struggle to defend children is, at the same time, a struggle to defend all victims of a system that puts corporate profits above all else.

— 10 —

The Body and Sexuality in Curriculum

LISA W. LOUTZENHEISER

> Sexuality—both authorized and unauthorized—is an ever-present, even if invisible discourse of the school.
>
> —Magda Lewis

INTRODUCTION

We are culturally suspended in an age where, for better or worse, sex, sexuality, and body image are the currency of adolescent culture. Looks, body size, and sexual orientation are key elements in the make-it-or-break-it world of peer acceptance and popularity. As constructed as these social markers may be, they are the cultural capital of adolescent society. What is relevant to this chapter, then, are the ways in which youth navigate their various identities and how schools make visible the terrain of normative behavior and the unattainable standards set by the dominant culture. Also significant is the further propagation of these norms within the physical space of our classrooms and hallways, and the silent spaces of our curricula.

SOCIAL PRESSURES? POLITICAL PRESSURES? FAMILIAL PRESSURES? ACADEMIC PRESSURES? WHERE DO WE BEGIN?

Youth face a number of challenges both inside and outside of school. While it would be less difficult to discuss these issues as separate, self-contained challenges to adolescent life, in actuality, there are no isolated issues. There are, however, issues that intersect in multiple ways, spaces, and places where the mechanisms and measures of social acceptability and failure come together to form the frameworks, and seemingly unavoidable binaries, of cultural inclusion/exclusion, popularity/social stigma, and success/failure. Individual pressures range from grade point averages and SAT scores to team memberships, acceptance, belonging, sexual conquest, and fashion savvy, all of which contribute to the development of the individual's idea of "self." For the "out" queer kid, the "closeted" gay or lesbian youth, and the "questioning" teen, these already overwhelmingly complex challenges are compounded by the added layer of normativity enacted by the categorizations of gender and sexuality.

The ideology of gender—what a girl should look like, how a boy's masculinity is defined (and all the subsequent limitations that constitute similar gender binaries)—form the categorical parameters of social acceptance. For adolescents who do not fit neatly into the limited categorizations of the social world, these barriers are omnipresent and seemingly impenetrable. Commonly, gender is narrowly understood as the way in which sexism is perpetuated on women by men, and while this occurs and needs to be deconstructed as such, to leave the dialogue there does not address the larger issues that gender encompasses. What I am arguing for is an uncovering of the assumptions that are held about gender and the roles that gender play vis-à-vis discussions of sexism, heteronormativity, and constructions of femininities and masculinities.

Because of the salience that sexuality and the body hold for youth, and the particular backlash-oriented historical instant in which we are positioned, this moment is ripe for discussions in the classroom, at the school board, at dinner tables, in churches, and in grocery stores. The idea that adolescents are "too sexual" and/or that youth culture is violent and hypersexualized is an accusation hurled with increasing import. It is not that youth are too sexual, but that the ways in which the accepted modulations of sexuality are limited to gender stereotypes and heterosexual performance are problematic and exclusionary of youth whose identities are messy and defiantly Other. Most children and young people spend a large percentage of their waking hours within school walls. In part, this is the reason why there is such a common belief that schools and teachers can raise our children. Even though this is an unfair and unreasonable expectation, it does highlight the possibilities, even constrained by the current climate of standardized testing. Increasingly, schools are developing curricula, pedagogies, and policies centering on school culture to make schools more welcoming to lesbian, gay, bisexual, transgender, and queer (LGBTQ) students, and to educate their peers and teachers about issues of concern to sexual minority youth and adults.

However, the function and structure of the school can make change difficult. Magda Lewis and Barbara Karin speak of the ways that "schools have succeeded [in] containing the body as a site of knowledge and self-authority by the managing, contriving and regulation of bodies as sites of specific and allowable discourses writ large in the particular enactments of femininity and masculinity."[1] Self-esteem, self-worth, and self-knowledge are central to academic success; students who do not see themselves in curricula care far less about learning, and those who see themselves in a dominant way within the curriculum learn to judge those whose identities seem to fall outside of the curricular borders. The school space is not separate from the rest of the world—it is part of that world, and as such, we need to address what "it" is that shapes our educational policy, curriculum, and classrooms. Curricula, and students' reactions to what is included in or omitted from them, point quite clearly to the fallacy of a split between the public and the private sphere.

I have constructed two vignettes to draw out several of the issues that face sexual minority youth. Although Marion and George are fictional characters, they are constructed from the stories told to me as teacher, researcher, or professor. Each of the discussed events occurred to an individual, but I have brought the details together in slightly altered representations in order to make Marion and George unrecognizable. The stories attempt to synthesize a few of the experiences that sexual minority youth encounter. The vignettes offer a small, and very partial, view of sexual minority youth. Following each story is an analysis of the issues and a discussion of why public schools and public school curricula are well suited to work with them. Additionally, I ask what schools and communities might do to address the need for sexuality education. Even though the focus remains on those students who are often marginalized and poorly served by the current educational system, the ways in which LGBTQ bodies fight within current structures are important for majority-sexual youth (and adults) to explore.

CHANGING SPACES AND ALTERED VIEWING

"I'm 16, but sometimes I feel 30, and other days around 12. I mean, in some ways, I have had to grow up really fast but in others I'm socially stunted. I don't really know how to talk to guys like I want to, like my friends would talk to girls." George is a student at East Side Secondary, a high school in an urban center on the West Coast of the United States. He and his family have just moved to the city, after having lived in a rural area for fifteen years. In his small town, he knew everyone and everyone knew him. George was "the artistic one," and the one who was good with his hands. Everyone could see that he was not interested in sports, but if they wanted their bicycle or car worked on, or an actor for the school play, they came to him. He was different, and while occasionally reminded of it, he was mostly tolerated as the designated oddball who did not do as people expected (date lots of girls, play basketball, etc.) Because he was of relatively small build,

George could avoid the pull toward team sports, although every year the wrestling coach tried to encourage him to join the team.

George realized he liked boys more than girls early on, but kept that knowledge to himself. He did not know any gay people in his town and, until recently, did not have a computer and didn't feel comfortable accessing LGBTQ materials at the public or school library. No one ever really talked about such issues in school or out, unless it was hearing the words "fag" or "that's so gay," in the hallways. That wasn't the same as having someone or someplace where he could talk about it. Occasionally, George would hear students at school say "fag" under their breath as he walked by, or girls, who for some reason thought he was cute, half-mockingly question why he did not ask them out. His best friend, Miranda, offered him cover of sorts; they had been attending social functions together forever. He was not really trying to fool anyone, but just felt as if in this town it was easier to not make a point of who he thought he was.

Last May, his mom had found this great new job and they (his mom, his little sister, and George) had moved to a city on the other side of the country. In some ways, he was really excited to move; George had just discovered that he could talk to other gay teens through the Internet. He had a secondhand computer and was finally hooked up. It seemed like a lot of people who responded in the chat rooms lived in larger cities. He was surprised and relieved to know that there were other kids like him who had similar interests. George thought that in a city, he might have more freedom to be himself. If he was very lucky, there might be other gay teens at his school. But the reality was a huge disappointment.

For the first time in his life, he was targeted at school. Every day, he was taunted with shouts of "fag," people pushed him or, perhaps even worse, ignored him altogether. No one knew that he worked on cars and loved drama, and it seemed as if no one was very interested in finding out. All they could see was his difference, the ways in which he was not like them. He became "George the fag" and that was all that formed his public identity. He was shocked that teachers saw him being taunted, pushed, or laughed at and did nothing. Similarly, when openly antigay comments were made, most of the teachers overlooked them or glanced at him apologetically and shrugged. School became a series of incidents centered on navigating the halls, breaks, and lunchrooms, rather than being about learning. College, even graduate school, had been his goal, either in drama or psychology, but his grades dropped pretty drastically. It seemed as if it was hard to pay attention in class, or perhaps his grades fell because, on many days, he just left school at lunch to avoid the inevitable noontime display of homophobia.

Yet, despite the isolation and taunting from his peers, things were opening up for him. He had found a gay and lesbian center where there was a youth group. It was one and a half hours away by bus, and it seemed to take him forever to get there, but once there it was a veritable haven. There were kids and adults, including a volunteer who was a teacher, and it was more than a group of people sitting around socializing. They were involved with doing things in the community or going to demonstrations. But, unfortunately, because of the distance and bus fare, he could get there only two or three times a month. The rest of the time, he was pretty much on his own.

Not an Easy Road

Schools are difficult places for lesbian, gay, bisexual, transgender, and queer youth. In a recent survey of youth who identify as sexual minorities, The Gay, Lesbian, and Straight Education Network (GLSEN) found that 84 percent of LGBTQ students reported being verbally harassed because of their sexual orientation, including 92 percent who heard remarks such as "faggot," "dyke," and "that's so gay" used frequently or often.[2] Students of color felt increased harassment almost half as much (45 percent) and stated that they were verbally taunted because of their sexual orientation and race/ethnicities.

Just as George felt that teachers let homophobic slurs and teasing pass without comment, youth in the research conducted by GLSEN noted that teachers and staff were not very adept at responding to these remarks, as 37 percent of students said that the faculty "never" intervened when hearing these comments, and 46 percent felt that faculty responded only some of the time. Only 14 percent reported that faculty responded most of the time. The lack of teacher and staff response is problematic on many levels. Of greatest concern, however, is the modeling that teachers, parents, and community members provide students. Thus, the behavior of individual teachers, be it action or inaction, may impact the response and behavior of any or all of the children or youth who witness it.

George experienced an escalation of this harassment, from verbal to physical, as did 40 percent of the youth in the GLSEN study, who note that they have been shoved, pushed, or otherwise physically abused due to their sexual orientation. Transgender students are most at risk, with a more than 30 percent greater risk for unwanted physical contact than lesbian, gay, or bisexual students. Similarly, LGBTQ students are more likely to have property stolen or damaged at school than their non–sexual minority peers (58 percent versus 35 percent). Almost two-thirds of all LGBTQ students report feeling unsafe at school because of their sexual orientation, and more than a quarter of them state that they missed at least one day of school because they felt unsafe. This percentage increases to 35 percent for LGBTQ youth of color.

George left school at lunchtime to avoid such harassment and, similar to many other LGBTQ youth, this affected his grades. GLSEN found that student grade point averages dropped from an average of 3.3 out of 4.0 for LGBTQ students who did not report frequent verbal harassment to 2.9 out of 4.0 for those who did. Dropout rates for LGBTQ students are above the national average, and those, like George, who experience frequent verbal harassment are more than twice as likely not to attend college than those who report rare or less frequent harassment.[3] Combine what occurs in schools with the pressures and systemic discriminations that LGBTQ students face in other areas of their lives, as well as in the media, and the outcomes become sadly predictable. Students often feel isolated and Othered, which, in turn, can lead to dropping out, self-medicating substance abuse, and, in some cases, even suicide. Studies have suggested that 30 percent of all youth suicides are committed by lesbian, gay, and bisexual youth; that they are three to five times more likely to attempt suicide than their heterosexual peers; and that they succeed in killing themselves more often.[4] This is not to argue that the majority of LGBTQ youth attempt suicide, fail at school, or drop out. There are many, of course, who do not; however, any percentage that falls out of the educational system because of sexual orientation, or because of the ways sexual orientation intersects with issues of race, is too high.

It is important to note that circumstances are equally difficult for those *perceived* to be LGBTQ, because harassment and teasing occur based on the perpetrators' perceptions of their target's sexuality. If they read the other student's body as "other than" or nonconforming in terms of gender norms, then often they interpret them as LGBTQ and direct their homophobia based on that assumption. Most often students are not beat up because they are known as gay but because they "look" or "act" gay. This is testimony to the pressure to conform, and, in the end, the limits of sexual conformity.

MISREPRESENTING GENDER AND SEX

The words *gender* and *sex* are often used and conflated but are rarely carefully defined or, when they are defined, are rarely positioned outside the binaries of boy/girl, male/female. Binaries consist of two separate elements considered in diametric opposition. Oftentimes, sex is considered to be the biological distinction between male and female, while gender is explained as a social construction. That is, gender is a performance of social norms understood to be either masculine or feminine in terms of their enactments rather than the presentation of some "true" manifestation of what is male or female. Some have argued that sex is that which we are born with, and gender is that which we gain or acquire. Accordingly, masculinity and femininity take on meaning through the social, political, and historical contexts in which they are located. However, the terms *gender* and *sex* remain ambiguous and contested; they are not easily distinguishable and, as some theorists argue, ought not be the subject of dichotomous or binary definitions.[5] Judith Butler, for example, argues that it is impossible to separate gender from sex, sex from gender, and gender or sex from sexuality. Equally unworkable are attempts to fundamentally erase binary definitions that presume a primal or originary biological sex.[6] Therefore, we ought to be questioning the certainty that sex and gender categories are useful and argue, instead, that the categories and meaning-makings of boy, girl, male, female, man, and woman are discursively constituted through both language and social interaction. That is, we are reliant upon understandings of language and its implications as unchanging in order to make meaning and sense of words, symbols, and the performance of words such as gender and sex. For example, if the word *man* is uttered, an image appears in the reader's mind. It might be different for different readers, but the language conjures up a representation, which, in turn, places more meaning on the word and the gendered performance of the term, and the interpretation of that performance.

Performance of Gender, Masculinity, and Sexuality

Gender is everywhere at school, whether it is discussed or silent, and therefore gender norms are also constantly in play. In addition, the pressures brought to bear on boys and men who do not meet the societal definitions or gender norms of an "authentic" masculinity are often underexplored. Connell argues that masculinity is not stationary or merely a linguistic or material given; rather, it is created, reinforced, and re-created as individuals and groups act and are acted upon. Male bodies, and those persons constructed vis-à-vis the male body, are acted upon by media and school structures that valorize a particular kind of maleness over those it considers lesser or weak.[7]

Indeed, as Epstein argues, dominant bodies are unavoidably heterosexual or assumed to be heterosexual because masculinity and femininity are intertwined and, thus, a "real" boy or girl is, and must be, assumed to be heterosexual.[8] In order to be considered authentically masculine, one must conform to certain gender ideals. Boys at the bottom of the student heap are considered less masculine, constructed more like a girl than a boy, and, therefore, not "fully" a man. One need only to walk the halls of any school to understand that the insults of choice between boys and young men are "fag" and "sissy." When a male does not conform to traditional gender role performances, he is assumed gay and this performance of gay (no matter the young person's sexual orientation) serves as a policing of the gender norms around him and to which he is expected to conform. The student is constructed as an Other, who is always held up as that which is not masculine. In these ways, gender and sex act as a regulatory agent for normative sexuality.

In the small, rural town where George spent most of his early years, he was accepted after a fashion. He was not overtly harassed. However, the price for that "tolerance" was that he did not stray too far from the heterosexual norm. The idea that there is a pervasive and systemic assumption of heterosexuality as the norm has been called "heteronormativity." Michael Warner describes how "heterosexual culture thinks of itself as the elemental form of human association, as the very model of inter-gender relations, as the indivisible basis of all community, and the means of reproduction without which society wouldn't exist."[9] The ramifications of heteronormativity are the silences LGBTQ students are forced to endure, the constant pressures to take on, as George did, the trappings of heterosexuality such as opposite-sex dating or joining the wrestling team.[10] If George, as someone who does not physically conform to stereotypical gender norms, fails to adopt some part of heteronormative attitudes—such as, he does not fix cars and bikes as well as act—he is more likely to be targeted as Other, or deviant. This is difficult for a youth to work through and with on an individual level, but on a systemic level it tells students and teachers alike that they do not belong and, through curricular and pedagogical silences, never have.

What might it mean to build pedagogies and curricula that interrogate the complicated nature of masculinities in classrooms? How do we create curricula that both invite an understanding of the powerful political, social, and historical positions of some men and explore how masculinities regulate all genders and sexualities?

George measures up against these norms enough to "pass." And when he lived in the small town, he chose to pass because it gave him freedom from harassment and exclusion. Yet there is a toll for this perceived assimilation. He felt as if he were living a lie and not standing up for himself. His fellow students lost the opportunity to see and hear a side of him that might encourage less Othering.

DEFENDING CHANGE IN PUBLIC SCHOOLS

There have been lengthy debates about the purposes of school and schooling. There are numerous beliefs ranging from the pursuit of knowledge for knowledge's sake, assimilation into a common culture or set of values, educating "good citizens," or training "the next generation of workers." No matter what the purposes may be, it is unquestionable that public schools in Canada and the United States have the largest block of early exposure to children and youth of any social institution. How we identify the roles of schools will likely define how we view teaching children to live within increasingly diverse societies. The school can be a powerful agent for social change, but more often it is an equal, if not more powerful, supporter of the status quo. Yet the possibility of change in schools leaves many of us hopeful about the changes that might be wrought if teachers were allowed to teach without the relentless pressure of standards, standardized tests, and "teaching to" said tests. As of yet, no standardized test has attempted to measure knowledge and reflection regarding issues of race, sexuality, gender, or class. We have to question what the role of the school can be in social change.

WHAT SCHOOLS AND COMMUNITIES CAN DO

There are a number of ways to combat heterosexism and homophobia in the classroom and school, yet I cannot offer one or two foolproof suggestions that are appropriate for each school because local context is vital in planning a strategy. However, changes can be accomplished at both the school board and classroom levels. One way that schools can respond to physical harassment is to develop a district or school board–wide policy that bans physical and verbal harassment. In one study of queer youth and literacy, a student talked about being unafraid at school because her peers knew that they would be expelled for fighting or hurting someone.[11] This was enough to protect the student from serious threats at school. The student also pointed out that this does nothing to change the homophobic response of other students. It is merely fear that keeps them in check, but at least she believed that the administration would not tolerate such behavior. Obviously, this is a stopgap measure that allows students some measure of safety but makes no progress toward systemic change in the school and classroom environments.

Teachers often ask what they should do to make their classrooms more welcoming for LGBTQ students. Generally, they do not desire to be unfair or exclusionary but have received little or no training and are fearful of parental responses. They are told that they decide how much and what they will feel comfortable tackling in their settings. However, there are some simple steps that can be taken by teachers, parents, and administrators. These include the encouragement, time, and structure for teachers and staff to explore how they, as individuals, the school, their classrooms and pedagogies, and their community organizations encourage and support heterosexism. It follows that if an educator has explored heterosexism, she or he will be better prepared to broach this topic with students in a manner that is not defensive or will not cause surprise at the content. When ready, nearly every teacher can include homophobic slurs in the prohibitions on language in her or his classroom rules. Just the conversation that occurs around the rules, and how homophobia and heterosexism might be defined, broaches a topic that many students have never discussed in a classroom setting. Also, it is up to parents and senior administrators to help support teachers as they attempt to educate their classes on the dilemmas of heterosexism. Another relatively easy method of altering school culture is to purchase curriculum materials for the school library that discuss LGBTQ issues. It is easy because it does not take a revamping of courses; however, it is also immensely difficult because school librarians can be rightfully concerned about community reaction. The school board and principals must proactively demonstrate their support for such materials.

The phrase "it takes a village to raise a child" has become worn and clichéd through overuse; yet responsibility for the complicated and overlapping concerns of making schools and other social institutions useful, productive spaces for LGBTQ students and teachers falls to a broad spectrum of individuals and systems. In order for these institutions and non–sexual minority individuals to learn about, and ally themselves with, the political and social concerns facing LGBTQ peoples, other heterosexually identified people must become proactive. This work falls not only to teachers and administrators but requires the active support of parents, grandparents, church leaders, and community members, whether they have children in the school system or not. This is not to argue that children and youth do not have agency or the ability to make changes on their own. On the contrary; but in a society that does not listen well to children, change must be attempted at numerous levels.

When was the last time you went to a school board meeting, worked with kids in the schools, or wrote a supportive letter to a school board or local newspaper? How many people are involved with the PTAs of their areas or form reading groups or diversity groups within or around the school community? How many heterosexually identified community and school members refuse to wait for those who identify as sexual minorities to take the lead and initiate discussions and/or pronounce their support of LGBTQ content, curricula, and pedagogies? How many people of any sexual orientation mentor an LGBTQ youth, encourage students to organize and advocate for what they need, or refuse to let those around them use "simple" phrases such as "that's so gay" without a response? If the only people or groups to show up at school board meetings about allowing sex education, condoms in the schools, books with LGBTQ content, or Gay-Straight Alliances are well organized groups who oppose such thinking on religious or ideological grounds, they seem to speak, then, as if with a united voice, when in fact they are the minority, and there is a huge silent majority. If individuals who are part of sexual minority communities attend and speak at these meetings, they are seen as "having an agenda" or "speaking without objectivity." Therefore, those who are heterosexual are in a much safer place and, unfortunately, in more often heard positions and, thus, can become catalysts for change where often LGBTQ individuals cannot. In order for things to begin to change beyond mere "window-dressing," individuals and groups who support sexual minority youth and teachers must make their thoughts and feelings known.

MOVING FOWARD, QUEERLY

Marion is 17 years old, biracial, and born and raised in the same large city, a city thought to be reasonably progressive. She identifies as queer. Her mom and dad have been supportive of her explorations and declarations regarding her sexuality, which started at 13 years old. They have encouraged her to speak up for herself, surround herself with good friends, and join whatever political and social groups interested her. She has a fairly large group of friends but only a few people in whom she confides. Her friends see her as the one to go to with a problem. Marion is an attentive listener, and she is appreciated for that. Her friends describe her as "fun," "loud," "talkative," and always "a really good friend you can count on."

When her attraction to both boys and girls became more apparent, she did not struggle with the idea of not being heterosexual. For Marion, the knowledge and ambiguity made everything just a bit more clear. Her parents nodded kindly, although Marion thought that she saw a bit of wistfulness in her mother's eyes, imagining a bubble forming above her head, reading "what might have been." Similarly, none of her friends pushed her away; she knew she was lucky. Nevertheless, she still sometimes worries about what the straight kids think or whether students or teachers treat her in a particular way because she is "out" on campus. She wonders if she loses out on anything, and that thought makes her feel very angry.

Marion does reasonably well at school, though everyone says she could do better. She is not very involved with school groups, although she was on the Student Council in grade nine. Marion has always been confused that adults, and maybe some students, see her as a leader when she has done nothing to validate this. No one gives her a particularly hard time at school, but no one except her queer friends ever seems to want to talk about the possibility of LGBTQ people existing at her school, or even out in the world. The exception to this is one of the English teachers, who declares the sexuality of each and every author he uses in class. It is almost as if he was told at some point that this was one way to talk about "it"; it, of course, being the incorporation of gay and lesbian content. But his intensely serious pronouncements have become a joke, with students looking at each other and laughing each time he does it. It seems as if teachers feel so uncomfortable with the idea of queer students that the possibility that they exist in their school is foreign. Perhaps if it is discovered, it ought to be kept quiet. The very use of the word *gay*, much less *queer*, makes adults squirm and change the subject, which Marion admits can be fun but not very helpful in the long run.

For a long time, Marion did not label herself as anything, in terms of her sexuality. Not that she didn't know that she liked boys and girls, but *lesbian* seemed old-fashioned, and *bisexual* was something that caused people to look at her derisively and argue that she was stuck on some invisible fence. None of the labels really fit, maybe because they were labels. Then, she started reading and hearing other people talk about "queer," which was kind of messy and didn't ask you to choose who you were each and every day. *Queer* seemed to state up front that it was political, a rejection of the old standard, in both the heterosexual world and that of older gays and lesbians. She liked it and was really surprised at her mother's vehemently negative response. "That's an awful word," she said. "Why would you want to call yourself something that people have used forever to harass gay people? Aren't you and your friends just being confrontational to be confrontational? How are people [meaning non-queer, non-gay] going to know when it is okay to call you a queer?"

WHY QUEER?

Queer as a term, as opposed to *gay*, *lesbian*, or *bisexual*, purposefully disrupts the notion that identity is fixed or immutable. It includes the desire to highlight the existence of, and to interrupt silent assumptions about, heterosexuality as normal and homosexuality as Other. In the classroom and in schools, this form of "ultimate" naming around which individuals are organized into groups results in students too often being viewed as universalized. For example, queer students whose queerness simultaneously disallows recognition as female, working class, differently abled, and/or of color. Understanding gender as singular silences the ways in which it functions for both women and men, and that race, sex, and sexuality, for example, have a regulatory function upon each other. The utilization of *queer* allows for an understanding of the individual more clearly met at the intersections of these myriad identities.

Each day in a typical classroom, there is regulation of student and teacher sex, gender, and sexuality. Butler argues that utilizing sex and sexuality not only operates and sets out the boundaries as a norm but also functions as part of a system or practice that both regulates what is normal and reproduces what is acceptable in relation to gender, sex, and sexuality through its very regulatory nature. What is male or female, in the ways constructed on biological terms, becomes an ideal that can never be made real but is articulated and circulated and rearticulated through bodies that attempt to, and are forced to, adhere to an impossible set of gender norms.[12]

Although the term *queer* has often been used as a pejorative—individually, theoretically, and politically—it has been reclaimed as a pedagogy, politics, and theory that dislodges the requirements of fixed identities, such as gay or lesbian and, subsequently, heterosexual. This invites an opening up of spaces where commonsense understandings of sex and sexuality are left messy and productively problematic. For educators, this affords the possibility of discussing sexuality as a site of social change in ways that demand that attention be paid to the intersectionality of races, genders, and sexualities.

A Fixed Curricular Identity—Add for Color and Texture

While many schools have instituted some form of multicultural or antiracism education program, the majority fail to incorporate the sexuality-related concerns of queer youth within the official curriculum. These missing discourses tell queer youth that they are not worthy of inclusion, that their lives are uncomplicated, and that they are and ought to remain invisible.[13] Contemporarily, curricular change focusing on sexuality has most often been focused on "add and stir" models. These models insert a lesson here or there on top of the "regular" lessons. This creates a curriculum that supplements the traditional guide to "include" women, people of color, and/or queer peoples without contextualizing or building interconnectedness with the rest of the content. Such lessons are generally developed with a desire for inclusion. However, little of the curricular or pedagogical planning is changed; the unit or essential questions are unaltered and the critical analyses of the roles of gender, race, and/or sexuality are left unexplored. It allows, though, the schools, teachers, and school boards to tick off the gender/or multicultural education box of curricular reform without altering the school culture or its explicit and hidden curricula.

What Is Queering and Queer Theory?

One method of reading texts, policies, and historical events in such a way as to problematize the "normal" utilizes similar reasoning as the use of "queer." Queer theory invites an opening up of spaces where commonsense understandings of sex and sexuality, the political, social, and historical relationships, and the contexts in which they function are left open, untidy, and difficult. That is, we can develop within education a theory that requires ways of teaching and learning, and that views identities as fluid and changing.

The queering of pedagogy and curricula is not a call to speak of sex, or sex acts, in the classroom. Nor is queer theory a call for the classroom to *become* gendered and (hetero)sexualized. It is, rather, a tool to uncover and analyze how the classroom is already sexualized and heterosexualized.[14] Daunting though it may be, it also encourages interrogations of all categories to which we seem drawn to organize. It is the work of these theories to disrupt the uncritical usage of categories and labeling, and require interrogations of when these constructions are useful and when they further stereotype, or merely encourage, a lack of complexity in favor of ease of understanding—that is, questioning the easiness of placing individuals, events, and solutions into established categories that make solutions and understandings more straightforward.

THE ROLES OF SCHOOLS AND COMMUNITIES IN SCHOOL-BASED CHANGE

Schools are fertile locations for both social change and the stagnation of stereotypes. Knowledge production and the lapses and inclusions of gender and sexuality in teaching and learning demand thoroughgoing and complicated analyses, as do the inclusion and exclusion of gender and sexuality in curricula. Without such analyses, there is a risk of a continuation and promotion of gender-based stereotypes. As noted above, the opportunities to develop nuanced understandings of the intersections and interdependencies of gender, sex, and sexuality are lost when each is considered in isolation. These conversations have particular salience in the classroom because ideals of democratic participation, citizenship, civil rights, historical accuracy, and social issues are laced throughout.

One method is to ask students to explore what is normative or heteronormative in popular culture, including movies, television, magazines, websites, and so on. This can be an invitation to analyze and critique the body, gender, and sexuality in pop culture, textbooks, and primary documents. While this obviously offers an entertaining entry point, it also has a far more serious purpose. It asks students to critically view the body and how it is manipulated. The realization of this manipulation offers a particularly poignant moment for viewing popular media. While one could analyze popular culture without a fluid notion of identity, this notion of identity would mean analyzing media of all types through a fluidity of identities.

COMPLICATING CONVERSATIONS

How might the vignettes and analyses presented above become more complicated? What has been left silent and unmarked? In the story of George, what do we know about him, and what do we assume? George's racial and ethnic background is completely ignored. When you viewed him in your mind's eye, did you see him as white? What would it mean to your understandings of the issues involved if I told you that at home he is called "Jorge" and that his parents came from Costa Rica? What if it were Mexico rather than Costa Rica? Would that change the story? Too often, when one identity is marked, such as sexuality, other identity markers are assumed to fall away under the weight of that which is most salient, even when the topic of the work is intersecting and fluid. However, if George were asked, he would likely say that he could not separate out the individual identity categories and discard them. Too often, we undercomplicate identity because it is easier and more manageable to work with one issue at a time. George tells us that it is impossible because neither he nor any other person is able to shave off one piece of him- or herself and understand it as monolithic, or the same as all others of that group, no matter their other identity intersections. The desire to move away from stable and unchanging identities is a piece of the growing field of queer politics and queer theory. While this complicating opens up possibilities, its very incarnation also causes concerns about the loss of political coalescing and training for differences in schools.

The challenges of these issues on the whole and of addressing them within the scope of a book chapter is not only to reveal the regulatory nature of gender, sex, sexualities, and heteronormativity occurring in schools and classrooms but also to trouble the ways in which these gendered mechanisms intersect with, and reinforce, other identity constructions in the classroom. Turning a critical eye toward the normative and normalizing and exploring their place in the classroom through a lens of queer, queer theories, fluidity, and nonessentialized identity categories may offer all of those who think and theorize about teaching and learning a productive path toward working with, among, and across differences.

— 11 —

When Race Shows Up in the Curriculum: Teacher (Self-) Reflective Responsibility in Students' Opportunities to Learn

H. RICHARD MILNER, LEON D. CALDWELL, AND IRA E. MURRAY

Public schools in the United States have faced harsh criticism over the last two decades.[1] Among the list of criticisms of schools and, consequently, teachers, administrators, and districts is that of poor student performance on academic measures, particularly among students of color. No doubt, students of color are not performing or achieving as well as their white counterparts. In particular, African-American and Hispanic-American students typically do not achieve at the same or similar levels as white students in most academic areas.[2] Steele reminds us that virtually every academic achievement measure shows, for instance, African-American students trailing white students in the content areas.[3]

There are those who make the argument that the causes of such academic disparities are related more to socioeconomics than race or other factors. However, Ladson-Billings and Tate maintain that:

> Although both class and gender can and do intersect race, as stand-alone variables they do not explain all of the educational achievement differences apparent between Whites and students of color. Indeed, there is some evidence to suggest that even when we hold constant for class, middle-class African-American students do not achieve at the same level as their White counterparts.[4]

These differences are consistent at every level of schooling (prekindergarten through grade twelve), and the predictors, as we have studied them, are not merely the results of socioeconomic status. Where issues of disparity are concerned, Ford wrote that:

> Black students, particularly males, are three times as likely as White males to be in a class for the educable mentally retarded, but only half as likely to be placed in a class for the gifted. Not only are Black students underenrolled in gifted education programs . . . Black students are over-represented in special education, in the lowest ability groups and tracks, and among high school and college dropouts . . . .[5]

Clearly, at a time when our nation's schools are under attack, we must think seriously about some of the academic disparities that still exist in them.

In this chapter, we discuss how race often "shows up" and influences the curriculum. By curriculum, we mean what students have the opportunity to learn under the direction of teachers and from the school itself. We discuss the importance of understanding race in the curriculum—particularly where teachers are concerned—and the roles of teachers in providing more meaningful learning opportunities for students of color as we attempt to bridge some of the gaps between students in the United States. We purposefully frame our discussion in an urgent fashion, as we have come to believe that without particular attention to some of these matters, we will find the situation of students of color worsening. Moreover, we present the discussion in a supportive manner for teachers because we realize the complex nature of their work. Indeed, teachers have enormous responsibilities and are usually working to the best of their abilities. Still, there is much work to be done. We conclude this chapter with methods teachers might employ in their work to better understand how race shows up in and influences the curriculum with the goal of providing better learning opportunities for students.

THINKING ABOUT RACE AND CURRICULUM

The specific concern regarding race and the curriculum has been present in the United States at least since the turn of the twentieth century, when W.E.B. Dubois, in *The Souls of Black Folk*, challenged America to consider an educational agenda that matched the political agenda of emancipation.[6] Carter G. Woodson, in the *Mis-Education of the Negro,* articulated as well an antiracist agenda.[7] In a similar fashion, the question of how to "civilize" (i.e., assimilate) Native Americans spurned the proliferation of Indian Schools in the mid-1800s. In more recent times the nation's historical struggle with race has continued to underlie arguments from school accountability to equal access to higher education.[8] The concept of race in primary and secondary education has been the struggle for both a racially inclusive curriculum and a culturally inclusive pedagogy. In fact, Ladson-Billings and Tate[9] asserted the notion of "critical race theory" in education with one major goal being to provide theoretical and empirical lenses through which to think about issues of race. Emerging out of the field of law, critical race theory attempts to show how race and systemic and institutional barriers surrounding race still cause racism and injustices. [10] Although some researchers in the field of education recognize the significance of thinking about race, Ladson-Billings reminds us of the seriousness associated with researching and theorizing about it.[11] Perhaps the serious nature of race helps illuminate why Ladson-Billings and Tate stress the point that race is still quite undertheorized in most disciplines and areas of research and study.[12] The undertheorization of race (particularly in the field of curriculum studies) necessitates that we think carefully about developing research designs and conceptual models to attend to race-based issues. The field of curriculum desperately needs to delve into some of these questions of race, always interrogating and keeping the seriousness of such concerns in mind. Race clearly has to be studied in a methodical and meticulous manner. Thus, thinking about curriculum with race as a central focus must be pursued in a careful, significant, and appropriate manner.

Defining Race in Curriculum

Race in curriculum refers to the implications of a person's skin color in relation to the historical, social, and structural issues that frame society and thus the contemporary, theoretical and applied, curriculum field. We recognize that race is socially constructed. That is, genetically, various racial groups of people are more the same than they are different. Thinking about race in curriculum, then, requires us to consider the links between society (on a macro level) and the school (on a micro level). To further illuminate, because race matters in the larger society for all individuals, regardless of skin color, it consequently matters in schools and in the curriculum.[13] One misnomer related to the importance of race has to do with who does and who does not benefit from racial implications—a notion that indicates to whom race really matters. That is, because of the systemic barriers that often stifle black American citizens' experiences, for instance, we often think only about race mattering to black people or to other groups of people that have been marginalized or oppressed. However, the benefits that white Americans obtain by virtue of their skin color and how their race has been socially constructed as "the right or normal race" privileges them. This points to an obvious significance, as race matters for all individuals in our country, not only people of color.

The privilege associated with white people's experiences enables them to experience the world (and schooling) at an advantage. Other groups of people, because they are not white, find themselves at a disadvantage. It is, therefore, paramount for all students to be introduced to and made cognizant of the experiences of other racial and ethnic groups of people within the safe confines of the classroom. White and nonwhite students will all benefit from sharing their experiences with one another, as it has become increasingly important for the future survival of a democratic United States. Citizens of American democracy will not be able to participate at a fully intelligent and engaged level if they are not "accurately informed concerning the problems and contributions of all members of . . . society. This correct information will make for tolerance and sympathetic understanding among the members."[14]

Race in Curriculum

Because race matters so significantly to all people in our country—whether white or not—it also matters in our schools. And, arguably, the curriculum is one of the most important aspects of schooling and society for everyone. If we think about the curriculum not only as what students have the opportunity to learn under the direction of teachers and schools but also in conjunction with who is interpreting the curriculum and who is implementing it, then race and the curriculum becomes an even more complex and overarching phenomenon. To be clear, we are suggesting that the teacher, his or her racial identity, and the nature of that teacher's interpretations and enactments of the curriculum are central to what students have the opportunity to learn. Elsewhere, for example, Milner has written about the influences of teachers as racial and cultural beings and stressed the necessity of the awarenesses of their own cultural-comprehensive knowledge bases.[15] In essence, Milner has reminded teachers that not only is it important for them to deeply understand Shulman's[16] categories of knowledge, but that they also need to be in tune with the bodies of knowledge related to who they are as cultural beings. Race, then, matters in the curriculum if we think about the enormous power and contributions teachers make in curricular decision making,[17] as, for instance, researchers consistently point to the huge influence teachers have in the curriculum and schooling more generally.[18]

TEACHERS AND THE RACIAL CURRICULUM

If teachers play an enormous role in the curriculum itself, then what a teacher decides to teach, the pedagogical approaches a teacher decides to employ, how a teacher interprets the curriculum itself, and the emphases teachers place on certain dimensions of the curriculum are all important to race and the teachers' control (at least on some essential levels). Thus, the nature of examples used in class, how much time a teacher spends on a particular topic, and whom a teacher calls on to respond (particularly regarding specific and critical topics) are all connected to that teacher's racial identity.[19] To clarify, because the teaching force in the United States is primarily white, middle class, and female, these subjective traits may connect to students' learning opportunities in fundamental and meaningful ways.[20] For many teachers have never had meaningful interactions or relationships with people of color outside of school.[21]

Teachers and Racial Identity

An often overlooked aspect of the teaching profession is the concept of racial identity. A significant research literature has been developed around whites' negative attitudes and behaviors toward African-Americans and other ethnic and racial minorities. Helms and Carter proposed the White Racial Identity Attitude Theory (WRIAT) that includes two phases: the abandonment of racism and the development of a positive white identity.[22] Helms's model suggests that white racial identity develops through six stages: contact, disintegration, reintegration, pseudo-independence, immersion, and autonomy. Each stage involves an introspective conception of self as a racial being and conceptions of others and oneself relative to other racial groups.

Rowe, Bennett, and Atkinson developed a White Racial Consciousness (WRC) model.[23] White consciousness is defined as one's awareness of being white and what that implies in relation to those who are not white. The WRC has two statuses: unachieved status or achieved status, which means the teacher, in this case, has or has not achieved a healthy positive identity. There are seven attitude categories: avoidant, dependent, dissonant, dominative, conflictive, reactive, and integrative. As previously stated, acknowledging the characteristics of racial identity is an important consideration for understanding race in the curriculum.

Unfortunately, teacher preparation programs, although offering courses in multicultural or urban education, create scant opportunities for students, especially white students, to reflect upon their racial history and socialization. The cumulative effects of this training gap are the perpetuation of white privilege, colorblindness, cultural bias, and aversive racism, to name but a few. Expecting that racially self-unaware preservice teachers will become racially aware practicing teachers is problematic. The scant discourse in teacher training programs around issues of racial identity and white privilege is essentially negligent.

The same may be true for teachers of color and their interactions with white people. For example, Cross provides a review of Black Racial Identity Theory, which argues that even when teachers (regardless of race) have had meaningful experiences with people outside of their own race, these experiences may reify stereotypes rather than shed light on more appropriate and accurate accounts of a group of people.[24] It is important to note that we are not suggesting here that if teachers live in a community with—and on some level understand—a group of Hispanic-American people outside of school, they will automatically understand all of the Hispanic-American students they encounter. The reality is that students (even within their various racial and cultural groups) are quite different, and the differences students possess must be taken into consideration when developing and implementing the curriculum. Thus, of course, it is dangerous to attempt to generalize about any groups of students based on preconceived assumptions and limited experiences with groups of people.

The emphasis, then, must be placed first on teachers themselves; teachers must understand who they are as racial beings and the influences they hold in and over the curriculum because of their inherent authority. Moreover, attention and critical consideration must be placed on individual students and the multiple life-world experiences that frame their learning and performances in and outside of school.

Thus, teachers' knowledges about students of color with whom they come in contact in schools is often nebulous and tenuous, at best. In essence, there is a racial and cultural mismatch between teachers and their students. Consequently, the curriculum does not connect to who the students are. Connecting to who students are means that teachers must take the whole student into their minds as they think about learning opportunities. Hooks wrote about this notion of holism and its significance in teaching and learning, and she links its potency to that of healing. Needless to say, attempting to bridge the divide between students and the curriculum, particularly where race is concerned, is very important and, for many, very difficult.[25]

Where enacting the curriculum is concerned, teachers may select examples in their teaching that do not line up with the experiences of their students of color. Our discussion of these racial and cultural mismatches is not meant to criticize teachers, as many of them have good intentions relative to the students they teach. However, our discussion is meant to stress the point that students of color are not white people with pigmented or colored skin.[26] Students of color experience the world in ways that are often inconsistent with their teachers' backgrounds and those of their white counterparts. And, because of this, students' learning styles, their behavior patterns, and their academic performances and achievement levels are quite different from those of white students'. Centralizing teachers' racial identities in the curriculum points, obviously, to whose knowledge is valued and thus valuable, as well as validated in society and in school.[27] If we believe that students' knowledge bases matter and are valuable, then the ways in which teachers approach the curriculum require a form of negotiation that forces teachers to (re)think who is actually the main arbiter of knowledge and why.[28]

The Curriculum and Color Blindness

Because students of color experience the world in very different ways from many of their teachers and white student counterparts, teachers should avoid

Dillard's notion of "white student" with colored skin.[29] There are deep-rooted issues in society that cause students of color to react to the curriculum in ways that cause teachers frustration and misunderstanding. Consequently, because of these students' out-of-school experiences around race, teachers should avoid color-blind ideologies in their interpretations of the curriculum and in their implementations of it. Color-blind ideologies focus on teachers' conscious efforts to "not see race" in their teaching.[30] We assert that color blindness is not only impractical but unethical. These ideologies are disadvantageous for students of color because so many of their life experiences are framed by who they are as racial beings. Moreover, as Johnson suggests, not seeing color will not allow teachers to see some of the systemic issues that often become commonplace in schools. These systemic issues that are often perpetuated when we do not consider the significance of race include disproportionate representation in special education and gifted education, as well as high numbers of black students being suspended and expelled.[31]

Indeed, some of the behavior "problems" that are attributed to (mostly male) students of color may in fact be consequences of the efforts of many teachers, administrators, and other school personnel to implement color-blind ideologies into their teaching methods. Ralph Ellison eloquently wrote about this premise in his classic novel *Invisible Man*. In discussing his "invisibility" to and in society, which can be appropriately applied to society's microcosm—that is school—he wrote:

> You wonder whether you aren't simply a phantom in other people's minds . . . . It's when you feel like this that, out of resentment, you begin to bump people back. And, let me confess, you feel that way most of the time. You ache with the need to convince yourself that you do exist in the real world, that you're a part of all the sound and anguish, and you strike out with your fists, you curse and you swear to make them recognize you. And, alas, it's seldom successful.[32]

Students of color can easily feel like Ellison's phantom in the collective mind of their teachers and their curricula and methods. Resentment may set in from the fact that they are excluded from the dominant academic experience, and in an effort to incorporate themselves into the classroom experience they may act out. And, as Ellison writes, it is very seldom successful.

Without a doubt, the absence of recognition in the classroom can have devastating effects, academic and disciplinary, on students of color. In addition, this absence has a negative effect on the accuracy of the educational experience for all students in American schools. The American classroom is a reflection of what citizens value most dearly. For black students in particular, inclusion is of the utmost importance because the history and experiences of African-Americans are so imbedded within the fabric of our society's traditions and life, so that "to leave out one would be to distort the other."[33]

If students of color, their history, and their experiences are not represented in the classroom, then how can they be expected to feel valued by society?

The Curriculum and Deficit Thinking

Because of how race is socially constructed, teachers often think about their students of color through "deficit" lenses. Deficit thinking often results in inaccurate perceptions of marginalized students that may prevent teachers from developing effective lessons that might better meet the needs of their diverse learners. Where cultural deficit theories are concerned, Ford wrote:

> These theories carry a "blame the victim" orientation, and supporters look upon Blacks and other minority groups as not only culturally but also intellectually inferior. According to deficit theories or perspectives, "different" is equated with deficient, inferior, and substandard.[34]

Thus, deficit thinking prevents teachers from realizing that all students are knowledgeable on some levels and bring a wealth of expertise into the learning context. Such thinking causes teachers to look upon students of color as liabilities rather than assets.

We are positing that the curriculum, then, may be developed through deficit orientations based on how teachers think about students of color and their potential to succeed. The research is clear that high expectations for and with students of color are more effective than low expectations.[35] So, what students have the opportunity to learn might be framed by teachers' negative perceptions of students' performance potential. This point connects to matters around the stereotype threat that Steele writes about concerning women and people (students) of color.[36]

Steele's work points to the psychological burdens that marginalized people have endured as a result of the systemic and socialized ways that such groups have been thought about throughout history. Consequently, certain groups of people (e.g., women in mathematics) and their performance is linked to their performance in domains that dominant groups have historically framed as inferior. Where curriculum is concerned, teachers have often developed these deficit theories about students of color based on the legacies that shape particular groups' performances. The curriculum, then, may be "watered down" because teachers believe that groups of students are incapable of success in some area of study. Interestingly, teachers may believe that they are being supportive of students of color because they are lowering their expectations and dumbing down the curriculum, when in reality they are hurting their students. This deficit thinking leads to incomplete, inaccurate, and "lower" learning objectives and consequently discriminatory outcomes for students of color and for all minorities.

METHODS IN TEACHER RACE REFLECTION FOR CURRICULUM APPROPRIATION

Because of the complex nature of curriculum development and because race may be such a central component in the nature of the curriculum, we must think seriously about methods teachers might use in their work to begin to address some of these issues in the (or their) curriculum. We suggest three activities that may prove effective: (a) racial identity assessment, (b) race reflective journaling, and (c) critically engaged racial dialogue.

Racial Identity Assessment

Assessing one's racial self-concept and understanding how it interacts with other races is an important consideration for teachers who may find themselves in diverse classrooms. Racial identity has direct implications for curriculum development. We suggest that teachers address their racial identity in order to uncover their biases and racial idiosyncrasies as they relate to others. These often subconscious attitudes can result in low expectations for nonwhite students, racially encapsulated curricula, and the perpetuation of stereotypes. These issues and others, we believe, prohibit the potential of teachers to meet the educational needs of all students. Racial identity, we assert, should be interjected into teacher preparation programs in addition to courses in multicultural education. Race in the classroom begins with racial self-consciousness.

We recommend that racial identity assessments be conducted periodically for teachers. Ponterotto and Pedersen provide an excellent overview of racial and social identity theories and assessments.[37] These assessments can be used to gauge the current level of racial self-awareness of teachers and to stimulate discussions regarding how race influences the student-teacher relationship.

Race Reflective Journaling

Race reflective journaling is one method for teachers to think through their experiences (past and present) around race. Race reflective journaling requires teachers to reflect on the racial influences of and on their work. By journaling, teachers might uncover aspects of who they are as racial beings. Such journaling does not have to be systematic. Instead, it might involve teachers writing down specific experiences relative to race when the opportunities and issues present themselves, and it may require that they use introspection to try to make sense of situations where their racial experiences are concerned. Ideally, teacher educators might introduce this notion of race reflective journaling in teacher education programs, and teachers would continue implementing (again, ideally) the practice into their daily work with students.

Because some teachers may find it difficult to reflect in this manner, teacher educators might find it helpful to develop tools that facilitate this type of reflection for their own (as teacher educators) and their students' (practicing and potential teachers') benefit. This may be especially important when teachers have not reflected in this manner in the past and when teachers even wonder about the appropriateness and necessity of this race reflection. To be clear, we are suggesting that instead of teacher educators requesting that teacher candidates and in-service teachers reflect in a general sense, there needs to be more emphasis placed on race and tools and typologies in order to make this happen. The writing/journaling approach could be most effective because it provides a "safe space" for teachers to think through often uncomfortable, complex, and challenging issues pertinent to race, so that they might be ready to discuss with or expose themselves as and/or to a group.

Several questions relative to curriculum development and enactment vis-à-vis race might be considered:

- How might my race influence the curriculum (or more specifically what students have the opportunity to learn)?
- How might my students' racial experiences influence their learning opportunities and their interactions with me (as teacher)?
- What is the impact of race on my beliefs around the curriculum?
- How do I, as a teacher, situate myself in the curriculum? And how do I negotiate the power structures and knowledges relevant to what students have the opportunity to learn?
- How might racial influences impact my and students' interests in the classroom? How might I enact the curriculum to address those interests?
- How do I situate and negotiate students' knowledge, experiences, expertise, and race with my own? In what ways do I incorporate this negotiation in the curriculum?

Critically Engaged Racial Dialogue

In addition to having race reflective journaling to address race in the curriculum, teachers may find it effective to engage in what we call "critically engaged racial dialogue." This method of "speaking about" or "talking through" racial issues and experiences (both positive and negative) could be a method that allows teachers to engage in conversations that they may not feel comfortable engaging in otherwise. This type of racial dialogue, additionally, could occur in small groups in teacher education courses or in larger group settings, such as discussion within whole classes. Teacher educators may find that teacher candidates and in-service teachers alike find it more effective to engage in this type of conversation in small groups, initially, as there may otherwise be levels of discomfort around such conversations. More important, teacher educators must promote spaces where students feel comfortable to have these conversations.[38] There is little room for antagonism—classes of individuals who blame others for years of racism or oppression that emerge from a myriad of experiences, persons, and institutions. Ideally, these conversations will lead teachers to pursue such discussions in their respective schools and classrooms. For such conversations have to start someplace, and the most obvious place seems to be in teacher preparation courses.

This type of dialogue has to be couched in teachers' experiences regarding their lives with respect to race. Here, hooks makes an important point where issues of voice, lived experience, and perspective are concerned:

> As a teacher, I recognize that students . . . enter classrooms within institutions where their voices have been neither heard nor welcomed, whether these students discuss facts—those that any of us might know—or personal experience. My pedagogy has been shaped to respond to this reality. If I do not wish to see these students use the "authority of experience" as a means of asserting voice, I can circumvent this possible misuse of power by bringing to the classroom pedagogical strategies that affirm their presence, their right to speak, in multiple ways on diverse topics.[39]

In this instance, experience is pedagogical and social theory. While in teacher education programs in higher education we want our students to couch their views and perspectives in theory and in research-based arguments, we must recognize that students' life experiences in terms of race and context will be foundational in developing more appropriate thinking and actions in preK–12 classrooms. Moreover, lived experience may be all that teachers have to rely on in light of the small number of studies that use race as a theoretical and empirical framework. The related questions may also be effective in guiding conversations around race and the curriculum as teachers engage in notions of critically engaged racial dialogue.

CONCLUSIONS

In short, we believe that teachers need to develop the skills and knowledges necessary to reflect on their own experiences where race and the curriculum are concerned. Strategies for introspection could lead teachers to place a greater emphasis on racially inclusive classroom contents and practices. Interventions addressing color blindness and assumptions of Eurocentric universality could prove effective as teachers grapple with ways to better meet the needs of racially diverse students (pedagogically and philosophically).

Indeed, students of color often operate in classrooms around the country that do not meet their affective, social, and intellectual needs.[40] As a result, many of these students become educationally marginalized, which exacerbates achievement gaps and myths of anti-intellectualism in nonwhite communities, especially African-American and Hispanic communities. However, the explication of race-based educational disparities infrequently includes discussions about the characteristics of teachers, such as their racial identities and racial attitudes. This chapter has attempted to shed light on this oversight and suggests strategies for increasing the awarenesses of race in the discourse of and on curriculum development. We framed our arguments purposefully in an urgent and pressing manner. With the ever-widening achievement gaps and their social and economic implications, educators can no longer afford to focus solely on the characteristics of the student without focusing on the characteristics of the teacher. That is our major, essential point.

— 12 —

Critical Multicultural Social Studies in the Borderlands: Resistance, Critical Pedagogy, and *la lucha* for Social Justice

MARC PRUYN, ROBERT HAWORTH, AND REBECCA SÁNCHEZ

In this chapter, we explore our attempted use of a critical pedagogy for social justice within both the social studies teacher education courses we teach and the K–12 classrooms where we most recently worked as teachers. We will review historically the foundations of the critical pedagogy movement and then lead readers empirically through our attempts to bring these notions of a critical pedagogy for social justice to our classrooms of both K–12 and preservice learners in the diverse U.S./México Borderlands of southern New Mexico.[1]

Marc began working as a bilingual public school teacher in the Salvadoran refugee neighborhood of Los Angeles known as Pico-Unión in 1987. He taught and learned at Magnolia Avenue Elementary for nine years. During his initial years as a teacher, he was driven to find a pedagogy that would be socially and culturally relevant to his students and to himself, a pedagogy that would allow him to go beyond the "banking" and teacher-centered approaches prevalent at the time. He was advised by colleagues going through similar professional struggles to read Paulo Freire's hallmark work, *Pedagogy of the Oppressed*.[2] He then began using Freire's ideas in his own work with both public school students and, later, with preservice teachers.

Rob grew up in southern California. He taught in public schools, working in special education, alternative secondary schools, and secondary social studies classrooms. Currently, he is a doctoral student and teaches social studies pedagogy courses in the teacher education program (TEP) of his institution. His current research involves youth culture, pedagogy, and how youth make meaning of the world outside of the classroom.

Rebecca is a native of the *frontera* in southern New México. She worked as a teacher for four years in a local public school, predominantly with Mexican immigrant and Mexican-American students. She is a graduate of the same TEP program in which she now teaches, one that emphasizes critical multiculturalism. Rebecca dedicated herself to exploring democratic and empowering pedagogical practices in the classroom as a result of her experiences as both a student in this program and as a classroom teacher. Also turning to Paulo Freire for inspiration, she drew upon students' experiences and critical inquiry as a basis for instruction.

Individually and collectively, in our separate teaching and learning experiences, and in our shared work as teacher educators, we have tried to explore a pedagogy of possibility that draws on the work of Freire and other social justice activists. How successful have we been in this endeavor? That is what this chapter is about. In the following pages, we share and critique our experiences as critical educators (still—and hopefully continually—in formation). These experiences are drawn from our work with both K–12 youngsters and with adults (preservice teachers).[3] But we do not feel this is enough. Now, more than three decades after the first publication of Freire's *Pedagogy of the Oppressed* in English, and as his final books published in English are enjoying unprecedented popularity,[4] we seek here to re-explore the work and legacy of Paulo Freire and reflect on how his ideas have influenced how we teach and how we have come to understand our pedagogical work through the lens of "critical multicultural social studies" (CMSS). We would like to remind the reader, and ourselves, of some of the original notions Freire outlined and hold them up as if to a mirror, a counterpoint, to our analyses of our pedagogical practices.

THEORETICAL AND POLITICAL ROOTS: FREIRE, SOCIAL JUSTICE, AND SOCIAL STUDIES

El Abuelito: Paulo Freire

To some, Paulo Freire was a critical theorist, to others, a radical resistance theorist, and to yet others, a neo-Marxist revolutionary. We feel he was all these things. As McLaren puts it, "the work of Brazilian educator Paulo Freire places him in the front ranks of that 'dying class' of educational revolutionaries who march behind the banner of liberation to fight for social justice and educational reform."[5] Freire was born into a middle-class family in Recife, Brazil, on September 19, 1921. He and his family later fell into poverty as the Great Depression sent shock waves throughout Latin America and the entire world. He taught from the 1940s through 1964 in Brazil, and at one time served as the director of the National Literacy Campaign.

When the military leaders of a United States–backed *coup d'état* came into power in 1964, he was accused of being a "subversive"—for teaching peasants how to read and write—and imprisoned for two months before being sent into exile. He briefly stayed in Bolivia but then settled in Chile, where he made his home with his wife Elza and their five children until 1970. While in Chile, he taught at the University of Santiago, was a UNESCO consultant with the Agrarian Reform Training and Research Institute, and did literacy work for elected socialist president Salvador Allende—who was later overthrown by another United States–sponsored coup in 1973. In 1969, Freire was appointed to Harvard University's Center for the Study of Development and Social Change, and in 1970 he and his family moved to Switzerland so Freire could work as a consultant to the office of education of the World Council of Churches. He returned from exile to Brazil in 1981 to teach at the Pontifica Universidade Católica de São Paulo. He later served as the Minister of Education in São Paulo.[6] He died in 1997.

Freire believed that we must realize our potential, our *vocation*, to become more fully human. He noted that "Humanization . . . man's [*sic*][7] vocation . . . is thwarted by injustice, exploitation, oppression, and the violence of the oppressors; it is affirmed by the yearning of the oppressed for freedom and justice, and by their struggle to recover their lost humanity."[8] This process, the recovery of our "lost humanity," is not only a means to an end—the end being the ability to read and transform our reality—but it is also a means to a means: it's a *process*. And this process, the thinking about thinking, the action with reflection, *is* the changing. This is a process that, once begun, is ongoing. According to Freire, thus begins the development of *conscientization*.

"Reading the world," says Freire, "always precedes reading the word, and reading the word continually implies reading the world."[9] Reading the world means seeing and understanding one's world, one's reality, and reading the word means applying this world understanding to one's written word, one's literacy. Freire believed that this should be done simultaneously. He commented that "Reading does not consist merely of decoding the written word of language; rather it is preceded by and intertwined with knowledge of the world."[10] Reading the world and the word simultaneously is dialogical cultural action. This action is a liberating and humanizing approach to be used by teachers and revolutionaries. This type of action and teaching puts the teacher/student/revolutionary together with the community so that all work jointly in reading their *collective* world and word in order to transform their oppressive realities.

"Dialogical communication [and education]," notes McLaren, "should prompt educators to draw upon the cultural capital of the oppressed in order to allow the oppressed to 'read' the world in both immediate and wider contexts."[11] Critical and investigative teaching and learning of this nature are at the heart of Paulo Freire's educational method. Learning to read and write one's world and word through dialogic pedagogical experiences is also intimately tied to the development of one's critical consciousness, or *conscientization*. *Conscientization* is "learning to perceive social, political, and economic contradictions, and to take action against the oppressive elements of reality. . . . The role of critical pedagogy is not to extinguish tensions. The prime role of critical pedagogy is to lead students to recognize various tensions and enable them to deal effectively with them."[12] This, according to Freire, is *conscientization*; this is "critical consciousness."[13]

Using Freire in New Ways: Critical Multicultural Social Studies

There is a growing body of literature detailing the importance and occasional inclusion of critical multicultural themes in social studies education.[14] This work, however, remains in the distinct minority within mainstream social studies and educational journals[15] and organizations.[16]

The National Council for the Social Studies (NCSS) offers a definition of the "primary purpose" of social studies that many in the criticalist tradition of social education would consider "conservative."[17] They hold that the main goal of social studies is to "help . . . young people develop the ability to make informed and reasoned decisions for the public good as citizens of a culturally diverse, democratic society in an interdependent world."[18] We believe that the goal of social studies (and education more generally) should involve much more than simply assisting "young people [in] develop[ing] the ability to make informed and reasoned decisions for the public good as citizens."[19] While this is laudable, it does not go nearly far enough. We have always understood social studies as the study of social interaction between human beings, and between human beings and their socially constructed environments. In drawing from critical pedagogy and multicultural education,[20] we hold that social studies should have as one of its central objectives the development of students who are not solely "informed citizens" but also cultural, political, social activists who are encouraged to manifest their beliefs with the ultimate goal of fighting oppression and furthering social justice, that is, a social studies guided by critical pedagogy.[21]

Several researchers/theorists within the social studies community have specifically called for combining critical pedagogy and social studies. Alquist holds that it is only through a "critical social studies" that we can foster "moral critical thinking" within both teacher education and with K–12 students. This approach must be "interdisciplinary, global in perspective, contextual, controversial, and help students employ critical thinking to solve real problems."[22] Poindexter posits that democratic values will be fostered through an approach to social studies education that emphasizes social justice and equity.[23] Seixas argues that we should move beyond the notion of the teaching of "social studies" to one of teaching "cultural studies"—

not just the study of culture, but the understanding and ability to deconstruct and then reconstruct culture such that the ends of social justice are served—in the critical tradition of Stuart Hall.[24] In more recent years, the cutting edge theoretical and empirical work in the area of critical social studies has been forwarded most notably by Kincheloe, Ross, and Hursh and Ross.[25]

In addition to critical pedagogy, numerous researchers and theorists would like to see the full inclusion of multicultural education in the social studies. Houser's research suggests that the use of multicultural literature within social studies education can help to promote social development, "sociocultural understandings," and "critical self-examination" within teacher education students.[26] The research of both Titus and Boyle-Baise indicates that the inclusion of multicultural educational themes in social studies curricula can improve instruction and raise student interest.[27] So the notion of combining within social studies education approaches and content from critical pedagogy and multicultural education—critical multicultural social studies or CMSS—is not new, although some argue that "mainstream" social studies organizations tend toward the more conservative approach of teaching "citizenship" over social activism.[28]

It is from these researchers, theorists, and traditions—beginning with Freire—that we have been drawing in our own teaching (in terms of content and pedagogy) and that now informs our pedagogical work in social studies and social justice.

WHERE THE RUBBER MEETS THE ROAD: CONNECTING THEORY AND PRACTICE

We teach and study in the Chihuahuan borderlands of the southwestern United States—where the states of Chihuahua, New México, and Texas converge across history, politics, geography, language, conquest, resistance, and time. All three of us are instructors in the teacher education program at our institution. We were all public school teachers. And we all learn with and from each other and our colleagues within our department in the college of education (in the sense of being "students/teachers" and "teachers/students" and members of a learning and cultural community of praxis). In this section of our paper, we share insights we have gained through our experiences as teachers (of adults and young people alike) in trying to implement CMSS and a social education for social justice.

"Throw Out the Paradigms, Theories, and Political Agendas": Marc's Experiences as a Professor

Jonathan, a former conservative military man—now with long hair, worn Levi's, and a liberal political orientation—was a student in Marc's teacher-education social studies pedagogy course. Two-thirds of the way through the seventeen-week semester, he raised his hand and asked, with a wry grin on his unshaven face, "Dr. Pruyn, when do we start learning about social studies?" This was during Marc's first year as a professor. Because of his attempted focus within social studies on critical multiculturalism, he has been often accused of "hating whites" and even of being a "race traitor." Several years later, a student actually rose and unabashedly asked the doctoral student (working with Marc) teaching one of our social studies education sections, "What does *race* have to do with social studies?" Indeed.

In analyzing the data[29] from Marc's preservice students over an eight-year period, it appears that many more of the TEP students accepted rather than rejected Marc's attempts at promoting social justice through CMSS (by a ratio of 4:1). But those who composed the numerical minority, the "resisters," often purported to speak for a great "silent majority" of students. Whether this was completely accurate in terms of representation (analyses of the data seem to challenge the veracity of this), they did so quite vociferously. And they "resisted" in several ways. First, they often objected to the content of the course. The alternative histories[30] and themes of critical multiculturalism—language, ethnicity, gender, class, and sexual orientation—were often points of contention for this group. They felt that Marc was "white bashing," "male bashing," and "America bashing" through his inclusion of these opposing/differing ways of viewing North American history and social events. These mostly white, female, middle-class students seemingly felt that issues of ethnic and gender oppression had no bearing on their own lives or in the lives of their future students. Many even indicated that such concerns were beyond their own lived experiences.

The following lengthy, excerpted example from one student's evaluation of Marc's course summarizes well the difficulty this small (albeit vocal) resisters group had with a pedagogy that asked them to reflect on and then coconstruct with the instructor a set of (hopefully) useful social studies knowledges that would take into account the real capitalist/classist, racist, sexist, and homophobic world in which we live:

- This class has been an excellent example of: how to waste students' valuable and limited time and effort; how to, sometimes not very subtly, impose one's values on students; how to present questionable and/or false information to students as fact; how to inspire resentment and ill feelings—an "us vs. them" atmosphere; and how to dismiss, challenge, and subject to ridicule certain viewpoints of many students.
- . . . if this is asking too much, consider, at least, providing a more balanced selection of required reading material and video selections. The reading material was so heavily weighted toward the radical & liberal perspectives that each weeks' [*sic*] assignments were nothing more than monotonous, boring, and redundant wastes of our time . . .

- . . . Lastly, the best and most experienced teachers I have ever met and observed are true educator[s], who illustrate the success of their teaching methods and worthwhile curriculum content through their students' academic and social successes. They don't know what a "paradigm" is, don't know if they have one or not, and they don't care. Their first and foremost concern is the success of each individual student—success achieved on their own and not on the back of someone else. Throw out the paradigms, theories, and political agendas. Schools are better off without them!! . . . (emphases Marc's).

Analyses of these data appear to indicate that those students who were resisting were doing so because they were being asked, in essence, to *re*socialize themselves to a new way of learning—and this was, perhaps for some of them, too overwhelming a challenge. Toward the end of each semester, even some of the more resistant and conservative students indicated that, while they benefited from the course, it was "difficult and new" for them "to be taught and to learn in this student-centered way" that did not tell them what to teach as future social studies teachers.

The majority of students (80 percent), the "supporters," on the other hand, would frequently speak out in favor of the alternative content and approach Marc was attempting to use in the course, and would consistently provide counterarguments to the resisters. But they would also report privately that they felt intimidated by the largely white and often "angry" resisters.

The following student comments give voice to this majority of the student body, the supporters, who felt positively about the way the course was organized (both in terms of content and pedagogical approach):

- [The course] forced me to really consider topics that I have previously avoided. It was comfortable and all opinions were [encouraged]. The information was presented in a useful manner, and many ideas were given regarding classroom implementation.
- Very positive! Dr. Pruyn is an excellent professor who respects [and] considers other's feelings! He gives us a lot of his own views, but lets us make our own judgments and does so in a caring and respectful manner!
- I think [the instructor] was very open minded and listened to everyone's ideas even if they were different [from] his. He is the *only* professor I have had that doesn't give lower grades for expressing different opinions [from] theirs.
- I think Dr. Pruyn is a great instructor. I especially liked his points and [the] respect which he had for us.

Another student shared that the pedagogy and content of this course helped to broaden her social perspective as a preservice teacher:

> I have probably never read this much in one semester. I'm glad I had a chance to improve my vocabulary. However, I'm most happy about the fact that I have

expanded my knowledge on so many issues. These class discussions have helped me both eliminate misconceptions about certain issues and also strengthen my beliefs about others. I now feel I am a stronger person and I also know I have a lot more research and learning to do. I am also excited to go and teach what I have learned.

And what of students' reactions to the inclusion of multiculturalism and critical pedagogy as *content areas*—beyond what was shared in their evaluations? Did the students accept the radical subject matter—a subject matter that asked them to question their assumptions about life, oppression, and potential liberation—offered in course readings and films?

When the students were asked what role multiculturalism should play in the teaching of social studies, over 95 percent said it should play a central role—indicating that even some of the resisters must have felt that certain elements of multicultural education were appropriate. They made comments in their surveys and course evaluations such as "multiculturalism should be integrated into social studies" and "multiculturalism *is* social studies." Two students noted:

- Multiculturalism MUST have a major role in our teaching of social studies. Our world is diverse, and students are diverse: we need to educate them about others and we do need to recognize and respect differences! It's a MUST!!!
- Keep up the good work and thank you for acknowledging us as "Mexican-American," "Latinos" . . . thank you for the respect that we desperately need. . . .

When asked about the role critical pedagogy should play in social studies, over 53 percent felt it should play an important and substantive role. They shared responses such as:

- It should be used to empower students. They should know that they can have a positive impact on their communities.
- It should "challenge students to think critically about the information they receive from school, peers, T.V., family and community."
- I have learned that being critical of things being taught is great. We need to look at everything in a way that will not harm others.

It is, of course, a sign of hope that a strong and relatively sizable majority of students represented in this qualitative documentary of Marc's social studies courses has been supportive of his attempts at CMSS. But this is an ongoing and always challenging (and exhilarating!) pedagogical, cultural, and political struggle, one that is still being developed, documented, and analyzed. And it is a struggle that has been (and continues to be) attempted by others, in different contexts and with variations of nuance, inspiration, and success.

Next we share Rob and Rebecca's experiences in teaching and using CMSS for social justice.

Rob and Rebecca: Lessons from Elementary School to the University

Rob and Rebecca's experiences with CMSS education in K–16 settings have proved to be both challenging and successful. At the university level, they found it important to study the students' backgrounds and experiences in social studies classrooms. In two of the social studies methods classes that they teach, they surveyed students regarding their own learning experiences in schools as well as their feelings toward CMSS. Most respondents gave similar responses in terms of their own social studies/social justice experiences: "It [social studies] was mostly memorizing names and dates"; "My social studies teacher made us read the chapter and answer the review questions." One of Rob and Rebecca's respondents even noted that one of her social studies teachers made sure that students wrote out the review questions but "graded much of our work on penmanship." These comments, and the experiences they reflect, while troublesome, are far from uncommon.

Preservice teachers come to classes informed by critical multicultural social studies with many questions about the "magic formula" for instruction. The beauty of CMSS lies in its illusive, nonformulaic, and contextually adaptable nature. Bill Bigelow, in his article entitled "Social Studies Standards for What?" offers alternative suggestions for how students and teachers can contextualize social studies differently:

1. Consistently seek out explanations for social phenomena and learn to distinguish between explanation and mere perception.
2. Recognize how their individual actions affect human and biotic communities throughout the world, reflecting on how every action they take has global social, and ecological implications.
3. Question the ecological sustainability of key economic and cultural practices, and consider alternatives to practices that are deemed unsustainable.
4. Evaluate the role that racism has played—and continues to play—in shaping the experiences of social groups, especially with respect to economic and political power.
5. Appreciate the impact social movements have had in addressing injustice of all kinds, and evaluate the effectiveness of those efforts.
6. See [how they are] capable, both individually and collectively, of contributing to social and ecological betterment.[31]

From these six suggestions, we would like to turn the discussion to how preservice teachers and teachers in the field engage in social studies and social justice work (or do not). Acknowledging differences of ideology and practice is an important element in seeking out and understanding the difficulties of implementing CMSS. Teachers and students become empowered in a classroom environment that is participatory, dialogic, and reflective. In spite of the benefits of using CMSS, many teachers continue to resist and rely on a pedagogy of regimentation. What prevents teachers from engaging in critical pedagogical practices under the guise of CMSS? The following section describes some common sentiments about CMSS and a discussion about how to integrate the approach.

Using a CMSS Pedagogical Approach Is Difficult and Too Time Consuming!

This is a valid concern. Critical multicultural education in any subject can be challenging. School districts provide textbook materials, standards, and curriculum guides that map out an entire school year for a teacher. Many teachers are comfortable utilizing the same textbook-driven curriculum that shaped their own education, even if such an approach is boring or meaningless to today's students. CMSS requires the constant shaping and construction of curriculum based on the diversity of the classroom. Our experiences have informed us that CMSS, while intense, is rewarding for both the students and the teacher.

In our classroom experiences with students from kindergarten through high school, we have found that opening up discussions to students allows for greater participation. In his book *Empowering Education: Critical Teaching for Social Change*, Ira Shor describes how dialogic pedagogy (a cornerstone of CMSS) redefines educational power structures and allows democratic instruction and learning to occur.[32] Conversations and observations by the students in our classrooms indicate several things about critical multicultural social studies education. First, students are able to identify and discuss complex issues and problems through dialogue. Second, through critical inquiry, they are able to make sense of what is happening in their own lives and also in the larger community. The students are prepared for action to become players in their own lives and to counter the hegemonic discourses surrounding them outside of the classroom. Initially, the dialogue process may appear foreign to students. They are reluctant to speak up because, for many, it is the first time they have been asked and given the forum to participate. After a time, they open up and begin the process of educational reclamation. The energy created by the students is an energizing force for us as teachers.

What about "Standards"?

Preservice teachers and teachers in the field often argue that "standards" and "benchmarks" prevent them from implementing CMSS. As professionals, we have read the standards and recognize the flexibility, creativity, and possibility that exist within them. However, standards should not control classrooms, classrooms should control standards. For example, one of our state social studies standards in New México for all grades is that students are required to make and understand connections among historical events, eras, and people. In many classrooms, this standard is taught using the traditional textbook approach. "It was mostly memorizing names and dates" is a response many of us can relate to from our own K–12 history courses. Howard Zinn and many other historians have used the term "address book history" to describe this pedagogical practice of memorization.[33] This term can also be connected to Freire's "banking education," which was discussed earlier in this chapter. Unfortunately, this has been the ongoing practice of social studies in our public schools in order to accommodate the standards. Understanding this, we encourage our classes of preservice teachers to reflect critically on mainstream history, to investigate other contributors, to identify what the not-mentioned (e.g., women, African-Americans, Latinas/Latinos, Native Americans, Asians, working-class folks, lesbians/gays/bisexuals/transsexuals) were doing during any given period. These learning experiences are well within the "objective" benchmark described above, but students are exposed to a more meaningful and connected history. The connections from these investigations contextualize and add meaning to contemporary realities and dilemmas observed by students.

CONCLUDING THOUGHTS

Marc received an e-mail several years ago from a former CMSS supporter. She had entered the course as a self-identified "non-political Hispanic" (as someone who drew her cultural heritage more from Europe and Iberia than from México, more white than *Raza*). Throughout the semester that she was in Marc's class, he saw her slowly evolve into a more engaged political being. In her e-mail, she informed him that she had learned much from the course and the experiences they collectively shared as part of it. These experiences had caused her, she wrote, to reflect on her ethnic, linguistic, and class backgrounds more deeply than she ever had before and that she felt a need to act to make the world a better place, for *Raza* (Mexican-Americans and Latinas/Latinos more generally) and for all people. Indeed, although she was licensed and working as a bilingual elementary school teacher in New México, she wanted to go on to earn a law degree so that she could affect the lives of more people than she felt she could as a teacher. She asked Marc for a letter of recommendation. He, of course, supplied one. But what struck him most about this exchange was the automatic signature line she included on the bottom of her e-mail, along with her address and phone number. It read: "¡*Xicana* to the Bone!" This originally self-identified "non-political

Hispanic" had become a *Chicana*, a Chicana who wanted to fight for social justice not just in the classroom,also via the legal system.

This gives us hope in our continued use of (and reflection upon, and modification of, and praxis around) a critical multicultural social studies for social justice, a social studies influenced by critical pedagogy, Paulo Freire, and the desire to create collectively a world based in and on mutually informative notions of love, dignity, respect, and justice for all *seres humanos.* And whether we are struggling as a community of preservice teachers/instructors in the United States, or as second graders living in poverty in Brazil, we should keep in mind something else *compañero* Freire has noted: "Freedom is acquired by conquest, not by gift."[34]

— 13 —

Schooling and Curriculum for Social Transformation: Reconsidering the Status of a Contentious Idea

WILLIAM B. STANLEY

Cultural transmission is fundamental to the survival of human society. Indeed, the capacity for cultural transmission is the distinguishing characteristic of the species. Of all the many sources of cultural knowledge, schooling is the most systematic and formal institution of cultural transmission. Schooling is compulsory, supported by taxation, and regulated by state and federal departments of education. Education credentials and the curriculum taught in K–12 schools are subject to government (federal, state, and local) review and approval. For most people, then, cultural transmission *is* the major purpose of schooling.

Given the reality described above, it is reasonable to ask why it might be justifiable to advocate for an approach to education as cultural transformation. One response to this question might be that social change is an unavoidable and inevitable feature of all human societies. At some level of social change, educators (as a result of internal or external forces) will be pressured to reconsider the value of the current curriculum and how it might be changed to address the new social reality.

However, we must distinguish between educational reforms enacted to address social change and those advocating education for social transmission. The former has occurred throughout history (e.g., education to help assimilate new waves of immigrants, promote racial integration, serve the interests of students with special needs, improve public health, combat drug abuse, prepare students to use new technologies, and increase American economic productivity in the face of foreign competition). None of these goals (with the possible exception of desegregation) promoted radical social change. In such instances, social change has led to educational reform.

In contrast, education for social transformation reverses the process by advocating the use of education to bring about fundamental changes in and to the social structure. Perhaps the most obvious examples of social transformation have occurred during revolutions. One can understand the potential for revolutions (for better or worse) to bring about radical social change, but it is more difficult to conceive of public education, an institution that normally serves to transmit the dominant culture, as the source of social transformation. As noted earlier, it is far more likely that social change will result in the transformation of K–12 schooling by powerful social groups rather than the reverse.

Nevertheless, support for an approach to education for social transformation has persisted as a minority voice in curriculum reform debates throughout much of the last century. Proponents of social transformation have largely been on the Left politically. Not surprisingly, the criticism of education for social transformation has most often (but not exclusively, as we will see) been a conservative critique. However, some have argued that the current standards-based education reform (SBER) movement is an instance of *conservative social transformation* in terms of its focus on a conservative version of "official knowledge" and its neglect of, if not hostility toward, strong forms of deliberative democracy. It is the continuing tension between conservative and progressive visions of education for social transformation that is the focus of this chapter.[1]

Although the views expressed here can be applied to educational reform in general, my primary focus is on social studies education, the curriculum area most concerned with citizenship education and social theory. First, I summarize the genesis and development of progressive arguments to use schooling for social transformation. Social reconstructionists, a relatively small but influential group on the left wing of the progressive education movement, were the most vocal proponents of social transformation. Second, I examine the role of ideology and theories of knowledge, as each bears on the issue of social transformation. In particular, I want to illustrate why schooling can never be fully neutral or apolitical and what follows from that assumption. Third, I summarize Dewey's critique of the social reconstructionist position to use education for social transformation via a process of countersocialization. Dewey's critique illustrates the deep divisions among progressives and remains relevant as a basis for criticizing current proposals for a critical pedagogy based on countersocialization. Fourth, I explore the theoretical dimensions of the current conservative cultural and political restoration as these relate to and challenge progressive views of education and education reform, especially vis-à-vis the current conservative critique of social studies education as it relates to education for democracy. Fifth, I critique progressive arguments for countersocialization as the preferred progressive approach to education for social transformation. Finally, I suggest an alternative progressive approach to curriculum and education policy.

ORIGINS OF PROGRESSIVE APPROACHES TO EDUCATION FOR SOCIAL TRANSFORMATION

The general failure of K–12 schooling to have a significant impact on the dominant social order has given credence to progressive and radical educators who have long argued that our schools are deliberately organized to help preserve or achieve a conservative cultural, social, and economic agenda. Nevertheless, there have been occasions in our history (the Depression in the 1930s is perhaps the best example) when, in the face of significant social change, a large segment of society lost faith in the existing social institutions and was open to a consideration of radical proposals for change. At such times, the public has been somewhat more receptive to proposals by progressive educators and their supporters who have promoted an educational program for the purposes of helping create a new and improved social order along more egalitarian and democratic lines.

The roots of the progressive vision of education for social transformation can be traced to the last quarter of the nineteenth century. Historian Herbert Kliebard provides an excellent account of how a curriculum tradition for social meliorism emerged in the decades following the Civil War.[2] The social meliorists were located on the political Left and shaped by significant intellectual developments in philosophy, science, and the new social sciences (e.g., biology and Darwinism), pragmatism, psychology, and sociology. The political goals of social meliorism were promoted by progressive political movements, which emerged in the late nineteenth and early twentieth centuries. The Progressive Education Association (PEA), founded in 1919, was a response by progressive educators to institutionalize the social meliorist mandate to use education for transformation of the current social order.

Although progressive educators were generally on the liberal side, or Left, politically, the PEA never reached consensus on the best approach to education reform. The influential "child-centered" wing of the movement disclaimed any social or political agenda and argued that the child's interests should be the central concern of education. As the president of the PEA explained in 1930, "Although our association has never promulgated or approved anything like a program . . . we do endorse, by common consent, the obvious hypothesis that the child rather than what he [*sic*] studies should be the center of all educational effort and that the scientific attitude toward educational ideas is the best guarantee of progress.[3]

In stark contrast, the social reconstructionist faction on the far left wing of the PEA were the most outspoken proponents of using educational programs for radical social transformation. At the annual meeting of the

Progressive Education Association in 1932, George Counts, a leading social reconstructionist, gave a provocative talk entitled "Dare the School Build a New Social Order?" The audience sat in stunned silence when the talk ended. Counts had been a student of Albion Small, an early advocate of the social meliorist position in curriculum theory. He believed that the impact of the Great Depression in the 1930s demonstrated that our society was in a state of crisis and argued for the creation of a new social order based on a fundamental redistribution of economic and political power. His goal was to push progressive education reform as a way to radicalize American society.

In 1932, such power was largely held by a relatively small class or group. Until this was changed, "the survival or development of a society that could in any sense be called democratic is [or was] unthinkable." Counts claimed that the capitalist economy of the United States would either have to be eliminated "or changed so radically in form and spirit that its identity will [or would] be completely lost." Counts's economic views gradually moderated over time. He eventually came to accept the retention of capitalism in *some* form, which left room for an accommodation with various "liberal" reform proposals. Yet Counts believed there was ample evidence to indict capitalism on moral grounds, and the Depression of 1929 provided evidence of the profound failure of capitalism in economic terms.[4]

Counts admitted that progressive educators had accomplished much in the first decades of the twentieth century. They were right to place more emphasis on the interests of the child than did those who advocated a subject-centered curriculum, and they were correct when they argued that "activity lies at the root of all true education." Learning should, as the progressives argued, be related to "life situations" and character development. But while this was an excellent beginning, it was not a sufficient program for education. For an educational movement to be truly progressive "it must have orientation; it must possess direction." The very term *progress* implies moving forward, and this "can have little meaning in the absence of clearly defined purpose." Thus, the chief weakness of progressive education was its failure to develop a theory of social welfare, "unless it be that of anarchy or extreme individualism." Counts believed that the overemphasis on individualism in our culture reflected the view of the upper middle class, many of whom sent their children to progressive schools. The members of this class seemed "entirely incapable of dealing with any of the great crises of our time." They had become too fond of their material possessions and, in a crisis, would likely "follow the lead of the most powerful and respectable forces in society and at the same time find good reasons for doing so."[5]

Counts was also concerned with the pervasive influence of a philosophic uncertainty in much progressive thinking, which functioned to block the development of a theory of social welfare by promoting relativism under the guise of objectivity and academic freedom. Counts believed that philosophic uncertainty, combined with the instrumentalism of most progressives and the narrow scientific approach of other educators, had resulted in the general tendency to avoid resolving pressing social problems.

It was necessary, therefore, for progressive educators to free themselves from philosophic relativism and the undesirable influences of an upper-middle-class culture. Such freedom would permit the development of "a realistic and comprehensive theory of social welfare" and "a compelling and challenging vision of human destiny." The construction of an educational program oriented by such a vision and theory of social welfare would also entail freeing progressive education from its apparent fear of imposition and indoctrination. Put another way, progressive educators must come to accept "that all education contains a large element of imposition, that in the very nature of the case this is inevitable, that the existence and evolution of society depend upon it, that it is consequently eminently desirable, and that the frank acceptance of this fact by the educator is a major professional obligation."[6]

Counts contended that our schools, oriented by a new, truly progressive curriculum, could and should be in the vanguard of a movement to make fundamental changes in our political and economic system. The new curriculum should be designed to expose the antidemocratic limitations of a market economy and promote a more collectivist economy to reduce disparities of income and wealth and a strong version of participatory democracy.[7]

While the reconstructionists reflected the shift toward the political Left during the 1930s, most orthodox Marxists, and the American Communist Party in particular, rejected their position as naïve, since schooling was a tool of the capitalist political structure. Marxists in the 1930s were certainly not opposed to using the schools to promote their political agenda. However, they believed that the social order itself would need to be changed by direct political action before any real change in education could take place.

The reconstructionist legacy prompted a significant conservative backlash in the 1930s and 1940s, culminating in the banning of, and in several cases groups publicly burning, copies of reconstructionist Harold Rugg's highly popular social studies textbook series for its allegedly anti-American content. The intense patriotic impact of World War II, followed by the repressive political climate promoted by the Cold War and Senator Joseph McCarthy in the late 1940s and 1950s, had a chilling effect on progressive education, prompting the firing of many K–12 teachers and professors in higher education and suppressing the expression of liberal and radical ideas in teaching and curriculum materials. Although the progressive legacy regained some influence in the 1960s and early 1970s, the past three decades have been marked by a conservative restoration that has been motivated by a generally successful effort to discredit the entire (liberal to radical) progressive legacy.

THE ROLE OF IDEOLOGY AND THEORIES OF KNOWLEDGE IN EDUCATION REFORM

The current SBER movement is only the most recent example of a long struggle to determine "what" and "whose" knowledge is of most worth in the process of curriculum development and teaching. The approach taken when answering such questions will always have a direct impact on education policy, curriculum, classroom practice, and the design of teacher education programs. Central to the struggle over the K–12 curriculum is the critical relationship between knowledge and power. The power-knowledge relationship is captured in Orwell's claim in *1984* that "Those who control the past control the future. Those who control the present control the past." The power to determine the nature of schooling and the curriculum is a direct concern of all political groups in our society.

Of course, some political groups have always had far more influence on the shape of curriculum and instructional practice than others. Still, the relationship of power to knowledge is rarely simple. Like Orwell, we generally tend to think in terms of the power to control knowledge, but Foucault has called our attention to the intricate and complex relationship between power and knowledge. For Foucault, just as power undoubtedly shapes the social construction of knowledge, so too does knowledge shape how power is employed.[8]

While political power and, on occasion, even brute force are employed to shape public knowledge, Foucault described how indirect, discursive methods have been far more influential in the production, reproduction, and deployment of particular forms of knowledge and power. As defined by Foucault, a "discourse" functions to determine the way we think and the very boundaries of knowledge we might consider legitimate. Thus, a dominant discourse will influence, often unconsciously, our conceptions of what knowledge is, how knowledge might be produced, and what we should value when constructing a K–12 curriculum.

The views expressed here are also influenced by the way ideology has been employed by James Gee to illustrate how dominant school discourses better serve the needs of certain groups of students as opposed to others. Ideology refers to the complex set of ideas, symbols, beliefs, norms, customs, and practices used to represent and legitimate cultural and social systems. Defined this way, ideology is a fundamental component of any culture but always something less than the totality of the culture it seeks to represent. More specifically, ideology is generally used to legitimate "beliefs about the appropriate distribution of social goods, such as power, prestige, status, distinction, or wealth."[9]

There is a pervasive tendency to view ideology in negative terms. Although our negative conceptions of ideology have many origins, there are two developments in intellectual history that have played a major role in this regard. First, Marxist theory has emphasized a view of ideology as "false consciousness," that is, a system of ideas and practices used by dominant groups to control subordinate groups by making cultural and social conditions appear as natural, neutral, and normal. A second and related source of ideology as a negative concept is the modern conception of science. For science, reality is something we can discover and know by using scientific methods of inquiry. Ideology would refer to unscientific conceptions of reality as opposed to the "truth" or scientific description of reality.

We should recall that Marx believed his method for economic and social analysis was scientific. In the current debates over educational reform, proponents of opposing positions (e.g., professionalism vs. the privatization of schooling) usually claim their views are derived from research-based (scientific) arguments and attempt to discredit opponents by describing their views as merely ideological (i.e., not based on research). We need to examine both of these positions (false consciousness and the scientific conception of the realist) as each relates to the debate over education for social transformation.[10]

Clearly, we can conceive of situations wherein a person or group is a victim of false consciousness. But unless we define ideology as a tautology (i.e., ideology *is* a false conception of reality) and assume that we can always know with certainty what social reality is at any given time (something I would argue is impossible), the definition of ideology as false consciousness only captures a limited version of how the concept can be applied to social inquiry. If we consider Gee's description of ideology, we might also ask how any social system could function absent some ideological dimension used to justify its existence.

Consequently, while false consciousness is often a feature of a given society or social group, ideology itself can never be reduced to mere false consciousness because it is always a necessary component of any movement that defends or seeks to undermine a social order. Protestations aside, both Marxism and modern conceptions of science have an ideological dimension. The point to keep in mind is that no one has the capacity to stand outside and analyze society from a position that does not represent an ideological perspective. As such, ideology is something we, as human beings, cannot live without. I am not asserting that we have no way to adjudicate knowledge claims or that all knowledge claims are equal (a radical form of relativism or even nihilism). I do claim, though, that humans have no access to certain knowledge regarding such things as values, theories of social welfare, social reality, and the reality that we assume exists independent of our knowledge of it. What we do have as humans is the capacity to develop the competence to make judgments concerning how we ought to live to maximize our potential. Although such judgments are never certain, some are more defensible than others.[11]

The view of ideology and social knowledge as I have described it also has important implications for our conceptions of knowledge and education. Both conservative and progressive educational theorists have tended to hold a conception of knowledge developed during the Enlightenment. Although challenged by various postpositivist theorists, the development of modern science has enabled the Enlightenment conception of knowledge to become the "taken-for-granted" view that shapes most educational discourse and practice. This view of knowledge holds that reality has an independent, objective existence, which we can come to know (at least in part) through scientific inquiry. It is this assumption of a scientific access to "truth" or an "objective" account of reality that has become the bedrock for most curriculum and educational reform discourse on both the Left and Right.[12]

The term *science-based* research is employed to support the No Child Left Behind (NCLB) legislation and as a filter to determine which educational research will be used to support the Bush administration's educational initiatives. Progressive critics of NCLB generally claim that proponents of conservative education reform are motivated by ideology and promote an agenda that is not, in fact, well supported by the best educational research; the conservative education reformers make the same claim against progressives. Both Cochran-Smith and Simcox provide a helpful analysis of this discursive impasse.[13]

Because the conservative proponents of standards-based reform assume we can distinguish clearly between "real" knowledge and other more ancillary goals, such as citizenship education, critical thinking, self-esteem, and multiculturalism, they feel justified in enacting state and federal legislation to shape K–12 curriculum and practice. Their progressive opponents claim the conservatives have both the science and the social theory wrong and believe we need to promote a counterreform to use education (among other things) to discredit and reverse the current standards-based movement. The more radical progressives would go further, recommending an educational program for social transformation. Within this context, arguments for social transformation amount to what Engle and Ochoa describe as countersocialization, an attempt to use education to bring about fundamental changes in our economic and political systems. Although Engle and Ochoa would accept a social welfare system that was characterized by strong forms of participatory democracy and a more equal distribution of income and wealth, certain Marxist educators argue that a truly democratic society is not possible until we have abolished our current capitalist system.[14]

To the extent that one accepts the position described in the preceding paragraphs, it follows that the task of education is not to eliminate ideology or bias from analysis but to reveal how these essential elements of being human work to shape our practice as educators and citizens in a democratic society.[15] Beyond that, we need to use education to cultivate the practical competence required to function effectively as members of a democratic society. Competence needed to function as a citizen in a democratic society is not an educational "frill" but something essential to our full development as humans. In contrast, arguments for a "scientific" (conceived as an objective and nonideological) approach to schooling should be greeted with a great deal of skepticism, as they will always disguise as objective what, in fact, is ideological.

In short, the arguments for social transformation via an educational program promoting countersocialization (either progressive or conservative) are ill conceived and even counterproductive. Accordingly, I reject the strong form of the social reconstructionist education program promoted by Counts and others. I continue the argument against social transformation as countersocialization in the next section, where I present an analysis of Dewey's pragmatic alternative to social reconstructionism.

DEWEY'S CRITIQUE OF THE SOCIAL RECONSTRUCTIONIST POSITION

Given their radical political agenda, it is not surprising that conservatives and even many liberals reacted negatively to the social reconstructionist reform proposals. But we might expect that Left-progressives like Dewey would have supported a program to use the schools to help bring about democratic social transformation. Dewey is often considered as part of the reconstructionist movement.[16] Dewey did agree that the school should have a definite social orientation. As he stated, "[it] is not whether the schools shall or shall not influence the course of future social life, but in what direction they shall do so and how."[17] He acknowledged that the way the schools actually "*share* in the building of the social order of the future, depends on the particular social forces and movements with which they ally."[18] Teachers cannot escape the responsibility for assisting in the task of social change (or maintenance), and this requires a particular social orientation. According to Dewey, education "must . . . assume an increasing responsibility for participation in projecting ideas of social change and taking part in their execution in order to be educative." The changes espoused by Dewey and Childs included a more just, open, and democratic society.[19]

Considering such sentiments, it is not surprising that Dewey has been considered a social reconstructionist.[20] Richard Rorty has argued that Dewey at least exhibited a seeming ambivalence on this issue.[21] However, it is a mistake (or at least an oversimplification) to lump Dewey's ideas with those of reconstructionism, a point Dewey himself took great pains to make clear. Although Dewey did believe that the schools should assist in the reconstruction of society, his view of this process differed significantly from that of Counts. Rather than indoctrinating students with a particular theory of social welfare, Dewey wanted the schools to participate in the intellectualization of society—in other words, the "method of intelligence" (i.e., equipping students with the critical skills necessary for reflective thought applied to the analysis of social problems).[22] For Dewey, the central aim of education was "to prepare individuals to take part intelligently in the management of conditions under which they will live, to bring them to an understanding of the forces which are moving to equip them with the intellectual and practiced tools by which they can themselves enter into direction of these forces."[23]

Dewey's insistence on a commitment to the method of intelligence was posed as just that—a commitment to a method and not to any specific social outcome as a result of employing that method. He never suggested that the schools should seek to indoctrinate students to promote a particular theory of social welfare, although he realized that schools could not help transmitting some social values. A key problem was the lack of any single system of social values existing in complex modern society. To attempt to indiscriminately follow all the values of the current society would be to abandon the method of intelligence.[24]

Dewey thought that educators had three basic choices. First, they might accept the present state of social confusion and conflict and drift in an aimless fashion. Second, "they may select the new scientific, theological, and cultural forces that are producing change in the older order; may estimate the direction in which they are moving and their outcome if they are given freer play, and what can be done to make the schools their ally."[25] The third choice was the conservative option that strives to use the schools to help maintain the old social order against forces of change. In this case, a choice was made to support the values of the status quo that function to secure special privileges for certain dominant groups. Dewey obviously rejected the first and third choices and opted for the method of intelligence by which the schools seek to help students acquire the understandings and insights to enable them "to take part in the great work of construction and organization that will have to be done, and to equip them with the attitudes and habits of action that will make their understanding and insight practically effective."[26]

Dewey understood human intelligence as a capacity or competence to help clarify and achieve desirable social ends. But a commitment to this approach did not entail the recommendation of any particular social end save the necessary social conditions under which the method might survive and be applied. Thus, Dewey would only recommend that teachers hold to an orientation that emphasized the application of intelligence to social problems. This commitment to intelligence could be conceived as instrumental, empirically grounded, and designed to draw tentative conclusions. To go beyond that point would be indoctrination, which Dewey rejected.

Dewey was quite specific in his response to reconstructionist critics who attacked his instrumental approach as neutral. He did not believe it was neutral, mechanical, aloof, or "purely intellectual" in analyzing social conflict. Those who had concluded that modern advances in science and technology "were creating a new type of social conflict" did so not through indoctrination but by the "intelligent study of historical and existing forces and conditions."[27] Dewey did believe that his method could not "fail . . . to support a new general social orientation."[28] In this sense, indoctrination was unnecessary. In due time, the application of the method of intelligences would reveal ways to improve the social order. "The upholders of indoctrination rest their adherence to the theory, in part, upon the fact that there is a great deal of indoctrination now going on in the schools, especially with reference to narrow nationalism under the name of patriotism, and with reference to the dominant economic regime. These facts unfortunately *are* facts. But they do not prove that the right course is to seize upon the method of indoctrination and reverse its object."[29]

Dewey defined indoctrination as the "systematic use of every possible means to impress upon [students] a particular set of . . . views to the exclusion of every other."[30] This is a more extreme view than the interpretations of indoctrination used by Counts and other reconstructionists who insisted on the open access to information, even though new knowledge might contradict the reconstructionist view of the "good society." In contrast to more authoritarian radical positions (e.g., orthodox Marxists who assumed they had a monopoly on the truth), the deliberate suppression or distortion of information was ruled out as a valid means of inculcation.

However, the limited reconstructionist qualifications regarding educational indoctrination were not enough for Dewey. The only form of indoctrination he entertained was the assertion that the method of intelligence was the preferred approach to education. "If the method we have recommended leads teachers and students to better conclusions than those which we have reached—as it surely will if widely and honestly adopted—so much the better."[31] It is fair to say Dewey believed that any attempt to inculcate preconceived conclusions regarding a preferred social order would ultimately work to subvert the method of intelligence, even if the open access to alternative views was maintained. Any such risk was not worth the effort, given Dewey's educational philosophy and optimism regarding the potential efficacy of his method if fully applied. We will return to this important insight when we examine more recent recommendations for progressive education as countersocialization.

CONSERVATIVE RESTORATION AND EDUCATIONAL REFORM

These discussions emphasize that education has always been a site of ideological and political struggle, and reform movements and debates over curriculum have been persistent phenomena throughout our nation's history. Curriculum is and should be contested terrain within a democratic society. While the education reform debates between various conservative and progressive groups have often been intense, until the last quarter of the twentieth century there remained a general consensus regarding the importance of public education to the survival of democratic society and the potential capacity of our schools to help solve social problems.

The conservative approach to the discourse on education reform made an important theoretical shift in the early 1980s. In part, this change represented an intensification of earlier movements emphasizing increased attention to accountability, teaching the basics, and instructional objectives, which arose in the 1970s in response to the perceived excesses of the progressive reforms of the 1960s. The hostile reaction of the 1960s and 1970s was an earlier example of what we have more recently come to call the "culture wars." The 1970s also produced a significant decline in the level of public support for many of our major institutions, including (among others) public schools. With the election of President Ronald R. Reagan in 1980, the stage was set for a new conservative restoration.[32]

The Reagan administration soon found an effective way to link education reform to economic policy. The president and members of his administration used a "bully pulpit" strategy, including advocacy, speeches, and commission reports to shape public opinion in support of a conservative educational policy. Government officials also worked closely with private foundations and think tanks to reshape the discourse on and public knowledge of education. Consistent with the conservative ethos of the Reagan administration, the escalation of education reform rhetoric coincided with the reduction of federal spending on education.[33]

The single most influential report on education reform from this period was *A Nation at Risk,* published by the National Commission on Excellence in Education, which was established by Terrell Bell, Reagan's first Secretary of Education.[34] The report had a dramatic rhetorical and political effect. It was widely (and uncritically) promoted by the media. The *Newsweek* headline "Can Our Schools Be Saved?" was typical of the mainstream reaction. The centerpiece of the new education reform rhetoric was the assertion that America was a "nation at risk" as a direct result of the failure of our public schools to educate our children properly. The failed public educational system was blamed for the decline of our economy, particularly in relation to Japan and Germany, as well as the corruption of our culture. Overnight, the discourse on education reform had been transformed.

The Reagan administration managed to create the perception of an educational crisis that seemed to surpass the earlier Cold War education crisis, which followed the Soviet launch of *Sputnik* in 1957.[35] The publication of the report coincided with a period of low public morale. The memories of America's military failure in Vietnam, followed by the oil crisis, stagflation, and the Iran hostage situation, shaped the national consciousness at the start of the 1980s. President James E. Carter had called our attention to an American "cultural malaise" shortly before leaving office. *A Nation at Risk* provided an appealing explanation for our perceived national decline. The report claimed that "Our once unchallenged preeminence in commerce, industry, science, and technological innovation is being overtaken by competitors throughout the world . . . [and the] educational foundations of our society are presently being eroded by a rising tide of mediocrity that threatens our very future as a Nation and a people."[36]

A Nation at Risk was soon followed by several similar reports from the Education Commission of the States, the College Board, the Carnegie Foundation, the National Science Board, and the Twentieth Century Fund. This education crisis rhetoric, although exaggerated and incorrect in many ways, formed the core of a conservative consensus (ideology) on education policy that has maintained much of its original power over the past two decades.[37] At the core of this ideology is the claim that a pervasive progressive and liberal approach to K–12 education, which has overemphasized educational equity at the expense of educational excellence, was the main reason for our educational and economic decline in the last decades of the twentieth century. Another important assumption in all these reports was that there is a direct link between the level of K–12 student academic achievement (i.e., on standardized test scores) and economic growth and competitiveness vis-à-vis other industrialized nations. According to conservative critics, American K–12 students were performing at lower levels than in the past and in comparison with students in other industrialized nations. These conservative claims regarding a "crisis" in education soon achieved the status of "official knowledge."

This conservative discourse, led by numerous "think tanks" and public intellectuals, was refined, expanded, and made more effective throughout the 1980s and 1990s. William Bennett, Harold Bloom, Lynne Cheney, Dinesh D'Souza, Chester Finn, E. D. Hirsch, Jr., and Diane Ravitch have been among the most prominent and influential of these conservative critics. The conservative argument has continued to expand to include increasing numbers of scholars in higher education, many of whom are funded by conservative foundations and think tanks. The work of these academics has provided an important theoretical and empirical research database with which to underpin the claims of the conservative critique of public education.[38] A good summary of this work can be found in two edited books published on the twentieth anniversary of *A Nation at Risk*.[39] The authors, with few exceptions, argue that the nation remains at risk and promote the conservative education reform agenda. Finally, in this respect and others, one must also give credit to the powerful influence of conservative talk-show hosts, such as Rush Limbaugh, who played (and continue to play) a key role in helping to disseminate this SBER agenda and ideology.

The think tanks and foundations of most influence include the American Enterprise Institute, the Fordham Foundation, the Free Congress Research and Education Foundation, the Heritage Foundation, the Hoover Institute, and the John F. Olin Foundation. Linda Simcox provides a good summary of how such think tanks influenced educational policy. Ronald Reagan was well aware of the importance of the conservative discourse as it related to policy change, noting that "Ideas do have consequences, rhetoric is policy, and words are action." The success and persistence of the current SBER movement is testimony to the continuing conservative dominance of education reform discourse and policy.[40]

THE NEOCONSERVATIVE CRITIQUE OF CITIZENSHIP EDUCATION

Although the establishment of common public schools took most of the nineteenth century to accomplish, Thomas Jefferson's argument that a well-educated citizenry is essential to the survival of a democratic culture and society now has a "taken-for-granted" quality for most people. While Jefferson's views regarding schools might seem self-evident, they also beg the question "What do we mean by democracy?" There is no consensus on how to answer this, yet the way we define democracy is central to any argument to use our schools for social transformation. The current conservative program for education reform is based on a more limited view of democracy than Jefferson's or that of most progressive educators. This point is critical to any understanding of the SBER movement, which should not be reduced merely to an argument over standardization and standardized testing.

Conservative critics of schooling have clearly grasped the potential inherent in combining their attack on education in conjunction with the promotion of their cultural and economic ideas. The conservative commitment to a "culture war" was a conscious policy recommendation by the Free Congress Research and Education Foundation's report "Cultural Conservatism: Toward a New National Agenda." While the business community had always had an interest in shaping public education, under the new SBER reform agenda, corporate executives were invited to participate directly in the development of educational policy.[41]

Neoliberal Theory and Education for Democracy

The conservative approach to education reform is deeply rooted in a set of powerful theoretical and ideological assumptions that developed in the mid-twentieth century and have been given increased legitimacy in the past two decades. Frederic Hayek and Milton Friedman, both colleagues at the University of Chicago in the 1950s, are among the best representatives of the core conservative theory and ideology that has had an increasingly powerful effect on educational reform. Hayek argued that our current social order was a spontaneous and natural result of human evolution and had developed the way it had for good reasons. In addition, human society was always far too complex to permit the sort of knowledge one would need for any central planning of our economy. Consequently, any attempt by government to interfere with the natural (evolved) social order would only make things worse.[42]

Hayek also argued that human values, like human intelligence, had evolved over time as the result of the multitude of individual social actions and interactions that take place. Thus, human liberty must always take precedence over general claims to social welfare, inasmuch as individual liberty was (and is) a prior condition for the creation of any concept of social welfare. For Hayek, the liberal or progressive emphasis on the need for a conception of "social justice" to drive public policy was among the most powerful threats to individual liberty to emerge in modern civilization. In his view, the current emphasis on social justice "inverts the original and authentic concept sense of liberty, in which it is properly attributed only to individual actions."[43]

Milton Freidman extended Hayek's ideas to his own economic theory, claiming that the original concept of liberalism had been corrupted in the twentieth century and confounded with the actions of a central government to improve the social welfare of its citizens. Such efforts were doomed to fail. Like Hayek, Friedman argued that true liberty requires individual economic freedom. A free market economy was inherently the best way to maximize both individual freedom and the potential of our social institutions, including schooling.

The Dewey-Lippmann Debate over Education for Democracy

Dewey, of course, had rejected the assertion that a free-market economic system was an essential component of a successful democratic society. Indeed, Dewey understood market economic theory as one of the major impediments to the quest for instituting a strong version of deliberative democracy consistent with his pedagogical theories. In contrast, the prominent journalist Walter Lippmann argued in the 1920s that the complex nature of modern industrial society, combined with the application of propaganda techniques through the mass media, undermined Dewey's conception of education to develop the reflective citizenship skills required to participate fully in modern political processes.[44] Modern society was far too complex to permit meaningful participation on the part of the average citizen, who did not have the time, ability, or access to acquire the knowledge necessary to make informed decisions regarding the best policy to deal with important social issues. The most we might hope for is to trust in the capacity of enlightened and competent political and technocratic elites, the only groups in position to make informed social, economic, and political decisions in the public interest.

While the average citizen could still play an important role in the political process in terms of public opinion, pressure, and voting to elect or remove politicians at the state and national levels, Lippmann had little faith in the competence of the masses to make wise decisions on public policy. Robert Westbrook, in his excellent and supportive biography of Dewey's views on democracy, argues that Lippmann got the better of Dewey in this debate.[45] To the extent that Lippmann's analysis was more right than Dewey's in the 1920s and 1930s, one could argue that his views should be even more persuasive in our contemporary modern culture, saturated, as it is, by mass media at a level Lippmann could glimpse only in part toward the end of his career.

Richard Posner's Type 2 Theory of Democracy

More recently, federal appellate court judge and public intellectual Richard Posner has provided a complex pragmatic critique of the strong form of deliberative democracy advocated by Dewey.[46] Interestingly, Posner never mentions Lippmann, but his views can be read as a theoretical extension of Lippmann's earlier position applied to our even more complex postindustrial society. Posner makes a case for what he calls Type 2 democracy, as contrasted with the stronger Type 1 form of strong deliberative democracy supported, albeit in different ways, by Jefferson, Madison, Dewey, and most contemporary progressive political theorists.[47] Posner draws on the work of Dewey, although he rejects his epistemological conception of democracy and education for democracy as naïve. His conception of Type 2 democracy is largely shaped by his own "practical" conception of pragmatism fused with the theories of conservative (Posner tends to view this work as falling within the scope of classical liberalism) scholars like Hayek and Schumpeter and liberal John Stuart Mill to develop an argument that rejects as unsophisticated any attempt, including educational reforms, to construct a strong form of deliberative democracy.

According to Posner, deliberative democracy is a quixotic and even counterproductive approach to governing modern societies. In an innovative application of market economic theory, Posner argues that our democratic political system functions much like a free market economy. Like Hayek, Lippmann, and Schumpeter, he considers modern society far too complex for the mass of humanity to understand. In fact, even elite technocratic groups never have access to the knowledge necessary for a full understanding of social issues. However, the market structure (think in terms of John Stuart Mill's "marketplace of ideas," wherein different views compete for attention and scrutiny) provides a structure for sorting and filtering political and technical information in a way that has the best potential to enable Democratic politicians to try to sell their candidacy to voters much as entrepreneurs do in terms of goods or services.

Posner does consider the right to vote to be a critically important element of democracy. Although the average person is unlikely to have the competence to make complex policy decisions, he or she is qualified to determine, over time, if elected officials are acting in the public interest. In this respect, he seems to have more faith than Lippmann in the competence of the masses to make good choices regarding their political representatives. However, even if a case could be made that the public often selects candidates unwisely, voting is a necessary condition for the success of Posner's model of democracy. If we follow the logic of Posner's argument, progressive approaches to education for social transformation would be a bad idea, especially if they focused on developing an illusionary conception of participatory democracy and dysfunctional restrictions on a market economy. Posner believes that Type 2 democracy is already functioning reasonably well in the United States. Thus, schools should help students move away from the progressive's naïve conception of Type 1 participatory democracy and secure a better understanding of how our current Type 2 democracy works, how it might be improved, and why it is the preferred political system.

Leming's Rejection of Social Studies as Problems-Based Citizenship Education

In a parallel but related development, social studies educator James Leming has made a case for removing what he sees as an emphasis on critical thinking, social problems, and citizenship education as core goals for social studies education.[48] Leming's most recent work has been supported by the conservative Fordham Foundation, which has been a leading voice in the current conservative attack on public education.[49]

Leming traces the first significant recommendation to focus on citizenship and social problems to the 1916 Report of the Social Studies Committee, part of the NEA Commission on the Reorganization of Secondary Education.[50] This approach also formed the basis of the more radical social reconstructionist program for countersocialization to promote social transformation in the 1920s and 1930s. But this general agreement on the need, or even the propriety, of countersocialization as a function of the social studies is not shared by the profession as a whole, according to Leming. He cites Engle and Ochoa as a good example of progressive social educators espousing an unhelpful "fringe position" on the definition of citizenship as a goal for the social studies.[51]

Leming first speculated, and then sought to demonstrate empirically, the hypothesis that the progressive critical position of college and university professors of social studies represents a distinctive academically oriented cultural ideology that is substantially at odds with the ideology and culture that pervades K–12 social studies classrooms, one that includes the vast majority of social studies educators. Leming also argues that the views of K–12 teachers are far more representative of the general population's views regarding education. He suggests that social studies academics should confine themselves to working within the profession's cultural mainstream. His most serious argument, however, challenges the basic validity of using social studies to promote countersocialization (and, by inference, social transformation) in a democratic society in which the public does not and would not endorse such a function for the public schools.[52]

Leming argues that defining "citizenship" as the rationale for social studies suffers from two serious problems.[53] First, any usably clear definition of citizenship would require substantive agreement on civic values and, perhaps, even a shared vision of the ideal society, which appears unlikely and perhaps undesirable. Furthermore, promoting a preferred view of social welfare is not something that could be or should be established for the society by social studies teachers. Second, he suggests that social studies instruction has proved to be ineffective in promoting even such limited aspects of citizenship as voting behavior. Leming has reviewed three major controlled studies of programs designed to promote students' critical thinking, thoughtfulness, and analysis of social problems as competencies central to citizenship education. He claims that none of the research supports a significant effect on student behavior. In fact, the emphasis on these goals is often counterproductive, resulting in higher levels of student frustration, hostility, and, consequently, wasting time better spent on more important goals.

Leming also cites the work of King and Kitchener to support his contention that reflective judgments regarding social issues (in effect, developing policy proposals) are beyond the cognitive capacity of the vast majority of public school students.[54] Contrary to what progressive social studies educators seem to assume, the level of cognitive development necessary to engage effectively in the reflective analysis of social problems is generally not achieved until age twenty-four. If Leming is right, most undergraduate college students also lack the necessary competence for high-level reflective thought. For Leming, forcing middle and high school students to engage in high-level reflective analysis of social problems is (a) an approach to social studies that is fundamentally undemocratic (given what the vast majority of people believe should be the goals of social studies), (b) an ineffective teaching method (given research results), (c) likely to cause student frustration, failure, and hostility, and (d) a waste of time better spent on more important social studies goals.

What should be the focus of social studies education? Leming argues that "[t]he development of an accurate knowledge of our American history, our traditions and the social world, should be the superordinate goal of social studies instruction. Our job as professionals should be to develop interesting, engaging, and effective means of achieving this goal."[55] Leming does not rule out teaching for thoughtfulness but argues that we need to reconsider what we mean by critical thinking and design a more modest focus for students to engage in thinking activities that does not ask students to go "beyond their abilities, yet [still] contribute to their future capacity for reflective thought."[56] Such an approach might include the study of policy debates as a component of American history and government courses, as well as developing a "rich and accurate store of information about our nation's history and institutions." Leming, like Hirsch, sees the acquisition of basic core knowledge ("cultural literacy") as fundamental to any successful education program.

In any event, Leming has spelled out a rationale that does rule out the kinds of intellectual activity that progressive educators and others regard as absolutely essential for developing the ability of students to think critically. Leming's more limited approach to social studies is in direct opposition to any educational program for social transformation, as well as the more moderate progressive approaches to citizenship education described earlier. In his view, most progressive approaches to education are actually thinly disguised liberal or Left political agendas.

Viewed within the context of SBER and the neoconservative revival reflected in various education reports, think tank policy publications, and academic scholarship critical of public schooling coupled with the work of other "renegade" or "contrarian" social studies educators, Leming's work has made a significant in-house contribution to the conservative discourse on educational reform. In addition, Posner's recent critique of deliberative democracy (including citizenship education programs based on Type 1 democracy) has added a powerful theoretical argument for rejecting progressive political and educational ideas. Taken as a whole, the neoconservative political and educational reform agenda has constructed a persuasive theoretical basis and effective discourse for rejecting not only education for social transformation but also the virtual core of the progressive education tradition. We might well be witnessing a sea change in the intellectual history of American education.

The consequences of this conservative agenda have had far-reaching effects. First, an influential movement to deregulate and privatize public education has gained legitimacy.[57] While conservatives have always sought to influence the nature of public education, many are now arguing that public schooling is an institution whose time has passed. The call for charter schools, homeschooling, and vouchers are all elements of this move toward privatization. Second, the focus on a market economy as both the cornerstone of democracy and the best way to create educational excellence poses a direct challenge to the progressive conception of the role of schooling in a democratic society. The SBER focus on students as workers and consumers as opposed to citizens has already led to a reduction or elimination of citizenship education and the critical analysis of social issues, ideas central to the social studies curriculum tradition.[58]

The implications for social studies teacher education are clear. If one is obligated to start with the assumption that a free market economy is the precondition for individual liberty and democracy, all attempts to analyze alternative economic and political systems are reduced to an examination of why the alternative systems are inferior. Educational reform discourse is in danger of being reduced to a dogmatic monologue. Given the current political context of education reform, what response might we make to the conservative critique?

CONCLUDING THOUGHTS AND RECOMMENDATIONS

First, as challenging as I think the conservative critique of Type 1 democracy is, I would still reject key elements of Leming's and Posner's arguments. In the case of Leming, he has made a compelling case for his approach to social education. Evans's critique of Leming's position as an exaggerated and distorted view of social studies education is generally persuasive.[59] In addition, although not in direct response to Leming, Parker's case for a strong form of citizenship education as the cornerstone of social studies draws on a broad range of scholarship that undermines the more extreme elements of Leming's argument.[60]

In addition, Posner agrees with the argument of progressives like Parker who argue—correctly I think—that democracy has not been and is not now the natural human condition. It is rather easy to document how infrequently democratic societies (even loosely defined) have existed throughout history. Moreover, strong forms of deliberative democracy (Posner's Type 1) have been even rarer and are likely to be confined to local rather than national contexts. To acknowledge this fact seems, to me, a compelling reason to include the teaching of democratic citizenship in our K–12 schools. On this point Posner and various progressive proponents of citizenship education would agree. Democracy does not just happen; it must be cultivated and learned. Posner, of course, would have schools teach students about the inevitability and desirability of Type 2 as opposed to Type 1 democracy. I am not so sure about Leming, who would be more likely to deal with the issue indirectly via teaching "core" cultural knowledge as a scaffold for future participation in the democratic process.

I side with Parker on this point. Although I can acknowledge the power of the Leming, Lippmann, Posner (and so on) critique of progressive approaches to citizenship education, I am left asking what alternative would make sense. Let us assume, for the purpose of argument, that these conservative critics are largely correct (i.e., by and large, elites make the crucial complex policy decisions in democracies and the masses have the difficult, if not impossible, task of engaging in the sort of behaviors associated with Type 1 democracy). We must ask how it is that the members of the elite were able to rise to that position. Presumably—but only presumably— access to elite group membership is never reduced merely to a birthright. Our history is filled with numerous examples of former poor and working-class individuals who rose to positions of enormous influence. True, the children of elite families have an advantage, but that has never precluded a significant number of individuals from nonelite backgrounds from becoming members of elite political, economic, social, and policy groups. Unless we assume we can predict with a high level of certainty who among the masses has such potential, on what basis would we withhold a focus on strong forms of citizenship education from the education of all children?

Second, for both pragmatic and political reasons, it would be a mistake to dismiss the conservative education critique of progressive education. The current level of political support for the conservative education agenda represents a clear, if not overwhelming, majority. It is simply not possible for K–12 teachers and teacher educators to ignore the basic elements of SBER, whatever our misgivings. Indeed, schools of education that openly resist SBER could find themselves on the endangered species list. It would also be a mistake to dismiss the conservative critiques of progressive education. While the conservative education reform discourse has often been mean spirited, exaggerated, unfair, narrow, disingenuous, and simply wrong, much of the conservative scholarship has raised real issues that progressives should heed if they want to be taken seriously.[61]

I have been to far too many meetings at which progressive colleagues attack the conservative agenda and bemoan the current state of affairs. These laments are quickly followed by the secular equivalent of amen. We progressives are too often preaching to the choir, not listening to external criticism, and in danger of existing in an intellectual echo chamber. Ironically, progressives' pleas on behalf of critical thinking frequently degenerate into a form of closed inquiry. Too many of us are no better than our conservative critics when it comes to keeping an open mind—something intrinsic to truly critical thought.

Third, in the present political context—and this needs to be said—progressive proposals to use K–12 education for the purpose of radical cultural transformation are completely unrealistic. What is worse, they could easily be counterproductive in terms of undermining what credibility progressives have left. For all practical purposes, conservatives have won, at least temporarily, the current culture war. What has happened since Reagan's election in 1980 is equivalent to the ascendancy of Roosevelt's welfare state model from 1932 until well into the 1970s. Like all political victories, this one is no doubt a temporary phenomenon, but it does not, at this time, show any signs of receding. Indeed, the SBER movement is thoroughly bipartisan.[62] All major political candidates in both parties endorse SBER in principle and tend to quarrel only over costs and implementation issues. Major teacher associations have endorsed the basic elements of the SBER movement. Most of the critical reaction by teachers and teacher educators who do resist is typically dismissed as special pleading. Certainly, this is both an unfair and unhealthy political climate, and I am not arguing that we abandon thoughtful forms of resistance. In fact, it is our professional obligation to resist those ideas and systems we find antithetical to education for human betterment.

However, we should be both realistic and relevant in our critiques or few will have much interest in our ideas. We must constantly bear in mind that we are teaching "other people's children." Leming is not entirely wrong when he calls our attention to a tendency for progressive educators to act as if they know what is best for the masses, while simultaneously preaching about participatory democracy. This sort of behavior can quickly become just another form of elitism. For example, the idea that any significant number of K–12 teachers, much less the public at large, would support the sort of Marxist views and education proposals endorsed by critical teacher educators strikes me as both surreal in political terms and elitist in its rhetorical appeal to superior knowledge located in "sacred" texts. If only we all read the right books, we would understand clearly what must be done.

Fourth, beyond crassly pragmatic political constraints and antidemocratic elitism, there is a deeper intellectual problem at the heart of radical progressive arguments for social transformation. The problem was well described by Dewey over seventy years ago. Earlier, I described Dewey's reasons for rejecting the reconstructionist arguments for social transformation. I believe that Dewey's position, combined with newer scholarship in pragmatism, critical theory, and more recent philosophical traditions (e.g., philosophical hermeneutics and poststructuralist theory), provides an alternative to the reductionist arguments for countersocialization that have been directly linked to arguments for social transformation.[63]

When progressive educators argue that social studies should include some kind of balance between socialization and an opposing countersocialization, they typically are construing "socialization" as the inculcation of the dominant social order's established norms—that is, as a debilitating training for conformity rather than a habilitating, enabling, and empowering formation of competence to act effectively within a particular society. While I support many of the educational practices recommended by the advocates of countersocialization, it is not necessary to invoke countersocialization as the rationale for these practices. It makes more sense—both intellectually and pragmatically—to justify the practices required as central to the "socialization" students need for competence as effective citizens vis-à-vis democratic culture and society.

In a linguistic context, James Gee notes how development as a member of a language community or a society is fulfilled only at a stage where one is competent to improvise and to participate in fundamental transformations.[64] For example, we do not think that the socialization of young scientists should be limited to training in the replication of past findings or conventional procedures. Fresh thinking and the challenging of established paradigms are not regarded as antiscientific, and thus science students require some kind of "countersocialization" that is opposed to "traditional" socialization as members of particular disciplines. No more should we describe as "countersocializing" those educational experiences in which students acquire the abilities to challenge social norms or policies, for these abilities are not antisocial but are essential aspects of the educated democratic mind.

Fifth, we need to reconsider how we teach values within a progressive curriculum framework. Instead of treating democratic values as positive, a priori, given the attributes of individuals or of societies, to be "analyzed" and "clarified," or to be directly taught, observed, applied, and inculcated, "values" would and should be open to reflective and critical consideration as judgments that have been formed over time as to the real, demonstrable values of the principles or practices in question—or the value that commitment to those principles or practices is believed to have in relation to real personal and social human interests. Even such "core" values as freedom, justice, and equality should be open to questioning. Reaffirmation requires a faith in the value of reexamining our principles—a confidence that questioning would lead to a renewed demonstration of the value of those principles.[65]

Indeed, the experience of recognizing the critical pragmatic importance of these values when they are challenged on the basis of some genuine doubt is exactly the kind of educational experience in which these values really can be learned as part of the ongoing development of students' practical competence for citizenship. My fear is that the present dominant approach, one strongly reinforced by most conservative and a good number of progressive educators as well, too often teaches only "pious" ways of talking about values that are not truly believed—if they are even understood. Indeed, if core values are held but are immune from critical examination, this might even teach students that such values are being preached dogmatically out of an implicit anxiety that they could not withstand critical scrutiny.

When critical pedagogy advocates insist, either explicitly or through their rhetoric, that a preexisting value commitment to an insurgent social agenda must come first, before specifically pedagogical proposals can be considered, this unfortunately suggests that their proposals are of interest or value only to those who share such specific substantive value commitments in advance. This approach to education reform is counterproductive, because the curriculum and teaching practices proposed by such progressive reformers are more likely to succeed to the extent they are open to the critical reexamination of core values. Such an open reflective approach needs to be embraced by a broader community as the kind of pedagogy that would promote formation of the competencies for full participation in a democratic society.

Sixth, we need to move beyond the dominant conception of critical thinking that understands drawing distinctions between "facts" and "values" as a skill basic to critical thought. This is just one aspect of what happens in attempts to replace real critical thinking with something that has been reduced to merely technical procedures. Since real critical thinking cannot be reduced to technical analysis, artificial technical procedures are invented tailor-made for teaching, but without any use or relevance outside the phony teaching situation.

Typically, such artificially concocted "thinking skills" are then substituted for real practical abilities. One out of many possible examples is the "skill" of "identifying bias," whereby "bias" is operationally defined as characterizing statements or positions expressed (for example) in emotionally charged language—since it is easy to teach techniques for identifying emotionally charged language that make this an attractive definition of "bias" if, that is, the only relevant criterion is conduciveness to being taught as a technique requiring no practical judgment. The problem is that outside of such bogus teaching situations, bias refers to something different, something real and important, something that students do need to be able to recognize and deal with. Human understanding cannot emerge from a blank slate. Having biases is something that is an essential component of our human capacity to make sense of each other and the world. Human thinking is impossible without biases or prejudices.

Certainly we should cultivate an awareness of our biases to limit their potentially negative effects (i.e., the potential to limit our capacity to think critically). However, we must also help students to understand the necessary role biases play in enabling us to communicate with others. Our consciousness of how our predispositions, preferences, and prejudices can play a positive role in communication, interpretation, and understanding is a critical component of a complete education. The ability to discern how biases both facilitate and limit human understanding requires far more than the kind of technical analysis and criteria called for by either conservative critics or certain gurus of "critical thinking skills." Democratic education should aim for nothing less than the understanding and employment essential to the real mental competence for interpersonal communication and making practical social and political judgments required in a democratic culture. This argument is an extension of the positive analysis of ideology presented earlier.

Seventh, in the present SBER context, knowledge of the scholarly disciplines is promoted as one of the fundamental elements of effective teaching. I would agree with a renewed emphasis on disciplinary knowledge, but not in the way such knowledge is generally described by conservative critics. Dewey was, contrary to his critics, a strong supporter of disciplinary knowledge as a core curriculum component. Such knowledge does represent significant human achievements in our attempt to better understand the social and physical world. If the issue of defining social education centers on the question of what students need for social competence, then the necessary roles of social science disciplines as resources become apparent, although not as the ends of social education in itself.

What C. Wright Mills described as "the sociological imagination" is a good example of one form of social competence that is essential for developing competent democratic citizens.[66] Mills was troubled by the widespread lack of ability for people to understand the private troubles, circumstances, and affairs of individuals in terms of larger social and historical forces and processes that decisively determine the constraints and opportunities that impinge on them—or, conversely, to understand larger scale phenomena in terms of how they result from, and in turn affect, the practices of daily life—or, finally, even to conceive of how to act in ways that might effectively improve our situation and our prospects, taking both levels of our historical and quotidian lives into account. Analogues to Mills's approach could be applied to history and other social science disciplines as well.

The key point is to understand these disciplinary capabilities as aspects of practical competence participation in a democratic society, not as ends in themselves. When people think of their situations only in terms of their own immediate familiar circumstances, they might be faulted for being selfish or for lacking the "right" democratic values. Instead, we should be looking at the consciousness of social causes, consequences, and relationships as an attribute of social competence and the democratic mind that requires a social education informed by the social science disciplines.

Eighth, the position recommended here is directly influenced by Dewey's commitment to, and faith in, what he referred to as "the method of intelligence." Dewey, unlike the reconstructionists and many contemporary progressive educators, believed that it was possible to cultivate the formation of the democratic mind by attending to requirements of competence for social action without the need to direct instruction toward more specific social outcomes or a theory of social welfare. This approach to education also enables us to see the development of citizenship as something that can be meaningfully and fruitfully pursued in schools without the need to first come to a consensus on our substantive conceptions of democracy.

Much like Dewey, I believe that the only valid path to education for social transformation lies in enabling students themselves to develop the competencies for active participation in a democratic culture. Dewey was convinced that such efforts would surely result in a more democratic and egalitarian society. The best society is the one in which human potential has the opportunity to develop and flourish. Competent citizens, not progressive teachers alone, are in the best position to determine the shape of the democratic society to come.

Notes

GENERAL EDITOR'S INTRODUCTION

1. Portions of this section draw upon E. Wayne Ross, "Remaking the Social Studies Curriculum," in *The Social Studies Curriculum: Purposes, Problems, and Possibilities*, rev. ed., ed. E. Wayne Ross (Albany: State University of New York Press, 2001).
2. John Dewey, *Democracy and Education* (New York: Free Press, 1966), p. 87.
3. Robert W. McChesney, Introduction to *Profits over People: Neoliberalism and Global Order*, by Noam Chomsky (New York: Seven Stories Press, 1988).
4. Madison quoted in Chomsky, *Profits over People*, p. 47.
5. For an explication of these issues see Edward S. Herman and Noam Chomsky, *Manufacturing Consent: The Political Economy of the Mass Media* (New York: Pantheon, 1988).
6. Noam Chomsky, *Media Control: The Spectacular Achievements of Propaganda* (New York: Seven Stories Press, 1997).
7. A. A. Lispcom and A. Ellery, eds., *The Writings of Thomas Jefferson*, vol. 16 (Washington, DC: The Thomas Jefferson Memorial Association, 1903), p. 96.
8. Dewey quoted in Noam Chomsky, *Class Warfare* (Vancouver: New Star Books, 1997).

INTRODUCTION

1. Kevin D. Vinson and E. Wayne Ross, *Image and Education: Teaching in the Face of the New Disciplinarity* (New York: Peter Lang, 2003).

CHAPTER 1

1. Maxine Greene, *Variations on a Blue Guitar: The Lincoln Center Institute Lectures on Aesthetic Education* (New York: Teachers College Press, 2001).

2. Elliot W. Eisner, *The Arts and the Creation of Mind* (London: Yale University Press, 2002).

3. Ibid., p. 1.

4. Rita L. Irwin, Wendy Stephenson, Helen Robertson, and J. Karen Reynolds, "Passionate Creativity, Compassionate Community," *Canadian Review of Art Education* 28, no. 2 (2001), pp. 15–34.

5. Ibid.

6. Frances Rauscher and Gordon Shaw, "Key Components of the Mozart Effect," *Perceptual and Motor Skills* 86 (1998), pp. 835–41.

7. Rena Upitis and Katharine Smithrim, *Learning through the Arts National Assessment 1999–2002: Final Report to the Royal Conservatory of Music* (Kingston, Ont.: Faculty of Education, Queen's University, 2003), pp. 1–54.

8. Eisner, pp. 42–45.

9. Greene, p. 82.

10. John Dewey, *Art as Experience* (New York: Minton Balch, 1934).

11. Upitis and Smithrim, p. 2.

12. Gail Burnaford, Arnold Aprill, Cynthia Weiss, and the Chicago Arts Partners in Education, eds., *Renaissance in the Classroom: Arts Integration and Meaningful Learning* (Mahwah, NJ: Lawrence Erlbaum, 2001), p. 10.

13. Eisner, p. 3.

14. Lynne B. Silverstein, "Artist Residencies: Evolving Educational Experiences," in *Acts of Achievement: The Role of the Performing Arts Centers in Education*, ed. Barbara Rich, Jane L. Polin, and Stephen J. Marcus (New York: Dana Press, 2003).

15. Rita L. Irwin, Sylvia Wilson Kind, Kit Grauer, and Alex de Cosson, "Integration as Embodied Curriculum" (under review).

16. Brent Hocking, Johnna Haskell, and Warren Linds, eds., *Unfolding Bodymind: Exploring Possibility through Education* (Brandon, VT: Foundation for Educational Renewal, 2001).

17. John P. Miller, *The Holistic Curriculum* (Toronto, Ont.: OISE Press, 1988).

18. Burnaford, Aprill, and Weiss.

19. Ramon Gallegos Nava, *Holistic Education: Pedagogy of Universal Love,* trans. Madeline Newman Rios and Gregory S. Miller. (Brandon, VT: Foundation for Educational Renewal, 2001).

20. Upitis and Smithrim, p. 6, who are referring to James S. Catterall, Richard Chapleau, and John Iwanaga, "Involvement in the Arts and Human Development: General Involvement and Intensive Involvement in Music and Theatre Arts, 1999" (The Imagination Project, Graduate School of Education and Information Studies, Los Angeles: UCLA, 2004) http://www.gseis.ucla.edu/faculty/publications/l.

21. Eisner, p. 49.

22. Rita L. Irwin, "Towards an Aesthetic of Unfolding In/Sights through Curriculum," *Journal of the Canadian Association for Curriculum Studies* 1, no. 2 (2003), pp. 63–78.

CHAPTER 2

1. Robert D. Barr, James L. Barth, and Samuel S. Shermis, *Defining the Social Studies* (Washington, DC: National Council for the Social Studies, 1977), p. 1.

2. Joel Spring, *Education and the Rise of the Corporate State* (Boston: Beacon Press, 1973).

3. Herbert M. Kliebard, "The Rise of Scientific Curriculum Making and Its Aftermath," *Curriculum Theory Network* 5, no. 1 (1975), p. 28.

4. Barr, Barth, and Shermis, p. 19.

5. Ibid., p. 20.

6. Edgar. B. Wesley and Stanley Wronski, *Teaching Social Studies in High School* (Boston: D.C. Heath, 1958), p. 3.

7. William B. Stanley and Jack L. Nelson, "The Foundations of Social Education in Historical Context," in *Inside/Out: Contemporary Critical Perspectives in Education*, ed. R. M. Martusewicz and W. M. Reynolds (New York: St. Martin's Press, 1994), pp. 266–84.

8. Ibid., p. 276.

9. Larry Cuban, "The History of Teaching Social Studies," in *Handbook of Research on Social Studies Teaching and Learning*, ed. James P. Shaver (New York: MacMillan, 1991), pp. 197–209.

10. Carnegie Forum on Education and the Economy, *A Nation Prepared: Teachers for the 20th Century* (New York: Carnegie Corporation, 1986), p. 25.

11. Jane Bernard-Powers, "Gender in the Social Studies Curriculum," in *The Social Studies Curriculum: Purposes, Problems, and Possibilities,* ed. E. Wayne Ross (State University of New York Press, 2000).

12. Nel Noddings, "Social Studies and Feminism," in *The Social Studies Curriculum: Purposes, Problems and Possibilities,* ed. E. Wayne Ross (State University of New York Press, 2000), p. 174.

13. Diane Ravitch, "A Brief History of the Social Studies," in *Where Did Social Studies Go Wrong?*, ed. James Leming, L. Ellington, and K. Porter (Washington, DC: Thomas B. Fordham Foundation, 2003).

14. B. Frazee and S. Ayers, "Garbage In, Garbage Out: Expanding Environments, Constructivism, and Content Knowledge in Social Studies," in Leming, Ellington, and Porter. (Washington, DC: Thomas B. Fordham Foundation, 2003).

15. James Leming, "Ignorant Activists: Social Change, 'Higher Order Thinking,' and the Failure of Social Studies," in Leming, Ellington, and Porter, p. 135.

16. Diane Ravitch, p. 5.

17. H. G. Hullfish and P. Smith, *Reflective Thinking: The Method of Education* (New York: Dodd Mead, 1961); Robert Stake and J. Easley, *Case Studies in Science Education: Report to the National Science Foundation* (University of Illinois at Urbana-Champaign: Center for Instructional Research and Curriculum Evaluation and Committee on Culture and Cognition, 1978), no. 036 000 0037 and no. 0038 000 00376-3 (Washington, DC: U.S. Government Printing Office); K. Wiley, *The Status of Pre-College Science, Mathematics, and Social Studies Education 1955–1975.* Report to the National Science Foundation, Document no. 038 000 00363-1 (Washington, DC: Social Science Education Consortium/USGPO, 1978); James S. Shaver, O. L. Davis, and S. Helburn, "The Status of Social Studies Education: Impressions

from Three NSF Studies," *Social Education* 43, no. 2 (1979), pp. 150–53; and E. Wayne Ross, "The Struggle for the Social Studies Curriculum," in *The Social Studies Curriculum: Purposes, Problems, and Possibilities*, (Albany: State University of New York Press, 2000).

18. Richard J. Paxton, "Don't Know Much about History—Never Did," *Phi Delta Kappan* 85, no. 4 (2003), p. 270.

19. Ibid., p. 273.

20. John I. Goodlad, *A Place Called School: Prospects for the Future* (New York: McGraw-Hill, 1984).

21. Ibid., p. 212.

22. James W. Loewen, *Lies My Teacher Told Me: Everything Your American History Textbook Got Wrong* (New York: Simon and Schuster, 1996).

23. D. Helfand, "Mr. Harts's Teachable Moment," *Los Angeles Times,* November 19, 2002.

24. Perry M. Marker, "Thinking Out of the Box: Rethinking and Reinventing a Moribund Social Studies Curriculum," *Theory and Research in Social Education* 50 (2001).

25. C. A. Bowers, *Mindful Conservatism* (Lanham, MD: Rowman & Littlefield, 2003).

26. Perry M. Marker, "High-Stakes Testing in Teacher Education: The California Teacher Performance Assessment," *Workplace* (July 2003), http://www.louisville.edu/journal/workplace/issue5p2/marker.html.

CHAPTER 3

1. Nila Banton Smith, *American Reading Instruction* (Newark, DE: International Reading Association, 1965).

2. Luther C. Gilbert, "Effect on Silent Reading of Attempting to Follow Oral Reading," *Elementary School Journal* 40 (1940), pp. 614–21.

3. Harry Singer, "Research That Should Have Made a Difference," *Elementary English* 47 (1970), pp. 27–34.

4. Dolores Durkin, *Teaching Them to Read*, 4th ed. (Boston: Allyn and Bacon, 1983), p. 43.

5. Mabel V. Morphett and Carleton Washburne, "When Should Children Begin to Read?" *Elementary School Journal* 31 (1931), pp. 496–503.

6. Rudolph Flesch, *Why Johnny Can't Read* (New York: Harper Row, 1955).

7. Guy L. Bond and Robert Dykstra, "The Cooperative Research Program in First-Grade Reading," *Reading Research Quarterly* 32, no. 6 (1967), pp. 348–427.

8. National Center for Educational Statistics, http://nces.gov/nationsreportcard/reading/trendsnational.asp.

9. Jerome C. Harste, Virginia A. Woodward, and Carolyn L. Burke, *Language Stories and Literacy Lessons* (Portsmouth, NH: Heinemann, 1984).

10. Elizabeth Sulzby, "Children's Emergent Reading of Favorite Storybooks: A Developmental Study," *Reading Research Quarterly* 20, no. 4 (1985), pp. 458–81.

11. Yetta M. Goodman, "What Is Whole Language?," in *The Whole Language Catalog*, ed. Kenneth S. Goodman, Lois B. Bird, and Yetta M. Goodman (Santa Rosa, CA: American School Publishers, 1991), p. 4.

12. Patricia A. Alexander, "Knowledge and Literacy: A Transgenerational Perspective," in *47th Yearbook of the National Reading Conference*, ed. Timothy Shanahan and Flora V. Rodriguez-Brown (Chicago: National Reading Conference, 1998), pp. 22–43.

13. P. David Pearson and Diane Stephens, "Learning about Literacy: A 30-Year History," in *Theoretical Models and Processes of Reading*, 4th ed., ed. Robert B. Ruddell, Martha Rapp Ruddell, and Harry Singer (Newark, DE: International Reading Association, 1994), pp. 22–42.

14. National Reading Panel, *Teaching Children to Read: An Evidence-Based Assessment of the Scientific Research Literature on Reading and Its Implications for Reading Instruction*. Publication no. 00-4769 and Publication no. 00-4754 (Washington, DC: National Institute of Child Health and Human Development, 2000).

15. Martha Rapp Ruddell, "Of Stand-Up Comics, Statisticians, Storytellers, and Small Girls Walking Backward: A New Look at the Discourses of Literacy Research," in *48th Yearbook of the National Reading Conference*, ed. Timothy Shanahan and Flora V. Rodriguez-Brown (Chicago: National Reading Conference, 1999), pp. 1–16.

16. James W. Cunningham, "The National Reading Panel Report," *Reading Research Quarterly* 36, no. 3 (2001), pp. 326–35.

17. Gregory Camilli, Sadako Vargas, and Michele Yurecko, "Teaching Children to Read: The Fragile Link between Science and Federal Education Policy," *Education Policy Analysis Archives* 11, no. 15 (2003), http://epaa.asu.edu/epaa/v11n15.

18. Ibid., p. 4.

19. Ibid.

20. Ibid., p. 37

21. Martha Rapp Ruddell, *Teaching Content Reading and Writing* (4th ed.), (New York: John Wiley & Sons, 2005).

22. Bond and Dykstra, p. 426.

CHAPTER 4

1. On history see, among other sources, Joel H. Spring, *The American School: 1642–2000* (New York: McGraw-Hill, 2000).

2. National Council of Teachers of Mathematics [NCTM], *A History of Mathematics Education in the United States and Canada* (Washington, D.C.: NCTM, 1970).

3. National Education Association [NEA], *Report of the Committee of Fifteen on Elementary Education* (New York: American Book Co., 1895).

4. Mathematical Association of America [MAA], *The Reorganization of Mathematics in Secondary Education* (Washington, D.C.: MAA, 1923).

5. NCTM.

6. Ibid.

7. Ibid.

8. Stephen S. Willoughby, "Perspectives on Mathematics Education," in *Learning Mathematics for a New Century: National Council of Teachers of Mathematics 2000 Yearbook*, ed. Maurice J. Burke and Frances R. Curcio (Reston, VA.: NCTM, 2000).

9. Kathryn L. Braddon, Nancy J. Hall, and Dale Taylor, *Math through Children's Literature: Making the NCTM Standards Come Alive* (Englewood, CO.: Teacher Ideas Press, 1993), p. 1.

10. Ibid.

11. National Council of Teachers of Mathematics [NCTM], *An Agenda for Action: Recommendations for School Mathematics of the 1980s* (Reston, VA.: NCTM, 1980).

12. National Council of Teachers of Mathematics [NCTM], *Everybody Counts: A Report to the Nation on the Future of Mathematics Education* (Washington, D.C.: National Academy Press, 1989); National Council of Teachers of Mathematics [NCTM], *Curriculum and Evaluation Standards for School Mathematics,* (Reston, VA.: NCTM, 1989).

13. Braddon, Hall, and Taylor, p. 1.

14. National Council of Teachers of Mathematics [NCTM], *Principles and Standards for School Mathematics* (Reston, VA.: NCTM, 2000).

15. Willoughby.

16. Ibid.

17. National Research Council (NRC), *Adding It Up: Helping Children Learn Mathematics* (Washington, DC: National Academy Press/National Academy of Sciences, 2001).

18. Ibid., p. 36.

19. Ibid., p. 39.

20. Ibid., p. 44.

21. Ibid., p. 54.

22. Ibid., p. 57.

23. See E. D. Hirsch, Jr., *Cultural Literacy: What Every American Needs to Know* (Boston: Houghton Mifflin, 1987) and *The Schools We Need and Why We Don't Have Them* (New York: Doubleday, 1996). For opposing views see David C. Berliner and Bruce J. Biddle, *The Manufactured Crisis: Myths, Fraud, and the Attack on America's Public Schools* (Reading, MA: Addison-Wesley, 1995) and Alfie Kohn, *The Schools Our Children Deserve: Moving beyond Traditional Classrooms and "Tougher Standards"* (Boston: Houghton Mifflin, 1999).

24. No Child Left Behind (Executive Summary) (Washington, DC: USGPO, 2001), January 2002, http://www.ed.gov/nclb/overview/intro/execsumm.html. See also Kevin D. Vinson and E. Wayne Ross, *Image and Education: Teaching in the Face of the New Disciplinarity* (New York: Peter Lang, 2003).

25. Ibid.

26. *The Facts about Math Achievement* (Washington, DC: U.S. Government Printing Office, 2004), http:www.ed.gov.print/nclb/methods/math/math.html.

27. Ibid.

28. Ibid.

29. No Child Left Behind; *The Facts About Math Achievement.*

30. Vinson and Ross.

31. National Center for Education Statistics, *Trends in International Mathematics and Science Study: Highlights from the Third International Mathematics and Science Study-Repeat (TIMSS-R)* (Washington, DC: U.S. Government Printing Office, 2003), http://www.nces.ed.gov/timss/highlights.asp. See also Beth D. Greene,

Marlena Herman, and David L. Haury, *TIMSS: What Have We Learned about Math and Science Teaching? ERIC Digest* (Columbus, OH: ERIC, 2000), http://www.ericdigests.org/2003-1/timss.htm. See Gerald W. Bracey's chapter on international comparisons of student achievement in *Defending Public Schools: The Nature and Limits of Standards Based Reform and Assessment* for a more extensive analysis of the TIMSS.

32. Ibid.

33. Ibid.

34. Ibid.

35. National Center for Education Statistics [NCES], *Mathematics* (Washington, DC: 2003), http://nces.ed.gov/nationsreportcard/mathematics/results2003/natscalescore.asp (and variously linked Web pages).

36. NCTM, *Principles and Standards for School Mathematics*, pp. 2–3.

37. Ibid., p. 2.

38. Ibid.

39. NRC, p. 5.

40. Ibid., pp. 116–17.

41. Association for Supervision and Curriculum Development, "Improving Achievement in Math Science," *Educational Leadership* [special issue] 61, no. 5 (2004).

CHAPTER 5

1. F. James Rutherford and Andrew Ahlgren, *Science for All Americans: Project 2061* (Oxford, UK: Oxford University Press, 1991), p. ix.

2. American Association for the Advancement of Science (AAAS), *Benchmarks for Scientific Literacy* (Oxford, UK: Oxford University Press, 1994), p. 124.

3. Ibid., p. 12.

4. AAAS, *Blueprints for Science Education Reform* (New York: Oxford University Press, 1997); AAAS, *Atlas of Science Literacy* (New York: Oxford University Press, 1998). Note: All AAAS *Project 2061* materials are available at no cost online at http://www.project2061.org/tools/toolWeb.htm, and the NSES and its sister documents can be found at http://www.nas.edu/nrc/.

5. Thirty years later, in the mid-1990s, another group of researchers videotaped Harvard students on the day of graduation and asked them questions like, Why do we have seasons? or Where do the materials come from to turn a seed into a tree? The elaborate, yet ultimately wrong, explanations from these graduates is testimony to the resistance of even the brightest learners to reconstructing experience-based beliefs about the world, regardless of how "excellent" their education might have been. Note: *A Private Universe* videos may be obtained from the Annenberg/CPB Math and Science Project at http://www.learner.org/teacherslab/index.html.

6. See, for example, J. R. Mokros and R. F. Tinker, "The Impact of Microcomputer-Based Labs on Children's Ability to Interpret Graphs," *Journal of Research in Science Teaching* 24, no. 4 (1987), pp. 363–83.

7. J. Hawkins and R. D. Pea, "New Representations: Tools for Bridging the Cultures of Everyday and Scientific Thinking," *Journal of Research in Science Teaching* 24, no. 4 (1987), pp. 291–307.

8. National Research Council, *National Science Education Standards: Observe, Interact, Change, Learn* (New York: National Academy Press, 1995); AAAS, *Benchmarks for Science Literacy*; AAAS, *Atlas of Scientific Literacy*; and AAAS, *Blueprints for Science Education Reform.*

9. For an overview, see I. R. Weiss, E. R. Banilower, R. A. Crawford, and C. M. Overstreet, *Local Systemic Change through Teacher Enhancement, Year Eight Cross-Site Report* (Triangle Park, NC: Horizon Research, 2001), http://www.horizon-research.com/reports/2003/year8.php.

10. See O. Amaral, L. Garrison, and M. L. Klentschy, "Helping English Learners Increase Achievement through Inquiry-Based Science Instruction," *Bilingual Research Journal* 26, no. 2 (2002), pp. 213–39.

CHAPTER 6

1. Gordon G. Vessels, *Character and Community Development: A School Planning and Teacher Training Handbook* (Westport, CT: Praeger, 1998), p. 16.

2. Ibid., p. 17.

3. Don Trent Jacobs and Jessica Jacobs-Spencer, *Teaching Virtues: Building Character across the Curriculum* (Lanham, MD: Scarecrow Press, 2001), p. ix.

4. Patrick Slattery, *Curriculum Development in the Postmodern Era* (New York: Garland, 1995), p. 79.

5. Larry K. Brendtro, Martin Brokenleg, and Steve Van Bockern, *Reclaiming Youth at Risk: Our Hope for the Future* (Bloomington, IN: National Education Service, 1990).

6. J. Baird Callicot and Fernando J. Da Rocha, eds., *Earth's Insights: A Survey of Ecological Ethics from the Mediterranean Basin to the Australian Outback* (New York: SUNY Press, 1997).

7. Aristotle, *Nichomachean Ethics,* trans. M. Oswald (Indianapolis: Liberal Arts Press, 1962).

8. William J. Bennett, *The Book of Virtues* (New York: Simon & Schuster, 1995).

9. Ibid.

10. Vessels, p. 19.

11. Robert J. Nash, *Answering the "Virtuecrats": A Moral Conversation on Character Education* (New York: Teachers College Press, 1997), p. xi.

12. Lawrence Kohlberg, *Essays on Moral Development: The Philosophy of Moral Development*, vol. 2 (New York: HarperCollins, 1984).

13. Nel Noddings, *Educating Moral People: A Caring Alternative to Character Education* (New York: Teachers College Press, 2002).

14. Jacobs and Jacobs-Spencer; Don Trent Jacobs (Four Arrows), *Spirituality in Education: A Matter of Significance for American Indian Cultures* (Brandon, VT: Holistic Education Press, 2002).

15. Edward A. Wynne and Kevin Ryan, *Reclaiming Our Schools: Teaching Character, Academics, and Discipline,* 2nd ed. (Upper Saddle River, NJ: Merrill, 1997), p. 68.

16. Nash, p. xi.

17. Emile Durkheim, *The Rules of Sociological Method* (New York: Free Press, 1938).

18. Don Trent Jacobs, *Primal Awareness: A True Story of Survival, Awakening and Transformation with the Raramuri Shamans of Mexico* (Rochester, VT: Inner Traditions International, 1998).
19. Thomas Lickona, *Educating for Character: How Our Schools Can Teach Respect and Responsibility* (New York: Bantam Books, 1992).
20. Amitai Etzioni, *The Spirit of Community: The Reinvention of American Society* (New York: Simon & Schuster, 1993), p. 38.
21. Robert B. Westbrook, *John Dewey and American Democracy* (Ithaca: Cornell University Press, 1991), p. 466.
22. C. David Lisman, *The Curricular Investigation of Ethics: Theory and Practice* (Westport, CT: Praeger, 1996), p. 5.
23. Jacobs, p. 16.
24. Plato, *Phaedrus,* trans. Reginald Hackforth (Cambridge: Cambridge University Press, 1972).
25. Noddings.
26. Jamake Highwater, *The Primal Mind: Vision and Reality in Indian America* (New York: HarperCollins, 1982), p. 126.
27. D. H. Lawrence, *Lady Chatterley's Lover,* trans. Michael Squires (New York: Penguin, 1994).
28. E. M. Forster, *The Eternal Moment and Other Stories* (New York: Harcourt, Brace & World, 1970), pp. 441–75.
29. Jo Ann Boydston, ed., *John Dewey: The Later Works, 1925–1953* (Carbondale, Southern Illinois University Press, 1989), p. 166.
30. Rebecca Robbins, "John Dewey's Philosophy and American Indians," *Journal of American Indian Education* 22, no. 3 (1983).
31. Denise Lardner Carmody and John Tully Carmody, *Native American Religions* (New York: Paulist Press, 1993), p. 232.
32. Brendtro, Brokenleg, and Van Bockern, p. 34.
33. Stanley Coopersmith, *The Antecedents of Self Esteem* (San Francisco: Freeman, 1967).
34. Joan G. Miller, "Culture and Moral Judgment: How Are Conflicts between Justice and Interpersonal Responsibilities Resolved," *Journal of Personality and Social Psychology* 26 (1992), pp. 541–54.
35. R. S. Fabes, J. Fultz, N. Eisenberg, T. May-Plumlee, and F. S. Christopher, "Effects of Rewards on Children's Prosocial Motivation: A Socialization Study," *Developmental Psychology* 25 (1989), pp. 509–15.
36. Yvonne Germaine Dufault, "A Quest for Character: Explaining the Relationship between First Nations Teachings and Character Education" (master's thesis, OISE, University of Toronto, 2003), pp. 80–83.
37. Richard D. Mosier, *Making the American Mind: Social and Moral Ideas in the McGuffy Readers* (New York: Russell & Russell, 1965).
38. Vessels, p. 25.
39. Alfie Kohn, "How Not to Teach Values," *Phi Delta Kappan,* http://www.alfiekohn.org/teaching/hnttv.htm.
40. Jacobs and Jacobs-Spencer, p. 161.
41. Georgia House of Representatives, *House Bill 1207 QBE, Amendment to Part 15, Article 6 of Chapter 2 of Title 20 of the Official Code of Georgia,* January 25, 2000.

42. Richard T. Cooper, "General Casts War in Religious Terms," *Los Angeles Times,* October 16, 2003.

43. Don Trent Jacobs, *The Bum's Rush: The Selling of Environmental Backlash: Phrases and Fallacies of Rush Limbaugh* (Boise: Legendary Publishing, 1994).

44. Highwater, p. 156.

45. Alfred North Whitehead, *Science and the Modern World* (New York: Free Press, 1925).

46. Ryan and Wynne; and James Davison Hunter, *The Death of Character: Moral Education in an Age without Good or Evil* (New York: Basic Books, 2000).

47. James Leming, "Research and Practices in *Character Education: A Historical Perspective,*" in *The Construction of Children's Character,* ed. A. Molnar (Chicago: University of Chicago Press, 1997).

48. Highwater, p. 193.

49. Jacobs and Jacobs-Spencer, p. 18.

50. Brendtro, Brokenleg, and Van Bockern, p. 35.

51. Sam Keen, *Hymns to an Unknown God: Awakening the Spirit in Everyday Life* (New York: Bantam Books, 1995), pp. 186, 298.

52. Joseph Campbell, *Historical Atlas of World Mythology: The Way of the Animal Powers,* vol. 1 (New York: Random House, 1993).

CHAPTER 7

1. National Commission on Excellence in Education, *A Nation at Risk: The Imperative for Educational Reform* (Washington, DC: U.S. Government Printing Office, 1983).

2. Examples of these various forms and levels of reform ideas vary, and the literature is extensive. Examples, however, and critiques, include The No Child Left Behind Act of 2001 (Executive Summary), January 2002, http://www.ed.gov/nclb/overview/intro/execsumm.html; Robert E. Slavin and Nancy A. Madden, *One Million Children: Success for All* (New York: Corwin Press, 2000) and *Success for All: Research and Reform in Elementary Education* (Mahwah, NJ: Lawrence Erlbaum, 2001); Susan Ohanian, *One Size Fits Few: The Folly of Educational Standards* (Portsmouth, NH, 1999); and Kevin D. Vinson and E. Wayne Ross, *Image and Education: Teaching in the Face of the New Disciplinarity* (New York: Peter Lang Publishing, 2003).

3. Interested readers should consult several biographies of Maria Montessori, including E. M. Standing, *Maria Montessori: Her Life and Work* (New York: New American Library, 1984) and Rita Kramer, *Maria Montessori: A Biography* (New York: Putnam, 1976). In addition, several of the major organizations devoted to Montessori and the Montessori Method offer brief biographical sketches online, including the *Association Montessori Internationale* [AMI], http://www.montessori-ami.org/ami.htm, the American Montessori Society [AMS], http://www.amshq.org/montessori.htm, and the North American Montessori Teachers' Association [NAMTA], http://www.montessori-namta.org/home.html. Perhaps a reasonable—and readable—introduction to Montessorian views and methods is presented in John Chattin-McNichols, *The Montessori Controversy* (Clifton Park, NY: Delmar Publishers, 1991).

4. Maria Montessori, *The Absorbent Mind* (New York: Dell, 1984); *The Secret of Childhood* (Notre Dame, IN: Fides, 1966); and *The Discovery of the Child* (New York: Ballantine Books, 1986).
5. AMS, *AMS Philosophy and Practice*, http://www.amshq.org/print/montessori_philosophyPNT.htm.
6. *AMI*, http://www.montessori-ami.org/ami.htm.
7. Ibid.
8. NAMTA, http://www.montessori-namta.org/home.html.
9. Ibid.
10. Montessori, *The Absorbent Mind,* quoted in NAMTA, *The "Prepared Environment,"* the *Montessori Materials,* and *"Normalization,"* http://www.montessori-namta.org/generalinfo/terms.html.
11. Standing, quoted in NAMTA, *The "Prepared Environment,"* the *Montessori Materials,* and *"Normalization,"* http://www.montessori-namta.org/generalinfo/terms.html.
12. *AMI*, http://www.montessori-ami.org/ami.htm.
13. Ibid.; for an overview of the various levels of Montessorian education, see also http://www.montessori-namta.org/generalinfo/devcont.html.
14. Ibid.; see also http://www.amshq.org/montessori_philosophy.htm.
15. NAMTA, *What is NAMTA,* January 14, 2004, http://www.montessori-namta.org/generalinfo/devcont.html.
16. The conservative educational criticism literature is extensive, but classic examples include (among others): Susan Wise Bauer, *The Well-Educated Mind: A Guide to the Classical Education You Never Had* (New York: W. W. Norton, 2003); John E. Chubb and Terry M. Moe, *Politics, Markets and America's Schools* (Washington, DC: Brookings Institution, 1990); E. D. Hirsch, Jr., *Cultural Literacy: What Every American Needs to Know* (New York: Vintage, 1988) and *The Schools We Need and Why We Don't Have Them* (New York: Anchor, 1999); and Diane Ravitch, *Left Back: A Century of Failed School Reforms* (New York: Simon and Schuster, 2000).
17. Here, too, the relevant literature is immense, but for classic examples see (among others) Michael W. Apple, *Official Knowledge: Democratic Education in a Conservative Age* (New York: Routledge, 1999); Alfie Kohn, *The Schools Our Children Deserve: Moving Beyond Traditional Classrooms and "Tougher Standards"* (Boston: Houghton Mifflin, 1999) and *The Case against Standardized Testing: Raising the Scores, Ruining the Schools* (Portsmouth, NH: Heinemann, 2000); Ohanian, and Vinson and Ross, especially chapter three.
18. Vinson and Ross, see also David C. Berliner and Bruce J. Biddle, *The Manufactured Crisis: Myths, Fraud, and the Attack on America's Public Schools* (New York: Perseus, 1995).
19. See NAMTA, *Montessori: Creating a Paradigm Shift*, http://www.montessori-namta.org/generalinfo/paradigm.html.
20. See, for example, Vinson and Ross; Apple.
21. See NAMTA, *Montessori: Creating a Paradigm Shift*, http://www.montessori-namta.org/generalinfo/paradigm.html.

CHAPTER 8

1. All these issues are examined in depth in the companion to this volume: *De-*

fending Public Schools: The Nature and Limits of Standards-Based Reform and Assessment, ed. Sandra Mathison and E. Wayne Ross. (New York: Praeger, 2004).

2. See, for example, Bracey's chapter "International Assessment Studies: Findings, Critiques, and Imlications" in *Defending Public Schools: The Nature and Limits of Standards-Based Reform and Assessment.*

3. David C. Berliner and Bruce J. Biddle, *The Manufactured Crisis: Myths, Fraud, and the Attack on America's Public Schools* (Cambridge, MA: Perseus, 1995).

4. Susan Ohanian, *One Size Fits Few: The Folly of Educational Standards* (Portsmouth, NH: Heinemann, 1999).

5. See, for example, Sandra Mathison and E. Wayne Ross, "The Hegemony of Accountability in Schools and Universities," *Workplace: A Journal of Academic Labor* 5, no. 1 (October 2002), http://www.louisville.edu/journal/workplace/issue5p1/mathison.html.

6. Surely comparative test scores will enable us to verify disparities in achievement between and among different schools, districts, and states; these same scores will enable higher authorities to point a stiff finger at lower authorities for allowing "unequal teaching," but the solution for educational inequalities remains the political choice of those who control educational funding. So far, little has changed. In fact, an Appellate Court judge in New York State recently ruled that no change was necessary, as the *provision* of an eighth-grade education is sufficient governmental responsibility.

7. See the winter 2003 issue of *Teacher Education Quarterly* for a thorough examination and critique of the state regulation of teacher education in California, particularly articles by Christine Sleeter ("Reform and Control: An Analysis of SB 2042") and Ann Berlak ("Who's in Charge Here? Teacher Education and 2042"), http://www.calfac.org/teacher.html.

8. For an examination of various ways in which "militarization" and "corporatization" function in schools, see Kenneth J. Saltman and David A. Gabbard, eds., *Education as Enforcement: The Militarization and Corporatization of Schools* (New York: RoutledgeFalmer, 2003).

9. Rich Gibson, *The Fascist Origins of the SAT Test* (San Diego: San Diego State University, 2001), http:// www.rougeform.org; see also Sandra Mathison's chapter "A Short History of Educational Assessment and Standards-Based Educational Reform," in *Defending Public Schools: The Nature and Limits of Standards-Based Reform and Assessment.*

10. Stefan Kühl, *The Nazi Connection: Eugenics, American Racism, and German National Socialism* (New York: Oxford University Press, 1994).

11. Barry Mehler, "Eliminating the Inferior: American and Nazi Sterilization Programs," *Science for the People* (November/December 1987), pp. 14–18.

12. Gibson.

13. Robert J. Sternberg, "Ability and Expertise: It's Time to Replace the Current Model of Intelligence," *American Educator* (Spring 1999), pp. 10–12, 50–51.

14. Michael W. Apple, *Ideology and Curriculum* (New York: Routledge, Chapman and Hall, 1990).

15. D. David Noble, "The Corporate Roots of Science," in *Science and Liberation,* ed. Pat Brennan, Steve Cavrak, and Rita Arditti (Montreal: Black Rose Books, 1980), pp. 64–65.

16. Ibid., p. 65.

17. Ibid., p. 71.
18. Mann, quoted in Noble, p. 73.
19. Noble, p. 73.
20. Ibid., p. 74.
21. William Blum, *Killing Hope: U.S. Military and CIA Interventions since World War II* (Monroe, ME: Common Courage Press, 1995).
22. E. Wayne Ross, "Redrawing the Lines: The Case against Traditional Social Studies Instruction," in *Democratic Social Education: Social Studies for Social Change*, ed. David W. Hursh and E. Wayne Ross (New York: RoutledgeFalmer, 2000).
23. Sydney Lens, *The Military-Industrial Complex* (Philadelphia, PA: Pilgrim Press & Kansas City, MO: National Catholic Reporter, 1970).
24. Ibid., p. 23.
25. Ibid. p. 22.
26. Ibid., pp. 22–23.
27. James P. Shaver, O. L. Davis, Jr., and Suzanne W. Helburn, "The Status of Social Studies Education: Impressions from Three NSF Studies," *Social Education*, 43 (1979), pp. 150–53.
28. National Commission on Excellence in Education, *A Nation at Risk: The Imperatives for Educational Reform* (Washington, DC: U.S. Department of Education, 1983).
29. D. L. Clark and T. A. Astuto, "The Significance and Permanence of Changes in Federal Education Policy," *Educational Researcher* 15, no. 7 (1986), pp. 4–13.
30. See Barbara Miner, "National Education Summit," *Rethinking Schools* 14, no. 2 (Winter 1999/2000), pp. 3, 8.
31. E. Wayne Ross, "Resisting the Tyranny of Tests," *Z Magazine* 14, nos. 7/8 (July/August 2001), pp. 83–88, http://www.zmag.org/ZMag/articles/jul01ross.htm.
32. David W. Hursh, "Discourse, Power and Resistance in New York: The Rise of Testing and Accountability and the Decline of Teacher Professionalism and Local Control," in *Discourse, Power and Resistance: Challenging the Rhetoric of Contemporary Education*, ed. Jerome Satterthwaite, Elizabeth Atkinson, and Ken Gale (Stoke on Trent, UK: Trentham Books, 2003); David W. Hursh and Camille Martina, "Neoliberalism and Schooling in the U.S.: How State and Federal Government Education Policies Perpetuate Inequality," *Journal for Critical Education Policy Studies* 1, no. 2 (2003), http://www.jceps.com/?pageID=article&articleID=12.
33. See http://www.RougeForum.org.
34. See http://www.commonsenseineducation.org.
35. See http://www.timeoutfromtesting.org.
36. Michael W. Apple, *The State and the Politics of Knowledge* (New York: RoutledgeFalmer, 2003).
37. Ibid., p. 3.
38. This point is further exemplified by the lobbying attempts of Kati Haycock and the Education Trust to force higher education to adhere to established K–12 standards, an ironic twist from earlier times when colleges set the standards for the schools. See Kati Haycock, "The Role of Higher Education in The Standards Movement," in *1999 National Education Summit Briefing Book* (Washington, DC: Achieve, Inc., 1999), http://www.achieve.org/achieve/achievestart.nsf.

CHAPTER 9

1. Business Roundtable, *Continuing the Commitment: Essential Components of a Successful Education System* (Washington, DC: Business Roundtable, 1995), p. 1, http:// www.brtable.org.

2. Business Roundtable, *Workforce Training and Development for U.S. Competitiveness* (Washington, DC: Business Roundtable, 1995), p. 1, http://www.brtable.org.

3. *Report of the National Reading Panel: Teaching Children to Read: An Evidence-Based Assessment of the Scientific Research Literature on Reading and Its Implications for Reading Instruction* (Washington, DC: U.S. Department of Education, 2000); Duane Alexander (testimony before the Subcommittee on Labor, Health and Human Services, and Education of the Senate Appropriations Committee, U. S. Senate, 2000), http:// www.nichd.nih.gov.

4. Reid Lyon (testimony before the Subcommittee on Education Reform, Committee on Education and the Workforce, 2001), U.S. House of Representatives, http://www.edworkforce. house.gov.

5. Norman R. Augustine, Ed Lupberger, and James F. Orr III, *A Common Agenda for Improving American Education* (Washington, DC: Business Roundtable, 1996), p. 1, http://www.businessroundtable.org/search/index.aspx.

6. Report of the 21st Century Workforce Commission, *A Nation of Opportunity: Building America's 21st Century Workforce* (Washington, DC: U.S. Department of Labor, 2000).

7. Augustine, Lupberger, and Orr.

8. Norman R. Augustine, *A Business Leader's Guide to Setting Academic Standards* (Washington, DC: Business Roundtable, 1997), http://www.businessroundtable.org/publications.

9. "Business Group Is Force in Education," *The Baltimore Sun*, January 31, 1998, p. 1B.

10. Business Roundtable, *Workforce Training and Development for U.S. Competitiveness.*

11. Augustine.

12. Barbara Foorman and Jack M. Fletcher, "Correcting Errors," *Phi Delta Kappan* 84 (2003), p. 719.

13. Elaine M. Garan, *Resisting Reading Mandates: How to Triumph with the Truth* (Portsmouth, NH: Heinemann, 2002).

14. J. A. Krol, *Statement on Voluntary National Testing* (Washington, DC: Business Roundtable, 1998), http://www.brtable.org.

15. For an extensive discussion of this see Alan D. Flurkey and Jingguo Xu, eds., *On the Revolution of Reading: The Selected Writings of Kenneth S. Goodman* (Portsmouth, NH: Heinemann, 2003).

16. National Council of Teachers of English, *Position Statement on Reading* (Urbana, IL: NCTE, 2001), http://www.ncte.org/about/over/positions/level/gen/107666.htm; National Council of Teachers of English, *On Government Intrusion into Professional Decision Making* (Urbana, IL: NCTE, 1997), http://www.ncte.org/about/over/positions/category/gov/107476.htm.

17. Lyon's comments were made on November 18, 2002, as part of a major policy forum with U.S. Secretary of Education Rod Paige called "Rigorous Evidence: The

Key to Progress in Education?" A webcast of the panel, as well as transcripts of the panel, can be accessed at: http://www.excelgov.org.

CHAPTER 10

1. Magda Lewis and Barbara Karin, "Queer Stories/Straight Talk: Tales from the School Playground," *Theory Into Practice* 33, no. 3 (1994), p. 200.
2. Gay, Lesbian and Straight Education Network, "The 2003 National School Climate Survey," (Washington, D.C.: Author, 2003). All statistics in this paragraph are from this report.
3. Massachusetts Governor's Commission on Gay and Lesbian Youth, *Making School Safe for Gay and Lesbian Youth*, (Boston: 1993).
4. Robert Kourany, "Suicide among Homosexual Adolescents," *Journal of Homosexuality* 13, no. 4 (1987);, Gary Remafedi, "Risk Factors for Attempted Suicide in Gay and Bisexual Youth," *Pediatrics* 87, no. 6 (1991).
5. Deborah P. Britzman, *Lost Subjects, Contested Objects* (Albany, NY: State University of New York Press, 1998); Judith Butler, *Bodies That Matter: On the Discursive Limits of "Sex"* (New York: Routledge, 1993)..
6. Butler, *Bodies That Matter;* Judith P. Butler, *Gender Trouble: Feminism and the Subversion of Identity* (New York: Routledge, 1999); Linda J. Nicholson, *Feminism/Postmodernism (Thinking Gender)* (New York: Routledge, 1989).
7. R. W. Connell, *The Men and the Boys* (Cambridge, MA: Polity, 2000).
8. Margaret Smith Crocco, "The Missing Discourse about Gender and Sexuality in the Social Studies," *Theory Into Practice* 40, no. 1 (2001); Debbie Epstein, "Keeping Them in Their Place: Hetero/Sexist Harassment, Gender and the Enforcement of Heterosexuality," in *Sex, Sensibility and the Gendered Body*, ed. Janet Holland and L. Adkins (London: Macmillan, 1996).
9. Michael Warner and Social Text Collective., *Fear of a Queer Planet : Queer Politics and Social Theory, Cultural Politics*, vol. 6 (Minneapolis: University of Minnesota Press, 1993), p. xxi.
10. Dennis Sumara and Brent Davis, "Interrupting Heteronormativity: Toward a Queer Curriculum Theory," *Curriculum Inquiry* 29, no. 2 (1999), p. 193.
11. Mollie C. Blackburn, "Disrupting the (Hetero)Normative: Exploring Literacy Performances and Identity Work with Queer Youth," *Journal of Adolescent and Adult Literacy* 46, no. 4 (2002).
12. Butler, *Bodies That Matter.*
13. Crocco.
14. Sumara and Davis.

CHAPTER 11

1. For more information on the nature of this criticism, see A. R. Sadovnik, P. W. Cookson, and S. F. Semel, *Exploring Education: An Introduction to the Foundations of Education,* 2nd ed. (Boston: Allyn and Bacon, 2001); Joel Spring, *The American School 1642-2000,* 5th ed. (New York: McGraw-Hill, 2001); and Joel Spring, *American Education,* 10th ed. (New York: McGraw-Hill, 2002).
2. A. W. Jackson and G. A. Davis, *Turning Points 2000: Educating Adolescents*

in the 21st Century: A Report of the Carnegie Corporation of New York (New York: Teachers College Press, 2000).

3. C. M. Steele, "A Threat in the Air: How Stereotypes Shape Intellectual Identity and Performance," *American Psychologist* 52 (1997), pp. 613–29.

4. Gloria Ladson-Billings and B. Tate, "Toward a Critical Race Theory of Education," *Teachers College Record* 97, no. 1 (1995), pp. 47–67.

5. D. Y. Ford, *Reversing Underachievement among Gifted Black Students: Promising Practices and Programs* (New York: Teachers College Press, 1996), p. 5.

6. W.E.B. Dubois, *The Souls of Black Folk* (New York: Modern Library, 2003).

7. Carter G. Woodson, *The Mis-Education of the Negro* (New York: Hakims, 1993, reprint 1933).

8. J. E. Hale, *Learning While Black: Creating Educational Excellence for African-American Children* (Baltimore: Johns Hopkins, 2001).

9. Ladson-Billings and Tate.

10. D. Bell, *Faces at the Bottom of the Well: The Permanence of Racism* (New York: Basic Books, 1992).

11. Gloria Ladson-Billings, "Just What Is Critical Race Theory and What's It Doing in a Nice Field Like Education?" *Qualitative Studies in Education* 11, no. 1 (1998), pp. 7–24.

12. Ladson-Billings and Tate; W. F. Tate, "Critical Race Theory and Education: History, Theory, and Implications," *Review of Research in Education* 22 (1997), pp. 195–247.

13. Ladson-Billings and Tate"; Cornel West, *Race Matters* (Boston: Beacon Press, 1993).

14. J. C. Bruce, "Why and How We Teach the Negro about Himself in the Washington Public Schools," *Journal of Negro Education* 22, no. 1 (1937), pp. 38–43.

15. H. Richard Milner, "A Case Study of an African-American English Teacher's Cultural Comprehensive Knowledge and (Self) Reflective Planning," *Journal of Curriculum and Supervision* 18, no. 2 (2003), pp. 175–96; H. Richard Milner, "Teacher Reflection and Race in Cultural Contexts: History, Meaning, and Methods in Teaching," *Theory into Practice* 42, no. 3 (2003), pp. 170–72; and H. Richard Milner, "Reflection, Racial Competence, and Critical Pedagogy: How Do We Prepare Preservice Teachers to Pose Tough Questions?" *Race, Ethnicity, and Education* 6, no. 2 (2003), pp. 193–208.

16. Lee S. Shulman, "Knowledge and Teaching: Foundations of the New Reform," *Harvard Educational Review* 19, no. 2 (1987), pp. 4–14.

17. Milner, "A Case Study of an African-American English Teacher's Cultural Comprehensive Knowledge and (Self) Reflective Planning."

18. G. McCutcheon, *Developing the Curriculum: Solo and Group Deliberation* (Troy, NY: Educators' Press International, 2002); and William H. Schubert, *Curriculum: Perspectives, Paradigms, and Possibilities* (New York: Macmillan, 1986).

19. Milner, "Teacher Reflection and Race in Cultural Contexts."

20. James A. Banks and Cherry A. M. Banks, *Multicultural Education: Issues and Perspectives,* 4th ed. (New York: Wiley, 2000); and G. Gay and T. Howard, "Multicultural Teacher Education for the 21st Century," *The Teacher Educator* 35, no. 1 (2000), pp. 1–16.

21. R. Burke-Spero, "Toward a Model of 'CIVITAS' through an Ethic of Care: A Qualitative Study of Preservice Teachers' Perceptions about Learning to Teach Diverse Student Populations" (Ph.D. diss., The Ohio State University, 1999); and Milner, "Reflection, Racial Competence, and Critical Pedagogy."

22. J. E. Helms, *Black and White Racial Identity: Theory, Research, and Practice* (New York: Greenwood Press, 1990); J. E. Helms, "An Update of Helms's White and People of Color Racial Identity Models," in *Handbook of Multicultural Counseling*, eds. J. G. Ponterotto, J. M. Casas, L. A. Suzuki, and C. M. Alexander (Thousand Oaks, CA: Sage); and J. E. Helms and R. T. Carter, "Development of the White Racial Identity Attitude Inventory," in *Black and White Racial Identity Inventory: Theory, Research, and Practice*, ed. J. E. Helms (Westport, CT: Greenwood, 1990).

23. W. Rowe, S. K. Bennett, and D. R. Atkinson, "White Racial Identity Models: A Critique and Alternative Proposals," *The Counseling Psychologist* 22 (1994), pp. 129–46.

24. W. E. Cross, "The Psychology of Nigresence: Revising the Cross Model," in *Handbook of Multicultural Counseling*, eds. J. G. Ponterotto, J. M. Casas, L. A. Suzuki, and C. M. Alexander (Thousand Oaks, CA: Sage, 1995).

25. Ford; bell hooks, *Teaching to Transgress: Education as the Practice of Freedom* (New York: Routledge, 1994).

26. C. B. Dillard, "Cultural Consideration in Paradigm Proliferation." Paper presented at the annual meeting of the American Educational Research Association, New Orleans, April 24–28, 2000.

27. Michael W. Apple and N. King, "Economics and Control in Everyday School Life," in *Ideology and Curriculum*, ed. Michael W. Apple (New York: Routledge, 1990), 43–60.

28. Paulo Freire, *Pedagogy of the Oppressed* (New York: Continuum, 1970).

29. Dillard.

30. Milner, "Teacher Reflection and Race in Cultural Contexts."

31. Ford.

32. Ralph Ellison, *Invisible Man* (New York: Vintage, 1947), p. 4.

33. Bruce, p. 41.

34. Ford, *Reversing Underachievement Among Gifted Black Students*, p. 84.

35. Gloria Ladson-Billings, *The Dreamkeepers: Successful Teachers of African-American Children* (San Francisco: Jossey-Bass, 1994); M. Foster, *Black Teachers on Teaching* (New York: New Press, 1997); and J. A. Irvine and D. E. York, "Learning Styles and Culturally Diverse Students: A Literature Review," in *Handbook of Research on Multicultural Education*, eds. J. A. Banks and C. A. M. Banks (New York: Simon & Schuster/Macmillan, 1995).

36. C. M. Steele, "A Threat in the Air: How Stereotypes Shape Intellectual Identity and Performance," *American Psychologist* 52 (1997), pp. 613–29.

37. J. G. Ponterotto and P. D. Pederson, *Preventing Prejudice: A Guide for Counselors and Educators* (Thousand Oaks, CA: Sage, 1993).

38. Dillard.

39. Hooks, p. 84.

40. Ford; Hale; and H. R. Milner, "Affective and Social Issues among High-Achieving African-American Students: Recommendations for Teachers and Teacher Education," *Action in Teacher Education* 24, no. 1 (2002), pp. 81–89.

CHAPTER 12

1. Portions of the text of this chapter were adapted from Marc's article, "Paulo Freire and Critical Multicultural Social Studies: One Case from the Teacher Education Borderlands," which appeared in 2003 in *Taboo: The Journal of Culture and Education.*

2. Paulo Freire, *Pedagogy of the Oppressed* (New York: Continuum, 1970).

3. These experiences, these "data" (which were collected among TEP university students through interviews and open-ended surveys and final course evaluations) are part of a larger study we are conducting—"Contextualizing the Social Studies: *Un caso fronterizo*"—among preservice teachers, secondary social studies/history teachers and students, elementary teachers, and students and local activists. We have envisioned and are conducting this as a *community case study* in our México/United States border town that is focusing on participants' understandings, applications, and aspirations regarding the social studies in general and "critical multicultural social studies" in particular. See, e.g., Curry Malott and Marc Pruyn, "'Dirty Music,' 'Extreme Profanity' and 'Questionable Activities': A Case Study of Three Christian Fundamentalist Teacher Education Students." Paper presented at the College and University Faculty Assembly of the National Council for the Social Studies, Washington, DC, November 14–18, 2001.

4. Freire, *Letters to Cristina* (New York: Routledge, 1996); *Pedagogy of the Heart* (New York and London: Continuum, 1998); *Pedagogy of Freedom: Ethics, Democracy, and Civic Courage* (Landham, MD: Rowman & Littlefield, 2000), reprint; and *Teachers as Cultural Workers* (Boulder, CO: Westview Press, 1998).

5. Peter McLaren, *Life in Schools: An Introduction to Critical Pedagogy in the Foundations of Education* (New York: Longman, 1989).

6. M. Torrez, *Educación Popular: Un Encuentro con Paulo Freire* (Quito, Ecuador: Corporación Ecuatoriana para el Desarrollo de la Comunicación, 1986).

7. Freire's use of "man," "he," and "his" throughout *Pedagogy of the Oppressed* should not go without comment. This usage uncritically reflected the dominant linguistic patriarchal hegemony of the day. In most of his prodigious work since, however, this language has been changed to "humankind," "she/he," and "their," reflecting Freire's—and most theorists' on the left—growing understandings of gender oppression.

8. Freire, *Pedagogy of the Oppressed*, p. 28.

9. Paulo Freire and Donaldo Macedo, *Literacy: Reading the Word and Reading the World* (South Hadley: Bergin & Garvey, 1987), p. 35.

10. Freire and Macedo, p. 27.

11. McLaren, p. 196.

12. See Myra Bergman Ramos's translator's note from Freire, *Pedagogy of the Oppressed*, p. 19; also Freire and Macedo, p. 49.

13. Freire and Macedo.

14. Leslie R. Bloom, "The Politics of Difference and Multicultural Feminism: Reconceptualizing Education for Democracy," *Theory & Research in Social Education* 26, no. 1 (1998), pp. 30–49; Rudolfo Chávez Chávez and Jim O'Donnell, *Speaking the Unpleasant: The Politics of (Non)Engagement in the Multicultural Educational Terrain* (Albany: State University of New York Press, 1998); Rich Gibson, "Paulo Freire and Pedagogy for Social Justice," *Theory & Research in Social Educa-*

tion 27, no. 2 (1999), pp. 129–59; Colin Green, "La Guerra: Struggles in Living and Teaching Critical Pedagogy," *Theory & Research in Social Education* 29, no. 1 (1999), pp. 166–80; David W. Hursh and E. Wayne Ross, eds., *Democratic Social Education: Social Studies for Social Change* (New York: RoutledgeFalmer, 2000); James Loewen, *Lies My Teacher Told Me: Everything Your American History Textbook Got Wrong* (New York: Touchstone, 1995); Valerie Ooka Pang, Juan Rivera, and Maureen Gillette, "Can CUFA Be a Leader in the National Debate on Racism?" *Theory & Research in Social Education* 26, no. 3 (1998), 430–36; Avner Segall, "Critical History: Implications for History/Social Studies Education," *Theory & Research in Social Education* 27, no. 3 (1999), 358–74; Kevin D. Vinson, "National Curriculum Standards and Social Studies Education: Dewey, Freire, Foucault, and the Construction of a Radical Critique," *Theory & Research in Social Education* 27, no. 3 (1999), pp. 296–328; Kevin D. Vinson, "Connected Citizenship," *Theory & Research in Social Education* 29, no. 3 (2001), pp. 400–4.

15. A notable exception is the intellectual space created by editor E. Wayne Ross (coeditor of this volume) in the journal *Theory & Research in Social Education* (a publication of the College and University Faculty Assembly, CUFA, of the National Council for the Social Studies, NCSS), from the mid-1990s through 2001.

16. Another notable exception to this general rule, in our estimation, is the Commission of Social Justice in Teacher Education—of which Marc is a member. This Commission was formed by former Presidents Edi Guyton of the Association of Teacher Educators (ATE) and Susan Adler of the NCSS, respectively. This ATE and NCSS Commission is cochaired by Rudolfo Chávez Chávez, who is a professor at New México State University and a member of the ATE, and Richard Deim, a professor at the University of Texas at San Antonio and another former president of the NCSS. Recent years have also seen the formation of the Committee for Diversity and Social Justice within the CUFA of the NCSS, although its formation was membership-driven.

17. Roberta Alquist, "Critical Pedagogy for Social Studies Teachers," *Social Studies Review* 29, no. 3 (1990), pp. 53–57; Joe L. Kincheloe, *Toward a Critical Politics of Teacher Thinking: Mapping the Postmodern* (Westport: Bergin & Garvey, 1993); Peter McLaren, *Critical Pedagogy and Predatory Culture: Oppositional Politics in a Postmodern Era* (London: Routledge, 1995); Peter McLaren, *Revolutionary Multiculturalism: Pedagogies of Dissent for the New Millennium* (Boulder: Westview, 1997); Sonia Nieto, *Affirming Diversity: The Sociopolitical Context of Multicultural Education* (White Plains: Longman, 1996); Christine Sleeter, *Culture, Difference and Power* (New York: Teachers College Press, 2001).

18. While criticalists, ourselves included, might label this position "mainstream"—that is, one that does not actively seek to disrupt hegemonic structures of power—it is important to note that this definition of what constitutes "social studies" is probably ascribed to by a majority of the NCSS's predominantly secondary social studies/history, white, middle-class, public school teacher membership, despite what progressive elements within the organization's leadership might prefer.

19. National Council for the Social Studies, "What Is Social Studies?" in *Curriculum Standards for Social Studies* (Washington, DC: National Council for the Social Studies, 1996).

20. Freire, *Pedagogy of the Oppressed*; Antonio Gramsci, *Selections from the Prison Notebooks*, ed. and trans. Q. Medea and N. Smith (London: Lawrence & Wishart,

1971); McLaren, *Critical Pedagogy and Predatory Culture*; McLaren, *Revolutionary Multiculturalism*; Nieto; Sleeter, *Culture, Difference and Power*; Christine Sleeter, *Multicultural Education as Social Activism* (Albany: State University of New York Press, 1996).

21. For a more elaborate discussion of some of these notions, see, for example, Marc Pruyn, *Discourse Wars in Gotham-West: A Latino Immigrant Urban Tale of Resistance and Agency* (Boulder: Westview, 1999).

22. Alquist, p. 56.

23. Betty Poindexter and Herb Korra, "Practicing Democracy through Equity Education: Social Studies Curriculum Grades K–12, 1991–1997," ERIC document no. ED350206 (Indianapolis: Warren Township Independent School District, 1997).

24. Peter Seixas, "From Social Studies to Cultural Studies." Paper presented at the Annual Meeting of the American Educational Research Association, Chicago, 1997; Stuart Hall, "Cultural Studies and Its Theoretical Legacies," in *Cultural Studies*, ed. Lawrence Grossberg, Cary Nelson, and Paula A. Treichler (New York: Routledge, 1992).

25. Joe L. Kincheloe, *Getting Beyond the Facts: Teaching Social Studies/Social Sciences in the Twenty-First Century*, 2nd ed. (New York: Peter Lang, 2001); E. Wayne Ross, *The Social Studies Curriculum: Purposes, Problems and Possibilities*, rev. ed. (Albany: State University of New York Press, 2001); Hursh and Ross.

26. Neil O. Houser, "Multicultural Literature, Equity Education, and the Social Studies," *Multicultural Education* 4, no. 4 (1997), pp. 9–12.

27. Charles Titus, "Social Studies Teachers and Multicultural Education: A Pilot Study of Attitudes, Practices, and Constraints," ERIC Document no. ED 366 516, 1992; Marilynne Boyle-Baise, "Multicultural Social Studies: Ideology and Practice," *Social Studies* 87, no. 2 (1996), pp. 81–87.

28. Jack Nelson, "Curmudgeons and Critics: Does Social Studies Education Need Any More? Or Dare the Social Education Professors Build a New Social Studies?" Paper presented at the Annual Meeting of the American Educational Research Association, Chicago, 1997.

29. The examples from this section are drawn from the data of a larger study (discussed earlier) being conducted among the preservice teachers in Marc's classroom.

30. William Bigelow, "Once upon a Genocide: Christopher Columbus in Children's Literature," *Language Arts* 69, no. 2 (1992), pp. 112–20; Kincheloe; Loewen; Howard Zinn, *A People's History of the United States: 1492–Present* (New York: HarperPerennial, 1995).

31. William Bigelow, "Social Studies Standards For What?" *Rethinking Schools* 16, no. 4 (2002).

32. Ira Shor, *Empowering Education: Critical Teaching for Social Change* (Chicago: University of Chicago Press, 1992).

33. Howard Zinn, *A People's History of the United States: 1492–Present: Abridged Teaching Addition* (New York: New Press, 1997).

34. Freire, *Pedagogy of the Oppressed*, p. 31.

CHAPTER 13

1. Kevin D. Vinson and E. Wayne Ross, "In Search of the Social Studies Curriculum: Standardization, Diversity, and a Conflict of Appearances," in *Critical Is-*

sues in Social Studies Research for the 21st Century, ed. William B. Stanley (Greenwich, CT: Information Age Publishing, 2001), pp. 39–71; Michael W. Apple, *Democratic Education in a Conservative Age* (New York: Routledge, 1993) and *Cultural Politics and Education* (New York: Teachers College Press, 1996).

2. Herbert M. Kliebard, *The Struggle for the American Curriculum, 1893–1958* (Boston: Routledge and Kegan Paul, 1986).

3. B. P. Fowler, "President's Message," *Progressive Education* 7, no. 4 (1930), p. 159.

4. George S. Counts, *Dare the School Build a New Social Order* (New York: John Day, 1932), pp. 45–47.

5. Ibid., pp. 5–8.

6. Ibid., pp. 9–12.

7. William B. Stanley, *Curriculum for Utopia: Social Reconstructionism and Critical Pedagogy in the Postmodern Era* (Albany: SUNY Press, 1992).

8. Michel Foucault, *Power/Knowledge: Selected Interviews and Other Writings, 1972–1977*, ed. Colin Gordon (New York: Pantheon, 1980).

9. James P. Gee, *The Social Mind: Language, Ideology, and Social Practice* (South Hadley, MA: Bergin & Garvey, 1992), p. 142.

10. M. Cochran-Smith and M. K. Fries, "Sticks, Stones, and Ideology: The Discourse of Reform in Teacher Education," *Educational Researcher* 30, no. 8 (2001), pp. 3–15.

11. Stanley.

12. James A. Whitson and William B. Stanley, "Re-Minding Education for Democracy," in *Educating the Democratic Mind*, ed. Walter C. Parker (Albany: State University of New York Press, 1996), pp. 309–36.

13. Cochran-Smith and Fries; and L. Simcox, *Whose History: The Struggle for National Standards in American Classrooms* (New York: Teachers College Press, 2002).

14. S. H. Engle and A. S. Ochoa, *Education for Democratic Citizenship: Decision Making in the Social Studies* (New York: Teachers College Press, 1988); David Hill, Peter McLaren, Michael Cole, and Glenn Rikowski, eds., *Marxism Against Postmodernism in Educational Theory* (New York: Lexington, 2002).

15. Stanley, *Curriculum for Utopia*.

16. Ronald W. Evans, *The Social Studies Wars* (New York: Teachers College Press, 2004).

17. John Dewey, "Education and Social Change," *The Social Frontier* 3, no. 26 (1937), p. 236.

18. John Dewey, "Can Education Share in the Social Reconstruction," *The Social Frontier* 1, no. 1 (1934), p. 11.

19. John Dewey and John L. Childs, "The Social-Economic Situation and Education," in *Educational Frontier*, ed. William H. Kilpatrick (New York: D. Appleton-Century, 1933), pp. 318–19.

20. See Henry A. Giroux, *Schooling and the Struggle for Public Life: Critical Pedagogy in the Modern Age* (Minneapolis: University of Minnesota, 1988) and *Teachers as Intellectuals: Toward a Critical Pedagogy of Learning*, rev. ed. (South Hadley, MA: Bergin & Garvey, 1988); Evans; John Dewey, *Experience and Education* (New York: Collier, 1938).

21. See here, especially, Richard Rorty, *Contingency, Irony, and Solidarity* (Cam-

bridge: Cambridge University Press, 1989) and *Philosophy and the Mirror of Nature* (Princeton: Princeton University Press, 1981).

22. John Dewey, "The Need for Orientation," *Forum* 93, no. 6 (1935), p. 334.

23. Dewey and Childs, p. 71.

24. John Dewey, "Education and Social Change," *The Social Frontier* 2, no. 26 (1937), pp. 235–38.

25. Ibid., p. 235.

26. Ibid., p. 236.

27. John Dewey, "The Crucial Role of Intelligence," *The Social Frontier* 1, no. 5 (1935), p. 9.

28. Ibid.

29. Dewey, "Education and Social Change," p. 238.

30. Ibid.

31. Dewey and Childs, p. 72.

32. Ira Shor, *Culture Wars* (Boston: Routledge, 1986); John Goodlad, *A Place Called School* (New York: McGraw-Hill, 1984).

33. Simcox.

34. National Commission on Excellence in Education (NCEE), *A Nation at Risk* (Washington: USGPO, 1983).

35. Simcox; David Berliner and Bruce J. Biddle, *The Manufactured Crisis: Myths, Fraud, and the Attack on America's Public Schools* (Reading, MA: Addison-Wesley); NCEE, p. 5.

36. p. 5.

37. Simcox.

38. Dale Ballou and Michael Podgursky, "Reforming Teacher Preparation and Licensing: What Is the Evidence?" *Teachers College Record* 102, no. 1 (2000), pp. 5–27.

39. D. T. Gordon, ed., *A Nation Reformed: American Education 20 Years after "A Nation at Risk"* (Cambridge, MA: Harvard University Press, 2003); D. Ballou and M. Podgursky, "Teacher Training and Licensure: A Layman's Guide," in *Better Teachers, Better Schools*, ed. M. Kanstoroom and C. Finn (Washington: The Thomas Fordham Foundation, 1999), pp. 31–82; and Paul E. Petersen, ed., *Our Schools and Our Future: Are We Still at Risk?* (Stanford: Hoover Institution Press, 2003).

40. Simcox, p. 50.

41. William S. Lind and William H. Marshner, *Cultural Conservatism: Toward a New National Agenda* (New York: Rowman & Littlefield, 1988).

42. Frederic Hayek, *The Road to Serfdom* (London: Routledge, 1944) and *The Constitution of Liberty* (London: Routledge, 1960); Milton Friedman, *Capitalism and Freedom* (Chicago: University of Chicago Press, 1962).

43. Hayek, *The Constitution of Liberty*, p. 387.

44. Walter Lippman, *Public Opinion* (New York: Macmillan, 1950).

45. Robert Westbrook, *John Dewey and American Democracy* (Ithaca, NY: Cornell University Press, 1991).

46. Gerald Posner, *Law, Pragmatism, and Democracy* (Cambridge, MA: Harvard University Press, 2003).

47. Benjamin Barber, *Strong Democracy* (Berkeley: University of California Press, 1984); Walter C. Parker, *Teaching Democracy* (New York: Teachers College Press, 2003).

48. James S. Leming, "The Two Cultures of Social Studies Education," *Social Education* 53, no. 6 (1989), pp. 404–8; James S. Leming, "Ideological Perspectives within the Social Studies Profession: An Empirical Examination of the Two Cultures Thesis," *Theory and Research in Social Education* 20, no. 3 (1992), pp. 293–312; James S. Leming, "Correct, But Not Politically Correct? A Response to Parker," *Theory and Research in Social Education* 20, no. 4 (1992), pp. 500–6.

49. James S. Leming, L. Ellington, and K. Porter, eds., *Where Did the Social Studies Go Wrong?* (Dayton, OH: Thomas B. Fordham Foundation, 2003).

50. James S. Leming, "Ignorant Activists," in *Where Did Social Studies Go Wrong?* ed. James S. Leming, Lucien Ellington, and Kathleen Porter (Washington, DC: Thomas B. Fordham Foundation, 2003).

51. Leming, "Correct, But Not Politically Correct?"

52. Ibid.

53. Leming, "Ignorant Activists."

54. Patricia M. King and Karen Strohm Kitchener, *Developing Reflective Judgment: Understanding and Promoting Intellectual Growth and Critical Thinking in Adolescents and Adults* (San Francisco, CA: Jossey-Bass, 1994); Patricia M. King and Karen Strohm Kitchener, "Reflective Judgment: Concepts of Justification and Their Relationship to Age and Education," *Journal of Applied Developmental Psychology* 2 (1981), pp. 89–116; Patricia M. King and Karen Strohm Kitchener, *Reflective Judgment Scoring Manual* (Denver, CO and Bowling Green, OH: University of Denver and Bowling Green State University, 1985).

55. Leming, "Ideological Perspectives within the Social Studies Profession," p. 310.

56. Leming, "Ignorant Activists," p. 134.

57. Ernest R. House, *Schools for Sale* (New York: Teachers College Press, 1998).

58. Leming, Ellington, and Porter; Evans.

59. Evans, *The Social Studies Wars.*

60. Walter C. Parker, *Teaching Democracy: Unity and Diversity in Public Life* (New York: Teachers College Press, 2003).

61. Berliner and Biddle; Evans; William Stanley and Hope Longwell-Grice, "Ideology, Power, and Control in Teacher Education," in *Critical Issues in Social Studies Teacher Preparation*, ed. Susan Adler (Greenwich, CT: Information Age Publishing, in press); Kevin D. Vinson and E. Wayne Ross, *Image and Education: Teaching in the Face of the New Disciplinarity* (New York: Peter Lang, 2003).

62. Vinson and Ross, *Image and Education.*

63. Stanley.

64. James P. Gee, *The Social Mind* (New York: Bergin and Garvey, 1992).

65. Whitson and Stanley.

66. C. Wright Mills, *The Sociological Imagination* (New York: Oxford University Press, 1959).

Index

About the Editors

KEVIN D. VINSON is Assistant Professor of Teaching and Teacher Education at the University of Arizona. He received his Ph.D. in Curriculum and Instruction, with a specialization in Social Studies Education, from the University of Maryland. Currently, his work focuses on the philosophical and theoretical contexts of social studies, especially with respect to questions of power, image, culture, standardization, diversity, and social justice, as well as on the meaning and relevance of the philosophies of Michel Foucault and Guy Debord vis-à-vis the potential social and pedagogical relationships among surveillance, spectacle, image, and disciplinarity. His research has appeared in *Theory and Research in Social Education, The Social Studies,* and *Social Education,* and has been presented at the annual meetings of the American Educational Research Association, the American Educational Studies Association, and the National Council for the Social Studies. He has contributed chapters to such books as *The Social Studies Curriculum: Purposes, Problems, and Possibilities* (edited by E. Wayne Ross); *Critical Issues in Social Studies Research for the 21st Century* (edited by William Stanley); and *Education as Enforcement: The Militarization and Corporatization of Schools* (edited by Kenneth Saltman and David Gabbard). He recently published his first book (with E. Wayne Ross), entitled *Image and Education: Teaching in the Face of the New Disciplinarity.*

E. WAYNE ROSS is Professor in the Department of Curriculum Studies at the University of British Columbia in Vancouver, Canada. He is a former secondary social studies and day care teacher in North Carolina and Georgia and has held faculty appointments at the University of Louisville and the State University of New York campuses at Albany and Binghamton. Ross is the author of numerous articles and reviews on issues of curriculum theory and practice, teacher education, and the politics of education. His books include *Image and Education* (with Kevin D. Vinson), *The Social Studies Curriculum*, and *Democratic Social Education* (with David W. Hursh). He is the cofounder of The Rouge Forum, a group of educators, parents, and students working for more democratic schools and society, and the general editor of *Defending Public Schools*.

About the Contributors

CYNTHIA O. ANHALT received her Ph.D. from the University of Arizona in Teaching and Teacher Education with an emphasis in mathematics education and a minor in mathematics. Anhalt was a K–8 teacher in public schools for ten years. Her research participation has included Mathematics Intervention for Children ages five to fifteen with leukemia (project funded by the National Cancer Institute [NCI] and National Institute of Nursing Research [NINR]); Transition Toward Algebra (T^2A) Project designed for mathematics teachers of grades five to nine; and Mathematics and Parent Partnership in the Southwest (MAPPS) funded by the National Science Foundation (NSF). She has published articles with the National Council of Teachers of Mathematics (NCTM), the *Journal of Latinos and Education (JLE),* and the Research Council on Mathematics Learning (RCML). She has presented her work at annual meetings of the NCTM and the American Educational Research Association. Her research interests emphasize preservice teachers' conceptual understandings of mathematics and their use of mathematical representations when designing lesson plans.

LEON D. CALDWELL, Ph.D., is an Assistant Professor of Educational Psychology at the University of Nebraska, Lincoln. His research is in the area of school and community-based prevention and health promotion interventions for African-American and economically disadvantaged adolescents. He has published in the areas of African and African-American psychology, educational achievement motivation, and counseling psychology. Dr. Caldwell has also written and lectured internationally on the topics of student development and mental health. He teaches a summer exchange course in Ghana, West Africa, at the University of Winneba. He is a graduate of Penn State (Ph.D., Counseling Psychology) and Lehigh University (M.Ed., Secondary School Counseling, B.A., Economics).

STEPHEN C. FLEURY is Professor of Education at Le Moyne College in Syracuse, New York and codirector of the Syracuse Center for Urban Education. The themes of his professional writings and academic activities are in science, social studies, and teacher and urban education and emanate from his interests in the relationships between "how one knows and how one lives," relationships that necessarily entail personal, social, cultural, and political factors in their production and reproduction in the contexts of schooling.

FOUR ARROWS, aka Don Trent Jacobs, is Associate Professor at Northern Arizona University and a faculty member at Fielding Graduate Institute. He was formerly Dean of Education at Oglala Lakota College on the Pine Ridge Indian Reservation. His books include *Indigenous Worldviews: First Nations Scholars Challenge Anti-Indian Hegemony, American Assassination: The Strange Death of Senator Paul Wellstone, Teaching Virtues: Building Character across the Curriculum, The Bum's Rush: The Selling of Environmental Backlash,* and *Primal Awareness.*

ROB HAWORTH is a doctoral student at New México State University. Currently, he is an instructor for the elementary and secondary social studies methods courses in the Teacher Education Program. His areas of research include: youth culture, critical pedagogy, youth resistance, and globalization and anarchist pedagogy.

RITA L. IRWIN is Professor of Curriculum Studies and Art Education and Head of the Department of Curriculum Studies at the University of British Columbia, Vancouver, BC, Canada. Her most recent work combines her longstanding interest in qualitative forms of research with understanding pedagogy through self-study and a/r/tography (a methodology that unites image and text through theory, practice, and research). She is an artist, researcher, and teacher who is committed to the arts as living inquiry. As such, she continues to create art, conduct research, and practice her pedagogy in ways that are integrative, reflective, and full of living awareness.

BRUCE JOHNSON is Assistant Professor in the Department of Teaching and Teacher Education, Associate Faculty in the College of Science Teacher Preparation Program, and director of the Earth Education Research and

Evaluation Team at the University of Arizona. He teaches courses in elementary science methods, adolescent development and learning theory, environmental learning, and cognition in science education. Dr. Johnson began his teaching career as a middle school teacher, focusing on both science and mathematics. He later taught in an elementary school where his focus was on science for students in the upper grades. In addition, he served as an outdoor school director for several years. Johnson's research focuses on two areas of science education: classroom learning environments (including the perceptions of students and teachers) and environmental learning (including teacher and student understanding of ecological concepts).

LISA W. LOUTZENHEISER is Assistant Professor in the Department of Curriculum Studies at the University of British Columbia. Prior to pursing a doctorate, she taught in public alternative schools. She combines a fascination with curriculum, queer/gender, and poststructural theories, as well as the intersections of race, gender, and sexuality in schooling to look at the experiences of marginalized youth. A second strand of her research and activism flows from the statements of youth in alternative settings that they learn best when strong connections are made with teachers and with their own lives and identities. Therefore, she is also interested in exploring how sometimes difficult and controversial issues, such as heteronormativity and racism, can be brought into both K–12 and teacher education courses.

PERRY M. MARKER, Ph.D., has taught secondary social studies in Ohio, and he currently teaches social studies teacher education, curriculum theory and research, and history and philosophy of education in the School of Education at Sonoma State University, California, where he is professor and chairman of the Department of Curriculum Studies and Secondary Education. He was awarded a Fulbright Scholarship to study the history, education, and culture of Brazil in 1987. He has made presentations at international, national, and state conferences, coauthored a social studies methods textbook, and has written numerous articles related to democratic education and the ideas of Paulo Freire.

H. RICHARD MILNER, Ph.D., is an Assistant Professor in the Department of Teaching and Learning at Peabody College of Vanderbilt University. His research interests concern three interrelated areas: Curriculum Theory and Research, Academic Achievement, and Cultural and Racial Diversity. His work has appeared in *Teaching and Teacher Education, Race, Ethnicity and Education, the Journal of Curriculum and Supervision, Journal of Negro Education, Theory into Practice, The High School Journal, Teachers and Teaching: Theory and Practice, Journal of Critical Inquiry into Curriculum and Instruction, Action in Teacher Education, Teacher Education and Practice, Gifted*

Child Quarterly, and *Teaching Education*. He earned Ph.D. and a M.A. (Curriculum Studies) from Ohio State University, and an M.A.T. and a B.A. (English) from South Carolina State University.

IRA E. MURRAY is a graduate student in Human, Organizational, and Community Development at Peabody College of Vanderbilt University. His research interests focus on community development in disadvantaged areas. Originally from Columbia, South Carolina, he is a graduate of Florida A&M University.

ELIZABETH OBERLE began her Montessori experiences at the age of three in a Montessori school attached to the State University of New York at Stony Brook. She received her Montessori Children's House (three to six years) certificate through AMI–St. Louis Training Centre in 1994 and her master's degree from Loyola College in Baltimore in 1995. She has been teaching in the public Montessori system of the Kansas City School District since 1993.

MARC PRUYN earned his Ph.D. in curriculum at UCLA, and now works at New México State University as an associate professor of Social Studies Education and as the director of Elementary Education. His research interests include exploring the connections among education for social justice, multiculturalism, critical pedagogy and theory, and the social studies in the Chihuahuan Borderlands and beyond. His areas of expertise include curriculum theory, educational foundations, and research methodologies.

ELISABETH ROBERTS is a Ph.D. student at the University of Arizona and is a member of the Earth Education Research and Evaluation Team. As a research associate with MJ Young and Associates and WestEd, she conducted national program evaluations and teacher professional development for the NSF and U.S. Department of Education, and was a fellow in NSF's National Academy for Science and Mathematics Education Leadership. At TERC in Cambridge, Massachusetts, Roberts was a member of the team that created the *National Geographic Kids Network*, *IBM Personal Science Laboratory*, and *TableTop* and *TableTop Jr.* software and curriculum. She is a co-author of *Hands on Elementary Science*, a program that introduces elementary teachers to inquiry science and technology. Her research at TERC investigated how teachers used technology to support data collection and analysis and build learning communities. She currently studies how visual representations of ecology concepts, such as systems, contribute to students' cognition.

MARTHA RAPP RUDDELL is currently Interim Dean of the School of Education, Sonoma State University in Rohnert Park, California. Previously she taught in the secondary teaching credential program and the graduate Reading and Language advanced credential and degree programs. Ruddell taught for ten years in both rural and city schools in Missouri and Kansas. She is author of numerous articles and book chapters and a text about adolescent literacy titled *Teaching Content Reading and Writing* that is now in its fourth edition. She is past president of the National Reading Conference, an international educational organization devoted to research in language and literacy. In 1996, she was inducted into the California Reading Association Reading Hall of Fame, and in 2003 she was honored with the Albert J. Kingston Service Award of the National Reading Conference.

REBECCA SÁNCHEZ is a doctoral student in the Department of Curriculum and Instruction at New México State University. Her area of specialization is critical pedagogy. Her research interests include critical theory, teacher education, and social justice issues in education. She is the program coordinator for Project Literacy, a program dedicated to recruiting, retaining, and funding Borderlands teachers for M.A. degrees in bilingual education and TESOL.

WILLIAM B. STANLEY currently serves as Dean of Education at Monmouth University in New Jersey. He is a former social studies teacher who taught for fourteen years before moving on to higher education. He received a doctorate in Curriculum and Instruction from Rutgers University and has taught at Louisiana State University, the University of Delaware, and the University of Colorado, Boulder. He is the author of numerous articles, book chapters, two edited books, and *Curriculum for Utopia* (1992). His research and publications have focused on social studies education, curriculum theory, and educational reform. Among his most recent work is an edited book, *Critical Issues in Social Studies for the 21st Century* (2002). Over the past seventeen years he has served as department chairman and Interim Dean at the University of Delaware, as Dean of Education at the University of Colorado, Boulder, and as Founding Dean at the University of Redlands, California. He is a member of the Professors of Curriculum Association and currently serves on the NCATE Board of Examiners.

STEVEN L. STRAUSS is a neurologist at the Franklin Square Hospital in Baltimore, Maryland. His research interests are in the linguistics and neurology of reading and the politics of phonics. Previously, he served as Professor of Neurology at the University of Maryland Medical Systems in Baltimore and also as Professor of Linguistics at the University of New Mexico, where he was on the faculty of the educational linguistics doctoral program. He is a former Fulbright Scholar in linguistics and neurolinguistics in Vienna, Austria.

ROBIN A. WARD is Assistant Professor of Mathematics Education at the University of Arizona. Prior to receiving her Ph.D. from the University of Virginia in 1997, Dr. Ward spent seven years in industry working as an aerospace engineer. From 1997 to 2000, she served as an Assistant Professor of Mathematics at California Polytechnic State University in San Luis Obispo, California, where she taught elementary mathematics, precalculus, and technology courses, and received grants from the NASA Dryden Flight Research Center to develop web-based mathematics lesson plans for K–12 teachers that showcase a variety of NASA Dryden research projects. She has also received an Instrumentation and Laboratory Improvement (ILI) grant from the National Science Foundation providing for the establishment of a Mathematics Education Center on Cal Poly's campus equipped with state-of-the-art technology and a major technology grant from the U.S. Department of Education to train university of Arizona faculty and preservice teachers in effective uses of technology. Ward has written and presented papers at many national conferences, addressing the effective uses of technology in mathematics classrooms. She also works on K–8 preservice teachers' conceptual understandings of various mathematical topics, as well as their use of mathematical representations when designing lesson plans.